THE LATTER-DAY SAINTS
IN THE MODERN DAY WORLD

The Latter-day Saints
in the Modern Day World

AN ACCOUNT OF
CONTEMPORARY MORMONISM

(Revised Edition)

William J. Whalen

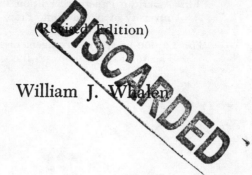

UNIVERSITY OF NOTRE DAME PRESS
Notre Dame, Indiana

Preface

THIS BOOK seeks to paint a portrait of contemporary Mormonism for the general reader. It is not a history of Mormonism although I have tried to sketch in enough historical background in the early chapters to enable the reader to understand the foreground.

Although this is probably not the kind of book which a Mormon missionary would loan to a prospective convert, I have tried to be objective and to sift out the fabrications and myths which characterize many anti-Mormon tracts. I did not write this book as an attack on the Church of Jesus Christ of Latter-day Saints although I have explored subjects which Church authorities would rather leave unmentioned.

During the past twenty years a number of first-rate studies have been published to acquaint Mormon and "Gentile" alike with various aspects of this faith, which now claims 2,400,000 adherents. The biography of Joseph Smith, Jr. by Mrs. Fawn Brodie is excoriated by Mormon scholars but is generally considered the best available life of the Prophet. Juanita Brooks has examined the famous Mountain Meadows massacre and the life of John D. Lee in a thoroughly scholarly fashion. Prof. Thomas F. O'Dea looked at Mormonism with the eyes of a trained sociologist.

I believe that an author should identify his own perspective when relevant to his subject matter. I am a Roman Catholic layman who has been writing about comparative religion for almost fifteen years. If I believed in the authenticity of the *Book of Mormon* and the claims of Joseph Smith, Jr., I would become a Mormon. Since I do not, my attitudes and some of my conclusions regarding the founder and the founding of the Mormon Church will differ from those of a committed Mormon. He in turn considers my Church and all Catholic, Protestant and Orthodox communions to be apostate and bereft of any authority to baptize or teach, so we are even.

Although I have tried to capture the spirit of contemporary Mormonism I would also be among the first to acknowledge the truth of an observation made by Sir Richard Burton more than a century ago. In his book, *City of the Saints,* which describes his visit to Salt Lake City he wrote: "But there is in Mormondom, as in all other exclusive faiths, whether Jewish, Hindu or other, an inner life which I cannot flatter myself or deceive the reader with the idea of my having penetrated."

The chapter on temple rites has been checked for accuracy by several former Mormons who have received their endowments in recent years. They prefer to remain anonymous but I would like to acknowledge their valuable assistance.

During the early stages of my research I received some cooperation from the LDS Church authorities. After August 1962, my letters to Church headquarters in Salt Lake City went unanswered. Since other non-Mormon writers have experienced the same treatment I suppose this is a defensive posture which the Church has adopted. I doubt if it accomplishes much good. I do appreciate the photographs supplied. Many people have assisted in my research or have been kind enough to review chapters of the manuscript. In particular I would like to thank Prof. Leland Negaard, Msgr. Jerome Stoffel, Rev. John P. Weisengoff, Rev. John L. Smith,

Elder Calvin Smith, F. Leon Edlefsen, Ammon Hennacy, and Edwin Butterworth. I would especially like to thank my colleague Prof. Eric Clitheroe, who first kindled my interest in Mormonism and who reviewed the entire manuscript and gave me the benefit of his long study of Mormon theology and practice. Of course, their assistance should not be construed as an endorsement of all my views nor should they be held accountable for my errors.

Moroni St. John prepared the illustrations and Mrs. Ruth Shaffer typed the manuscript. My wife also offered valuable comments and suggestions on the chapters as they were written.

Some readers may notice an apparent inconsistency in usage. The Utah Church hyphenates the word "Latter-day Saints" while the Reorganized Church prefers the form "Latter Day Saints." Most of the observations in this book pertain to the larger Utah Church; Chapter 18 examines the Reorganized LDS and smaller LDS bodies.

W. J. W.

Lafayette, Indiana

Contents

Illustrations

THE LATTER-DAY SAINTS
IN THE MODERN DAY WORLD

1. *Mormonism Today*

A CHURCH WHOSE MEMBERS were driven out of Missouri and Illinois, whose founder and Prophet was shot to death by a mob, and whose tenets aroused the nation in a moral crusade has become a respected religious denomination noted for its strict morals, patriotism, and wealth.

This same church, which began with only six members in 1830 in upstate New York, found a sanctuary in the Rocky Mountains and recently reported a worldwide membership of more than 2,400,000.

Its members once endured persecution, tarring and feathering, massacres, and charges of treason and immorality—but now members of this church are known as hospitable, sober, industrious, chaste neighbors and friends.

Largest of the three major indigenous American religions (including Christian Science and Jehovah's Witnesses), the Church of Jesus Christ of Latter-day Saints is better known by its nickname, the Mormon Church. Mormons themselves and residents of predominantly Mormon communities are more likely to refer to the Church and its practices as "LDS" for Latter-day Saint.

Although Utah and Salt Lake City have been identified with Mormonism, the Church also reports considerable strength in the neighboring states of Idaho, Arizona, Wyoming, Oregon, Colorado, New Mexico and Nevada. A small army of Mormons in government service has built up a substantial Mormon community in Washington, D. C., and the Mormons of California, centered around the Los Angeles area and San Bernardino Valley, are numbered in excess of 250,000. Mormon congregations, known as wards, have sprung up in college and university towns across the country, serving the unusual number of Mormons who have gone into teaching and research work.

Utah itself remains about 70 percent Mormon, although Salt Lake City now reports more non-Mormons (Gentiles) than Mormons: 53 percent to 47 percent LDS. The growth of industry in Salt Lake City will probably lower even further the percentage of LDS in the city they founded.

Salt Lake City is the Mormon Mecca, the center of Church life, and headquarters for all of the major Church departments. More than 1 million people a year visit Temple Square and tour the Mormon Tabernacle. About 140 Mormon business and professional men conduct free tours of the Tabernacle and grounds for the tourists and answer questions about their church's doctrines. Next door looms the impressive Mormon Temple whose doors are closed to all Gentiles and lukewarm Mormons.

This is only one of a dozen Mormon temples where secret rites for the living and dead clothe the Church in a veil of mystery. In recent years such temples have been built in Los Angeles, Switzerland, England, and New Zealand. There are others in the United States and Canada.

Mormons have won positions of prominence on the national scene and are stirring up interest in the church to which they give their allegiance. One of the Twelve Apostles of the Mormon Church (similar in rank to a cardinal of the Roman Catholic Church) served as Secretary of Agriculture in the Eisenhower cabinet: Ezra Taft Benson. He belongs to a pioneer Mormon family. Another Mormon who served as a missionary in England and as president of the Detroit stake (diocese) of the Church pulled the financially wobbly American Motors Corporation to profitability via the compact car. Now governor of Michigan, George Romney, has been mentioned as a possible Republican presidential nominee.

Romney was born in Chihuahaun, Mexico, in 1907. This was a colony founded by polygamous Mormons, although Romney's father had only one wife. When Pancho Villa chased the Saints out of this colony, the Romneys moved to Salt Lake City.

Four Latter-day Saints sit in the United States Senate—three belong to the Utah Church and one to the smaller Reorganized Church of Jesus Christ of Latter Day Saints with headquarters in Independence, Missouri. Five Mormons serve in the House of Representatives. Two are state governors.

Other Mormons in the public eye include Stewart Udall, Secretary of the Interior in the Kennedy and Johnson administrations; financier Marriner S. Eccles; television pioneer Philo Farnsworth. Dr. Harvey Fletcher is the author of 52 books on acoustics and electricity while Dr. Henry Eyring, a chemist, has been listed among the top ten American scientists. Winsome Mormon lassies have captured national beauty crowns as Miss America and Miss USA.

In 1966 Mormons were serving as presidents of the National Biscuit Co., Continental Illinois National Bank, Anaconda Co., and F. W. Woolworth Co.

Traditionally dedicated to education, the Mormon Church boasts that it furnishes a higher percentage of entries in *Who's Who in America* than any other denomination. (The Unitarians may dispute this claim.) The Church has produced an army of chemists, agronomists, sociologists, recreation specialists and educational administrators. Utah leads the nation in literacy and in the percentage of its college age young people actually enrolled in a college or university. The Church itself sponsors the largest church-related university in the country: Brigham Young University in Provo, Utah.

Growth of the Mormon Church surpasses 9 out of 10 other American churches. It has doubled its members during the past decade and only the aggressive Jehovah's Witnesses reveals a faster worldwide gain.

The Mormons dedicate a new ward chapel every week and in 1965 added more than 82,000 adult converts to their rolls. More than 12,000 missionaries, mostly young men of nineteen and twenty, seek converts to the Restored Gospel around the globe. This proselytizing program has been picking up momentum in recent years; by comparison the Church sent out only 525 missionaries in 1933 and garnered a mere 7,000 converts.

Since David O. McKay became president, prophet, seer, and revelator of the Church in 1951 the Church has doubled the number of stakes from 180 to 414. During the 93 years of McKay's life the Mormon church has multiplied in size 20 times. It is building a 30-story skyscraper in Manhattan to serve as eastern headquarters and a 25-story office building in Salt Lake City.

Long concerned about health reform, the Mormon Church insists that all members abstain from tobacco, liquor, tea, coffee and even cola drinks. It supports 15 hospitals which engage in research projects in heart disease, cancer, leukemia, and other diseases.

To maintain membership in good standing a Latter-day Saint must also attend church regularly and contribute 10 percent of his gross income to the Church. An additional 2 percent goes to support the local congregation. A Mormon family gives up two meals on the first Sunday of each month and sends the equivalent grocery money to Salt Lake City to finance an extensive welfare plan to aid needy Mormons.

The devout Mormon who has received his "endowments" in the temple will wear sacred temple undergarments at all times. Resembling a union suit, now abbreviated at the knees, the undergarments are worn by both men and women, awake and sleeping. It is said that older Mormons refuse to take off these garments completely even while taking a bath; they will hang one leg out of the tub so that they will never lose contact with the garments. Mystic signs are embroidered on them to remind the wearers of their temple obligations.

Perhaps the most tightly organized denomination in the country, the Mormon Church relies almost entirely on an unsalaried volunteer ministry. Some of the top officials receive stipends, but the 4,000 local bishops (corresponding to Protestant or Catholic pastors) support themselves by secular employment. They receive only a nominal allowance for stationery, postage, etc. What formal training in theology they have received has been in Sunday school and part-time educational centers; no Mormon pursues a seminary course such as would be required for a Catholic, Presbyterian, Lutheran, or Episcopalian clergyman. Typically the Mormon Church calls on successful businessmen to fill its top posts such as the office of apostle.

Almost every worthy Mormon male belongs to some grade of the priesthood. Most Mormon boys are ordained deacons at the age of twelve and advance through a series of grades to high priest by the time they are established as family men and citizens. The only men ineligible for ordination are those with any trace of Negro blood.

Every August the Church presents the largest outdoor pageant in the country on a hillside near Palmyra, New York. It dramatizes the discovery of the golden plates of the *Book of Mormon* by a young lad, Joseph Smith, Jr. He miraculously translated the plates, published the book, and founded the Church of Jesus Christ of Latter-day Saints. More than 100,000 people witness the four nights of the pageant.

Restoration of the Mormon city of Nauvoo, Illinois, is now under way. Once a model city of 20,000 Latter-day Saints, Nauvoo became a ghost town after the assassination of the Prophet and the flight of most of the Mormons to the West under the leadership of Brigham Young. Some Mormons hope to restore Nauvoo into a "Williamsburg of the Midwest." Archaeological work has been undertaken by a team from Southern Illinois University under a grant from the Mormon Church. Many of the old Mormon homes and buildings are owned by the Reorganized Church. The

Nauvoo temple itself was destroyed by vandals and by a tornado, but excavation of its site has begun.

From the Tabernacle come the programs of the world-famous Tabernacle Choir of 375 voices. Its Sunday morning concerts have been broadcast since 1929 and are now carried by 165 radio stations in the United States and Canada. Its 30 recordings, European tours, and television appearances have made it the best known choral group in the nation.

Among the Church's many business enterprises is a daily newspaper in Salt Lake City: the *Deseret News*. The Mormon newspaper avoids sermonizing and polemics. It publishes a Saturday supplement, *Church News,* which brings members up to date on activities of the Church and the Latter-day Saints. The chief Mormon periodical, *Improvement Era,* features color photography and modern typography, and reports a circulation of 225,000. The Mormon Church also owns 300,000 shares of the *Los Angeles Times.*

No one knows the full extent of the Church's financial holdings and business enterprises except the governing body of the Church. The income from tithes and profits has been estimated at $1 million a day but this may be conservative. If true, this income would make the Mormon Church the wealthiest church per capita in the United States if not in the world. Yet at one time the Federal Government stripped the Church of most of its property in its campaign to dislodge polygamy.

For more than 40 years the Mormon Church taught and authorized polygamy but since 1890 it has forbidden such unions where outlawed by the state. Several Church presidents supported multiple wives, and one Mormon patriarch married 45 women. Brigham Young himself married 27 women including several who were said to be widows of Smith. Today a Mormon exposed as a polygamist is immediately excommunicated by the Utah church. He may then choose to join one of the fundamentalist Mormon sects which continue the practice. The Reorganized Church denies that the Prophet ever countenanced polygamy and has never approved of plural marriage for its members.

Even if he has no other hobbies every Mormon is expected to become an amateur genealogist. So that their ancestors may be baptized by proxy and given an opportunity to accept the Mormon gospel in the next life, Mormons spend many hours preparing their family genealogies. The microfilm library at the Genealogical Society offices in Salt Lake City includes more than 500 million pages of records of births, marriages, deaths, etc. Information comes from official records, family Bibles, cemetery tombstones, military files, medical records, parish files of other denominations. Without doubt this has become the greatest genealogical collection in the world. Some Mormons have been baptized vicariously a hundred times or more for their dead relatives.

To protect genealogical records against any type of disaster the Church has recently completed a $1,704,000 storage vault at the mouth of Little Cottonwood Canyon. Tunnels have been blasted 600 feet into the side of the mountain and lead to three huge vaults.

Once pretty much confined to the intermountain area, the Mormon Church has come to the attention of the entire nation in recent years and to the attention of leaders of other churches. The *Christian Century* recently commented in an editorial:

Looking at the phenomenal growth of the Church of Jesus Christ of Latter-day Saints (Mormon) in recent years, other churches which view many Mormon beliefs and some Mormon practices as unbiblical and bizarre ask, "What does it have that we don't?" . . . The numerical and material success of the Church of Jesus Christ of Latter-day Saints will compel other churches to examine Mormon methods. Some of the beliefs and disciplines of the Mormons will have no appeal to other Christians. However, some of their procedures—long ago abandoned by other churches as tedious, undignified, ineffective or embarrassing—

may be worthy of reappraisal. Among them: a routine, continuous house-to-house evangelism; relief programs which care for the poor and the ill and provide education, recreation and employment for members who cannot provide for themselves; a discipline which requires each young man to give two years' service to the Church without compensation; a church structure which makes extensive use of laymen and which keeps to a minimum the number of professional church leaders. . . . It will be well to ask what the astonishing growth of the Mormon Church is saying to mainline Christian denominations.[1]

Leo Tolstoy once predicted that "if Mormonism is able to endure unmodified until it reaches the third or fourth generation it is destined to become the greatest power the world has ever known." Some modification and accommodation are already evident, especially in marital patterns, but other trends indicate that Tolstoy may have understood the power and potential of the Mormon Church better than many of his contemporaries.

In the following pages we will examine various aspects of contemporary Mormonism: religious, sociological, economic. Every informed American will be hearing and reading more about Mormonism in the years ahead. The Federal Government already recognizes four major religions: Protestantism, Roman Catholicism, Eastern Orthodoxy, and Judaism. The writer makes no claim to the gift of prophecy but he feels reasonably confident that within two decades the Latter-day Saints will be acknowledged as members of the fifth major American religion.

2. Joseph Smith, Jr.

Many of the world's religions have been started by men of humble backgrounds. The founder may be a carpenter or a camel driver or, as in the case of Mormonism, a young man with no particular occupation save hunting for buried treasure by means of a peep stone.

Joseph Smith, Jr., the man whom millions of Mormons have revered as the Prophet of God through whom the one true Church of Christ was restored, was born December 23, 1805, in Sharon, Vermont. He was shot to death in a jail in Carthage, Illinois, thirty-eight years later together with his brother.

His ancestors had lived in New England for more than one hundred years, moving about Vermont and New Hampshire. His grandfather, Solomon Mack, claimed to have experienced divine visions and published his account of these visions in a little book which he tried to sell to his friends and neighbors. Grandfather Mack was seventy-eight when his book was printed.

At the age of ten young Joseph accompanied his family to the city of Palmyra in western New York. His mother opened a cake and beer shop and his father did odd jobs. Later his father bought about a hundred acres of unimproved land south of Palmyra near the village of Manchester. The Smith family cleared the land and tapped the maple trees for sap to be used to make syrup and maple sugar. But the living was hard and the family lived on the outskirts of poverty.

This part of the country was known as the "burned-over

district" because it had been the scene of one religious revival after another. At numberless camp meetings evangelists and faith healers wrung the last drop of emotional sweat from the people of the area in efforts to convert them to a particular sect or induce a moral reform. Older denominations such as the Methodist and Baptist churches were rent by schism.

About thirty miles from Palmyra the Shakers, followers of Ann Lee, built a settlement. Their founder, who proclaimed herself the feminine reincarnation of Christ, prescribed celibacy and communism for her converts. Another female prophet, Jemima Wilkinson, built her colony of Jerusalem about twenty-five miles from the Smith homestead and ruled her subjects by means of a series of revelations. Some people listened to the message of the Swedish seer Emanuel Swedenborg, who claimed to have conversed with spirits who revealed among other things that the marriage relationship is eternal and was not severed by the grave. After Smith's departure from New York, William Miller left the Baptist Church to preach the imminence of the second coming. He warned Christians of other churches that they were all living in the latter-days and would soon see Jesus Christ return in power and glory to establish the millennial kingdom. Some of his followers would reorganize as the Seventh-day Adventists. In a cottage at Lily Dale, New York, the Fox sisters would give birth to the modern spiritualist movement. Some of these fruits of the burned-over district shriveled up as scandal rocked their communities or death claimed their founders. None achieved the material and statistical success of the church established by Joseph Smith, Jr.

Despite the highly charged religious atmosphere of upstate New York in those years we have little evidence that young Joseph was precociously religious. Like his father he apparently adopted a "plague on all your houses" attitude toward the rival preachers and sects. He preferred to try to locate buried treasures by means of his peep stone, a sort of crystal ball. Sometimes the treasure was Spanish gold and sometimes precious jewels buried in mounds by the Indians. Although he recorded no unusual finds with his peep stone his fame spread beyond the environs of Palmyra. A farmer, Josiah Stowell, invited Smith to search for a lost silver mine once worked by the Spaniards in Pennsylvania. He would provide free board and $14 a month for the seer's services.

In Harmony, Pennsylvania, Smith stayed at the home of Isaac Hale and soon became attracted to Hale's daughter Emma, who was a year older than he. One of Stowell's neighbors disturbed the treasure-hunting routine by swearing out a warrant for Smith's arrest on a charge of being "a disorderly person and an impostor." The trial was held in Bainbridge, New York, in March 1826 and the court record, the first published notice of Smith's career, indicates that the young man admitted:

...he had a certain stone, which he had occasionally looked at to determine where hidden treasures in the bowels of the earth were; that he professed to tell in this manner where gold mines were a distance under ground, and had looked for Mr. Stowell several times and informed him where he could find those treasures, and Mr. Stowell had been engaged in digging for them; that at Palmyra he pretended to tell, by looking at this stone, where coined money was buried in Pennsylvania, and while at Palmyra he had frequently ascertained in that way where lost property was, of various kinds; that he occasionally had been in the habit of looking through this stone to find lost property for three years, but of late had pretty much given it up on account of its injuring his health, especially his eyes—made them sore; that he did not solicit business of this kind, and had always rather declined having anything to do with this business.

Three defense witnesses testified at the trial that the defendant could "divine things" by "looking into a hat at his dark-colored stone." The court found him guilty but we have no record of the sentence. Smith lingered on at Stowell's house since he was now courting Emma Hale despite the strenuous opposition of her father. Finally the couple eloped and were married on January 18, 1827. They went to live with the groom's family in Manchester. Eight months after the wedding they returned to Harmony to face the father of the bride. He stormed at his son-in-law: "You have stolen my daughter and married her. I had much rather followed her to her grave. You spend your time in digging for money—pretend to see in a stone, and thus try to deceive people." Smith agreed to give up his treasure hunting and start to work for a living. With this promise Hale allowed the newlyweds to rejoin his household in Harmony.

Shortly after his marriage, rumors began to circulate that Smith had discovered the plates of a golden bible. The rumors were contradictory and confusing but the events leading up to the discovery were published by Smith himself in 1838.

Determined to find out which if any of the competing sects was true, Joseph Smith, Jr. had gone into the woods one day in 1820 to ask of God Himself the answer to his question. Smith's mother, brothers, and sister had joined the Presbyterian Church while Joseph himself inclined toward the Methodists. Two personages, identified as God the Father and Jesus Christ, visited him and told him that all churches were an abomination in the sight of God. One of the personages said, "They draw near to me with their lips, but their hearts are far from me, they teach for doctrines the commandments of men, having a form of godliness, but they deny the power thereof." This answer satisfied the lad, then fifteen years old.

In 1823, on the night of September 2, the boy was startled to see another heavenly personage standing in his bedroom, his feet off the floor. The angel wore a brilliant white garment and radiated light. He revealed that he was Moroni and was authorized to tell the young man that he would be privileged to receive a book, written on golden plates, and two stones in silver bows, the Urim and Thummim, with which to translate the text. This book contained the "fullness of the everlasting Gospel . . . as delivered by the Saviour to the ancient inhabitants."

The angel appeared two other times on the same night and repeated the marvelous message. On the next night the angel Moroni returned and instructed Smith to tell his father about the vision. Smith followed the angel's directions and discovered the plates and the Urim and Thummim in the Hill Cumorah not far from his home. He was forbidden to take the plates home with him. During a four-year period of probation he visited the spot where the plates were buried on the anniversary date of the first vision. Finally they were delivered into his keeping on September 22, 1827. For a while he hid them in a hollow log a couple of miles from his home, but some hoodlums tried to steal the plates and Smith ran home with them.

Smith described the plates as being about eight inches square, bound with three rings. If the plates were gold plates of the dimensions indicated they must have weighed between 175 and 225 pounds. His mother described the Urim and Thummim as "two smooth three-cornered diamonds set in glass and the glasses set in silver bows."

A sympathetic farmer, Martin Harris, loaned Smith enough money to go back to Harmony with his bride. His father-in-law breathed a sigh of relief when Smith agreed to abandon his treasure hunting but before long he discovered that Smith was busily engaged in translating the plates he had brought with him from Manchester. Emma served as his first amanuensis. Harris was willing to finance the publication of the wonderful book but wanted someone to verify the characters on the plates which, Smith explained, were written in the Reformed Egyptian language. Smith copied some of the characters and Harris took the paper to a professor of Greek and Latin at Columbia College—Charles

Anthon. He examined the characters but the verdict he rendered is interpreted differently by Mormons and Mormon critics. Mormons insist that Professor Anthon declared the characters were genuine. Yet in a letter to E. D. Howe on February 17, 1834, Professor Anthon wrote in part:

This paper was in fact a singular scrawl. It consisted of crooked characters disposed in columns and had evidently been prepared by some person who had before him at the time a book containing various alphabets. Greek and Hebrew letters, crosses and flourishes, Roman letters inverted or placed sideways, were arranged in perpendicular columns, and the whole ended in a rude delineation of a circle, divided into various compartments, decked with various strange marks, and evidently copied after the Mexican Calendar given by Humboldt, but copied in such a way as not to betray the source whence it was derived.

In the same letter Anthon wrote that he had decided the Reformed Egyptian hieroglyphics were either a "hoax upon the learned" or "a scheme to cheat the farmer out of his money." He flatly denied Mormon claims that he had verified the authenticity of the characters and called the claim "perfectly false." Harris was not dissuaded and he moved to Harmony in February 1828 to become Smith's secretary. Smith hung a blanket across the room and sat on one side

Facsimile of the characters engraved on the golden plates of the *Book of Mormon.*

with the plates and the Urim and Thummim while his scribe sat on the other side and took down his dictation. They worked together for two months and, with what Emma had copied down, completed 116 pages of foolscap.

Harris began to beg Smith to allow him to borrow the 116 pages to show his wife, who believed her husband was wasting his time and money on a harebrained scheme. Smith finally consented. He would regret the decision when he discovered that Harris had lost the manuscript. Mrs. Harris probably appropriated the manuscript and destroyed it, since it has never been found.

Smith went back to Manchester and confronted his scribe. Harris confessed the carelessness and cried, "I have lost my soul!" Smith himself groaned, "Oh, my God. All is lost. What shall I do?"

At the very least, more than several months' labor was lost. At the most, Smith's plan to present a translation of the golden plates by means of the magic spectacles was compromised. If he attempted to retranslate the same pages, he said, his enemies might alter the original version and try to expose him as an impostor. Mrs. Harris challenged him: "If this be a divine communication, the same Being who revealed it to you can easily replace it." Of course, the original manuscript was written in Emma's and Martin's handwriting so that any alteration in the text could be detected.

Smith's solution was to appeal to God for a revelation. The Lord told him to forget about retranslating the first 116 pages. A set of small plates called the plates of Nephi happened to cover the same ground as the missing pages.

Harris resumed his role as amanuensis in the winter of 1828–29 and the book known as the *Book of Mormon* began to take shape. It began:

I, Nephi, having been born of goodly parents, therefore I was taught somewhat in all the learning of my father; and having seen many afflictions in the course of my days, nevertheless, having been highly favored of the Lord in all my days; yea, having had a great knowledge of the goodness and the mysteries of God, therefore I make a record of my proceedings in my days.

Yes, I make a record in the language of my father, which consists of the learning of the Jews and the language of the Egyptians.

If Smith were composing instead of translating the book, he had had a year in which to work out his plot and characters and 116 pages in which to develop his style. In April 1828 an itinerant schoolteacher, Oliver Cowdery, called on Smith and within two days he had replaced Martin Harris as Smith's secretary. He had not met Smith before this but had been boarding at the Smith home in Manchester when he heard about the Golden Bible.

Smith never revealed the details of his translation. His own brother Hyrum asked him to elaborate on the method in a church meeting in 1831 but the Prophet would only say that the book was produced "by the power of God."

Emma reported in an interview in 1879 that her husband sat with his face buried in a hat containing a seer stone. The plates themselves lay on a table covered by a tablecloth. He apparently did not have to examine the plates themselves to decipher the meaning. David Whitmer, one of the three witnesses, published a booklet entitled *Address to All Believers in Christ* in 1887. He wrote:

I will now give you a description of the manner in which the *Book of Mormon* was translated. Joseph Smith would put the seer stone into a hat, and put his face in the hat, drawing it closely around his face to exclude the light; and in the darkness the spiritual light would shine. A piece of something resembling parchment would appear, and on that appeared the writing. One character at a time would appear, and under it was the interpretation in English. Brother Joseph would read off the English to Oliver Cowdery, who was his principal scribe, and when it was written down and repeated to Brother Joseph to see if it was correct, then it would disappear, and another character with the interpretation would appear. Thus the *Book of Mormon* was translated by the gift and power of God, and not by any power of man.[1]

What about the Urim and Thummim? Mormon scholars seem to believe that the first 116 pages were translated with the help of the Urim and Thummim but that after Harris had lost these pages the spectacles were taken away by an angel. Instead, Smith received the seer stone which Whitmer describes as a "strange, oval-shaped, chocolate-colored stone about the size of an egg."

Harris confirmed the use of the seer stone. He was interviewed in his later years when he was living in Utah. An account of his remarks appeared in the *Millennial Star* on February 6, 1882:

> By aid of the seer stone, sentences would appear and were read by the Prophet and written by Martin, and when finished he would say, "Written," and if correctly written that sentence would disappear and another appear in its place, but if not written correctly it remained until corrected, so that the translation was just as it was engraven on the plates, precisely in the language then used.[2]

From these statements we are led to understand that the presence of the plates themselves or the use of the Urim and Thummim were quite incidental to the translation of the *Book of Mormon* as it is now published. Smith simply stared at an egg-shaped stone in his hat and dictated the story to his secretaries Harris and Cowdery.

The organization of a church following the writing of the *Book of Mormon* was a logical step and one which Smith had wanted to take for some time. Cowdery, however, hesitated to endorse this plan because he was disturbed that Smith was not an ordained minister of the gospel. Accordingly the pair went into the woods one May afternoon in 1829 and later reported that John the Baptist had conferred on them the Aaronic priesthood. Each baptized and ordained the other.

Later, on another day, Peter, James and John bestowed the higher Melchizedek priesthood.

To complete the translation Smith and Cowdery went to the Whitmer home in Fayette, New York. Harris prodded Joseph into appointing the three witnesses who were to see the plates. The three selected were Harris, Cowdery and Whitmer. The three men accompanied Smith into the woods and prayed for a vision. Harris withdrew from the prayer circle because of his doubts and unworthiness and the others remained. Eventually an angel appeared and displayed the plates, turning over the pages so that the engravings were discernible. Smith went to Harris and he too received the vision.

Every edition of the *Book of Mormon* carries the testimony of the three witnesses and of eight other witnesses who swore that they had seen and handled the plates. Harris, Cowdery and Whitmer all left the Mormon Church and were damned by Smith, but Cowdery and Harris returned and were rebaptized. None of the trio ever denied his testimony but Harris later explained that he had seen the plates with the eyes of faith. Questioned by a lawyer, Harris replied, "I did not see them [the plates] as I do that pencil-case, yet I saw them with the eye of faith; I saw them just as distinctly as I see anything around me—although at the time they were covered with a cloth." [3]

Of the eight other witnesses three were members of the Smith family, four were Whitmers, and the eighth (Hiram Page) had married a Whitmer daughter. Mark Twain commented: "I could not feel more satisfied and at rest if the entire Whitmer family had testified."

Non-Mormons speculate that Smith was able to obtain these testimonies by means of his powers of suggestion and hypnosis. It is even possible that he fashioned some plates to resemble the golden plates and used these to convince the witnesses.

Harris had to agree to guarantee the sum of $3,000 which

the printer demanded for the first 5,000 copies of the *Book of Mormon*. Harris was a credulous man in a credulous age. He solemnly reported that he had seen and talked to Jesus in the form of a deer and had also seen the devil, who resembled a jackass with short, smooth hair like a mouse.[4] The book went on sale March 26, 1830.

Shortly after the book was released, Smith assumed the title "Seer, a Translator, a Prophet, an Apostle of Jesus Christ, and Elder of the Church through the will of God the Father, and the grace of your Lord Jesus Christ." Members of his family and a few friends began to sell the book from door to door.

The Church itself was established on April 6, 1830, with six members: Smith, his brothers Hyrum and Samuel, Cowdery, David and Peter Whitmer, Jr. The laws of New York required six members for incorporation. At its founding the Church was known simply as the Church of Christ. Four years later its name was changed to Church of the Latter-day Saints and in 1838 it adopted its present official name: Church of Jesus Christ of Latter-day Saints.

Within a month it had grown to a membership of forty. Cowdery attempted to receive revelations himself but Smith rebuked him and sent him out to convert the Indians. Missionaries approached a disaffected Campbellite preacher, Sidney Rigdon, who led a congregation and socialistic experiment in Kirtland, Ohio, which is now a suburb of Cleveland. Rigdon and his followers read the *Book of Mormon* and were baptized into the infant Mormon Church within three weeks. In one swoop the Church gained the 127 members of Rigdon's congregation. Headquarters of the Church moved from New York to Kirtland and by the next spring the Church counted more than 1,000 souls.

Rigdon was a popular preacher and formerly a close associate of Alexander Campbell, founder of the Disciples of Christ movement. Campbell sought to restore primitive Christianity. He urged an abolition of distinction between clergy and laity, baptism by immersion of believers, a weekly communion service, and adoption of a name which would identify the church as the Church of Christ and not a description of church polity (Presbyterian), a name taken from a reformer (Lutheran), or a distinctive practice (Baptist). Rigdon accepted most of these positions but urged the Campbellites to try a communistic way of life. No doubt he later influenced Smith, his junior by twelve years, to incorporate these Campbellite ideas in the Church of Jesus Christ of Latter-day Saints.

At this point the young Prophet could point to a church barely a year old but with a rapidly growing constituency, a book of scriptures which seemed to answer many of the theological questions of the day as well as to explain the origin of the American Indians, and a priesthood alleged to have been derived from God Himself. Before we follow the history of the Prophet as he and his Church move West, we will pause to examine the curious book which in the 1830 edition listed Joseph Smith, Jr. as "author and proprietor."

3. *The* Book of Mormon

WHATEVER JUDGMENT a reader may make about the *Book of Mormon*—an inspired revelation, a hoax, an early American epic novel, or a wicked scheme to deceive Methodists and Baptists—he must admit that the book is a remarkable document. It has influenced the course of history and has changed the lives of millions of men and women.

Tens of thousands of converts, mostly from the British Isles and Scandinavian countries, immigrated to the United States as a result of their acceptance of the claims of Joseph Smith and his book. Faith in the authenticity of the *Book of Mormon* led other thousands to follow Brigham Young to the Great Salt Lake Valley and to open new frontiers in the American West. Today millions of Latter-day Saints accept the book as a divine record and look to its pages for inspiration, religious doctrine, and answers to many of the mysteries of life. Copies of the *Book of Mormon* in many languages are distributed throughout the world by zealous Mormon missionaries; in a recent year more than 100,000 adults examined the book, accepted its miraculous translation, and asked for baptism in the Church of Jesus Christ of Latter-day Saints.

Yet despite its impact on history, especially American history, the *Book of Mormon* has practically been ignored by archaeologists, social historians, Protestant and Catholic theologians, linguists, and students of American literature. In fact the number of non-Mormons who have ever read the book through is probably infinitesimal.

Even Sir Richard Burton, who spent some time with the

Mormons in Salt Lake City and is generally well disposed toward the Mormons, wrote:

> Surely there never was a book so thoroughly dull and heavy; it is monotonous as a sage-prairie. Though not liable to be terrified by dry or hard reading, I was, it is only fair to own, unable to turn over more than a few chapters at a time, and my conviction is that very few are so highly gifted that they have been able to read it through at a heat.[1]

As published in its present form the *Book of Mormon* consists of 15 books: the First Book of Nephi, Second Nephi, the Book of Jacob, Book of Enos, Book of Jarom, Book of Omni, the Words of Mormon, the Book of Mosiah, Book of Alma, Book of Helaman, Third Nephi, Fourth Nephi, Book of Mormon, Book of Ether, and Book of Moroni. Each book is named after its principal author.

Its theme is that of faith in God, pride and fall, repentance. O'Dea calls it a "work of Christian imagination." Its theological understanding of God is monotheistic in contrast to the plurality of Gods taught by the Utah Church today.

The edition distributed by the Utah church comes to 568 pages (about 275,000 words) including Smith's version of receiving the plates, the testimony of the three and eight witnesses, cross-references, a synopsis of chapters, pronouncing vocabulary, and index. The original manuscript lacked paragraphs, punctuation and capitalization. Much of this was furnished by the publisher, E. H. Grandin of Palmyra, New York. An edition appeared in 1842 with the notation that it had been "carefully revised by the translator." Orson Pratt broke up the *Book* into books, chapters and numbered verses in 1879. Since 1920 the *Book of Mormon* has been printed in double columns and each book has been preceded by an abstract of its contents.

Although Mormonism now embraces ethical and social values of its own, its theological validity stands or falls on the basis of the authenticity of the *Book of Mormon*. In his book, *Divine Authenticity of the Book of Mormon*, Pratt declares:

This book must be either true or false . . . If false, it is one of the most cunning, wicked, bold, deep-laid impositions ever palmed upon the world, calculated to deceive and ruin millions who will sincerely receive it as the word of God, and will suppose themselves securely built upon the rock of truth until they are plunged with their families into hopeless despair. The nature of the message in the Book of Mormon is such that, if true, no one can possibly be saved and reject it; if false, no one can possibly be saved and receive it . . . If, after rigid examination, it be found an imposition, it should be extensively published to the world as such; the evidences and arguments on which the imposture was detected, should be clearly and logically stated, that those who have been sincerely yet unfortunately deceived, may perceive the nature of the deception and be reclaimed, and that those who continue to publish the delusion, may be exposed and silenced. . . .[2]

If it can be demonstrated that the *Book of Mormon* actually reveals the history of the aborigines of the Western Hemisphere as this history was revealed to a young man in New York State on plates delivered by an angel, every human being would have to give the book serious study and consideration. The religion based on the authenticity of this record and the claims of its translator would deserve the prayerful investigation of every man and woman in the world.

On the other hand, if the preponderance of evidence indicates that the book is the product of an imaginative writer in the early 1800's, both the book and the religion it inspired would lose their theological significance even though they might be studied from the point of view of sociology, history, comparative religion, etc.

Mormons well understand the crucial importance of establishing the authenticity of the *Book of Mormon*. Brigham

H. Roberts, one of the most capable Mormon historians and apologists, wrote in 1911:

> The Book of Mormon must submit to every analysis and examination. It must submit to historical tests, to the tests of archeological research, and also to higher criticism ... We proclaim it true and the world has the right to test it to the uttermost in every possible way.[3]

Critics of the claim of divine origin of the *Book of Mormon* have been forced to build their case on conjecture. If they maintain that someone other than Smith wrote the manuscript which became known as the *Book of Mormon* they find it impossible to prove beyond any reasonable doubt that Smith acquired such a manuscript from which he plagiarized the book.

Many Gentile scholars insist that Smith came into possession of a manuscript about the American Indians written by a Congregational minister, Solomon Spaulding. Perhaps Smith's first prominent convert and lieutenant for many years, Sidney Rigdon, acquired the manuscript, inserted the theological portions, and induced the young man to invent the tale of the golden plates. While his secretaries copied down his words as fast as they could write, Smith read the Spaulding manuscript behind the blanket stretched across the cabin.

Some friends of Spaulding insisted that they had seen the purloined manuscript and confirmed that many of the names such as Moroni appear in both publications. Eventually one of Spaulding's manuscripts turned up in possession of L. L. Rice of Honolulu. Rice had been state printer at Columbus, Ohio, and had once published a newspaper in Painesville where his predecessor obtained the manuscript from Spaulding's widow. The manuscript found in Hawaii bears little resemblance to the Mormon Bible. It remains in the library of Oberlin College. Those who continue to uphold the Spaulding theory maintain that Spaulding wrote more than one novel about the American Indians and that the one from which Smith plagiarized has never been recovered. How this missing manuscript got into the possession of Rigdon and Smith cannot be ascertained; the Spaulding theorists have been forced to rely on circumstantial evidence. The possibility that any new evidence may turn up regarding the movements of Smith and Rigdon prior to the appearance of the *Book of Mormon* grows dimmer with each passing year.

Another theory suggests that Smith stole his ideas from a manuscript written by the Reverend Ethan Smith, a Congregationalist minister of Poultney, Vermont. Ethan Smith's book, *Views of the Hebrews: or the Ten Tribes of Israel in America,* was published in 1823 and attempted to solve the problem of the origin of the American Indians by offering a theory of their Jewish ancestry. This book was widely read and commented upon five years before the appearance of the *Book of Mormon.* Some think that Ethan Smith was working on a companion volume which somehow got into Joseph Smith's hands and formed the basis for the *Book of Mormon.* This theory remains even more speculative than the Spaulding theory. That Ethan Smith's ideas find many parallels in the *Book of Mormon* is undeniable and there is every likelihood that the Smith family had access to a copy of *Views of the Hebrews* or to abridgments which appeared in a number of weekly newspapers.

At least one scholar, Prof. I. W. Riley, attributed the production of the *Book of Mormon* to the phenomenon of automatic writing induced by epilepsy but hardly anyone believes that Joseph Smith, Jr. was an epileptic. His occasional descriptions of bright lights and visions do not warrant a diagnosis of epilepsy. Nevertheless, this theory was also accepted by the German scholar Eduard Meyer in his 1912 study of Mormonism.

Today the majority of Gentile scholars who reject the miraculous appearance of the plates and their translation by means of the Urim and Thummin have come to believe that Smith himself could conceivably have concocted the *Book of Mormon*. That a young man with a lively imagination, a smattering of the Bible, a passable ability at reading, an acquaintance with the theological debates of the day and the anti-Masonic agitation could bring forth a book such as the *Book of Mormon* is not out of the question. The various revelations gathered in *Doctrine and Covenants* reveal a style much like that of the *Book of Mormon*. Much of the text is repetitious and monotonous; the phrase "And it came to pass" alone takes up 10,000 words. Large chunks of the King James Version of the Bible are quoted verbatim or slightly altered: the Ten Commandments appear in Mosiah 12 and 13; Third Nephi 12–14 includes a slightly different version of the Sermon on the Mount. Altogether Smith's book contains about 27,000 words from the Old and New Testaments.

The original manuscript was completed in only 90 days from the day Oliver Cowdery became Smith's amanuensis; this would average out to a literary production of approximately 3,000 words a day. Since this production did not involve the revision and rewriting by which authors usually polish their copy, the author/translator would be held back only by the ability of the secretary to take down the dictation.

Corroborative evidence that Smith possessed the ability to compose the book without outside assistance is given by his mother, Lucy Mack Smith, in her *Joseph Smith and His Progenitors*. In a book since suppressed by the Mormon Church she wrote:

During our evening conversations, Joseph would occasionally give us some of the most amusing recitals that could be imagined. He would describe the ancient inhabitants of this continent, their dress, mode of traveling, their buildings, with every particular; their mode of warfare; and also their religious worship. This he would do with as much ease, seemingly, as if he had spent his whole life among them.[4]

This storytelling was long before he had received permission to begin translating the golden plates and indicates that the same stories he told around the fireside could be written down by a secretary to form a substantial volume.

O'Dea inclines toward the belief that Smith himself composed the story of the *Book of Mormon:*

There is a simple common-sense explanation which states that Joseph Smith was a normal person living in an atmosphere of religious excitement that influenced his behavior as it had that of so many thousands of others and, through a unique concomitance of circumstances, influences and pressures, led him from necromancy into revelation, from revelation to prophecy, and from prophecy to leadership of an important religious movement and to involvement in the bitter and fatal intergroup conflicts that his innovations and success had called forth. To the non-Mormon who does not accept the work as a divinely revealed scripture, such an explanation on the basis of the evidence at hand seems by far the most likely and safest.[5]

To reinforce the claim that the writing of the *Book of Mormon* was a miraculous achievement, Mormon apologists have been tempted to belittle the Prophet's literary ability. One of the witnesses, David Whitmer, even wrote that Smith was "illiterate" at the time the *Book of Mormon* was produced. Yet by Smith's own statements we understand that he was able to read the Bible and probably newspapers and periodicals. His schooling was limited as was that of many people on the frontier but he certainly possessed a rudimentary knowledge of reading prior to the "translation" of the *Book of Mormon.* He may not have mastered the art of writing, which explains his employment of Emma, Martin Harris and Cowdery as secretaries.

Orson Pratt described the educational attainments of the Prophet at the time of the appearance of the *Book* as follows: "He could read without much difficulty, and write an imperfect hand, and had a very limited understanding of the elementary rules of arithmetic."

The *Book of Mormon* purports to describe a period from 600 B.C. to A.D. 421. The Book of Ether also relates the history of another group of people, the Jaredites, who left the Tower of Babel about 2200 B.C. and were exterminated by about the start of the period covered by the other books of the *Book of Mormon*—600 B.C. The last word written on the plates was composed about 1,400 years before the publication of the *Book of Mormon*.

Four sets of plates are involved in the translation. The plates of Nephi record secular history; the plates of Mormon are an abridgment of the plates of Nephi by Mormon and his son Moroni; the plates of Ether, also abridged by Moroni, tell the story of the Jaredites; and a fourth set, said to have been brought from Jerusalem by Lehi, contain extracts from the Hebrew scriptures up to Jeremiah.

In the first two books, First and Second Nephi, we read how a Jew named Lehi, a descendant of Joseph, along with his wife Sariah and his sons, left Jerusalem just before the Babylonian captivity and sailed to the shores of South America. The Lord directed him in his building of his ship and he was guided by a round ball called a compass. He sailed from an area bordering on the Red Sea, via the Indian and Pacific oceans. Along with Lehi's family were a man named Zoran, and Ishmael and his daughters. The latter married Lehi's sons—Laman, Lemuel, Sam, and Nephi.

Eventually two of the sons, Laman and Lemuel, rebelled and their descendants fell into wickedness and idolatry and were cursed by God with a dark skin; they are the ancestors of the American Indians known as Lamanites.

The next four books bring the story up to 130 B.C. The descendants of Lehi are now generally divided into the faithful Nephites and the wicked Lamanites. The Nephites migrated to North America and met a colony of people called the Zarahemlites who left Jerusalem about nine years after

Lehi. The Nephites and the citizens of the city Zarahemla joined forces. Another short book, the Words of Mormon, is said to be a statement by the compiler of the *Book of Mormon,* and was written about A.D. 385.

Mosiah, Alma and Helaman tell the story of the Nephites from 130 B.C. to 2 B.C. The Nephites of Central and North America waged many wars against the Lamanites of South America. The Nephites occasionally fell from grace and the Lamanites were reconverted, but the Nephites remained the heroes and the Lamanites the villains.

Third and Fourth Nephi describe the visit of Christ to this hemisphere after his resurrection and the establishment of his Church among both the Nephites and Lamanites. Jesus taught baptism by immersion and a memorial supper interpretation of the Eucharist. He appointed 12 disciples and ordained priests.

Fourth Nephi covers the period from Christ's visit to A.D. 321. The original Church of Christ had broken up into rival denominations. Some people revived the oaths of a secret society known as the Gadianton fraternal order which bears a strong resemblance to Freemasonry. By the year 300 both the Nephites and Lamanites had fallen away from the true religion and into sinful ways.

After a series of wars the Lamanites massed a huge army to attack a Nephite force of 230,000 soldiers near the Hill Cumorah in western New York State. The last great Nephite general, Mormon, left the plates to his son Moroni who buried them in the hillside. By A.D. 400, Moroni was the sole survivor of the Nephite race; he lived until his death as a hermit in the forests of New York.

The Book of Ether tells a separate story. The children of Lehi were not the first settlers of this hemisphere. The Jaredites had arrived much earlier (2200 B.C.). The Lord instructed them to build a peculiar sort of submarine in which to cross the ocean. The vessels were completely enclosed except for holes in the top and bottom which could be plugged up to keep out the water or opened to let in fresh air. To light the interior, Jared collected 16 stones "and they were white and clear, even as transparent glass." The Lord touched these and they continued to glow and provided light for the passengers in the eight barges. The small barges were tossed and turned on the seas for 344 days, but all landed on the same day at the promised destination. The Jaredites landed on the east coast of Central America, pros- pered for many centuries, but apostatized and were destroyed before the invasion of Lehi and his companions.

The *Book of Mormon* concludes with the Book of Moroni, which gives doctrinal and ritual instruction. Alexander Campbell reviewed the *Book of Mormon* the year after its publication and made this observation:

This prophet Smith, through his stone spectacles, wrote on the plates of Nephi, in his *Book of Mormon,* every error and almost every truth discussed in New York for the last ten years. He decided all the great controversies:—infant baptism, ordination, the trinity, regeneration, repentance, justification, the fall of man, the atonement, transubstantiation, fasting, penance, church gov- ernment, religious experience, the call to the ministry, the general resurrection, eternal punishment, who may baptize, and even the question of freemasonry, republican government, and the rights of man....[6]

The puzzle of the origin of the American Indians intrigued many people in early nineteenth-century America. A number of people such as Roger Williams, William Penn and Jona- than Edwards believed that the Indians were descendants of Jews, perhaps of the lost tribes of Israel. The existence of Indian burial mounds, the darker skin of the aborigines, the stories of Mayan and Aztec ruins, led to speculation. The *Book of Mormon* claimed to solve these and other questions.

Unlike the Old and New Testaments the *Book of Mormon* has never been subjected to the rigorous criticism of biblical scholars. Believing Mormons do not question its authenticity and few Mormons have the academic equipment to apply the critical methods used in examining the Christian scriptures. Protestant and Catholic scripture scholars have not bothered to examine the internal evidence of the *Book of Mormon,* although the remarkable growth of Mormonism may prompt a thoroughgoing examination of its basic book.

It is possible, however, for the layman to question many of the anachronisms of the *Book of Mormon.* For example, if a book purportedly written in the year 1000 tells of a political movement led by a Fuehrer, symbolized by a swastika, and arrayed against a coalition known as the Allies, we might suspect that the writer was contemporary of the Nazi movement.

Many words appear in the text which were unknown at the dates ascribed to the composition of the *Book of Mormon.* The Nephites worship in *synagogues,* a Greek word signifying an institution which developed after the Nephites had left Palestine. Other words which the Nephites could hardly have known are *baptize, church, gospel, barges,* etc.

The Greek word *biblia* from which we derive the word *bible* was first used as a name for the scriptures in the fifth century after Christ. It means "books" or "booklets" and is used to designate a collection of inspired writings bound in codex form. But in 2 Nephi 29:3 we read, "Many of the Gentiles shall say: A Bible! A Bible! We have got a Bible, and there cannot be any more Bible."

The point of view of the Nephites puzzles the non-Mormon reader since the Messianic hopes of the Nephites are so clearly identified with the person of Jesus Christ, his atonement, baptism, death by crucifixion, and resurrection. Nothing anywhere so specific and prophetic appears in the Old Testament. Verses in 2 Nephi 31:6 and 8, allegedly written between 559 and 545 B.C., refer to Jesus Christ in the past tense: "Now, I would ask of you, my beloved brethren, wherein the Lamb of God did fulfil all righteousness in being baptized in water? . . . Wherefore, after he was baptized with water the Holy Ghost descended upon him in the form of a dove." Again in 2 Nephi 33:6 the Nephite prophet exclaims: "I glory in my Jesus for he hath redeemed my soul from hell." These sentiments would have a more genuine ring if we were told they were expressed by a frontier revivalist than by a Nephite writing six centuries before the birth of Christ.

Biblical scholars would be startled to discover the invented word *Jehovah* in the Nephite scriptures. In 2 Nephi 22:2 we read:

Behold, God is my salvation; I will trust and not be afraid; for the Lord JEHOVAH is my strength and my song; he also has become my salvation.

With one minor change this is a transcription of Isaiah 12:2 in the 1611 version. The problem for Mormon scholars is that the word *Jehovah* was made up from the Jewish tetragrammaton—JHVH—long after the plates of the *Book of Mormon* were buried in A.D. 420. The Jews did not pronounce the name of God but used these four letters in their scriptures. The true pronunciation was lost but Christian scholars inserted the vowel points from the word *Adonai,* which means the Lord. They came up with "Jehovah" but this was certainly not the correct name. It was probably closer to "Yahweh" and recent Bible translations have dropped "Jehovah" for this reason. The word could not have existed before the invention of Hebrew vowel points in the sixth century after Christ, but it appears in the *Book of Mormon.*

By examining the extensive selections corresponding to those in the Bible we can also arrive at a judgment as to the date at which the *Book of Mormon* was actually composed. For example, the ending of the Lord's Prayer, "For thine is the kingdom, and the power, and the glory, forever"—which appears in the King James Version as Matthew 6:13 and in the *Book of Mormon* as 3 Nephi 13:13—is certainly an interpolation. Scripture scholars agree that this liturgical addition was introduced around the fifth century and mistakenly incorporated into some versions of the New Testament. Recent versions eliminate the interpolation. That a Nephite scribe on another continent could come up with the identical interpolation stretches credibility.

The King James Version renders Isaiah 5:25 incorrectly as "and their carcasses were torn in the midst of the streets." The Hebrew word *suchah* means "refuse" not "torn" and modern Protestant versions correct this error so that it reads "And their corpses were as refuse (offal) in the midst of the streets." The *Book of Mormon* in 2 Nephi 15:25 perpetuates the King James error.

A serious problem for Mormon scholars is that of Isaiah. The *Book of Mormon* quotes 21 complete chapters of Isaiah and parts of other chapters. But few Christian scripture scholars continue to attribute the entire book of Isaiah to the Prophet Isaiah. They believe at least nine other unknown prophets contributed to the Book of Isaiah and many of these wrote their passages at least sixty years after the Nephites were said to have left Jerusalem. Lehi and his family presumably lost all contact with their homeland after their voyage to the New World. How then could the Nephites incorporate the sayings of these unknown prophets into the *Book of Mormon?*

An odd discrepancy appears in 3 Nephi 25:2. The Mormon passage reads:

But unto you that fear my name, shall the Son of Righteousness arise with healing in his wings; and yet shall go forth and grow up as calves in the stall.

In all other Protestant and Catholic versions this appears as Malachi 4:2, but the translation is "sun of righteousness" not "Son of Righteousness." Had the translator been reading from a copy of the Bible it is understandable that Cowdery should have written "Son" instead of "sun." The Mormons must insist that this is the correct rendering since the translation proceeded only after the spirit ascertained its correctness.

Several *Book of Mormon* passages defy understanding. In the Book of Ether we read: "And it came to pass that after he had smitten off the head of Shiz, that Shiz raised upon his hands and fell; and after that he had struggled for breath, he died" (15:31). How anyone with his head cut off could struggle for breath is left a mystery. In Helaman 9:6 we learn that a judge was "stabbed by his brother by a garb of secrecy." But the strangest malapropism appears in Alma 46:19. "And when Moroni had said these words, he went forth among the people, waving the rent [part] of his garment in the air, that all might see the writing which he had wrote [written] upon the rent [part] . . ." The words in brackets have been added or altered in recent editions but the original edition seems to give the impression that a "rent" is something on which a man can write!

Most critics of the *Book of Mormon* make reference to the anachronisms in the text. Laban draws a sword and Nephi observes that "the blade thereof was of the most precious steel." No one believes that steel was available to Laban or anyone else in 592 B.C. The ship taking Lehi and his family and friends to the New World is guided by a compass which was invented many centuries later. In Alma 20:6 the writer mentions horses, which all archaeologists agree were extinct on this continent by that period and were not introduced until the coming of Spanish settlers. The Jaredites were provided with a catalogue of anachronisms:

. . . having all manner of fruit, and of grain, and of silks, and of fine linen, and of gold, and of silver, and of precious things, and also all manner of cattle, of oxen, and cows, and of sheep, and of swine, and of goats, and also many other kinds of animals, which were useful for the food of man; and they also had horses, and asses, and there were elephants, and cureloms, and cumons, all of which were useful unto man, and more especially the elephants and cureloms, and cumons (Ether 9:17-19).

Nobody knows what "cureloms and cumons" might be although the *LDS Reference Encyclopedia* ventures a guess: "Useful animals known to the Jaredites. By some these were thought to be the Mastodon, by others the Llama or Alpaca." [7]

Textual changes since the original 1830 edition of the *Book of Mormon* number more than 2,000. Nevertheless, the Prophet insisted that "the *Book of Mormon* is the most correct of any book on earth, and the keystone of our religion, and a man would get nearer to God by abiding by its precepts, than by any other book" (1841). Here are a few samples of textual changes:

1830 edition, p. 25.
"Behold, the virgin which thou seest, is the mother of God."
1 Nephi 11:18.
"Behold, the virgin whom thou seest, is the mother of the Son of God . . ."
1830, p. 25.
"And the angel said unto me, behold the Lamb of God, yea, even the Eternal Father!"
1 Nephi 11:21.
"And the angel said unto me: Behold the Lamb of God, yea, even the Son of the Eternal Father!"

1830, p. 32.
"that the Lamb of God is the Eternal Father . . ."
1 Nephi 13:40.
"that the Lamb of God is the Son of the Eternal Father . . ."

1830, p. 200.
". . . king Benjamin had a gift from God."
Mosiah 21:28.
". . . king Mosiah had a gift from God."

1830, p. 303.
"Yea, decreeth unto them that decrees which are unalterable . . ." Completely deleted in current edition (see Alma 29:4).

Numerous grammatical errors mar the original printing:

They was added, page 192.
The priests was, p. 193.
And this he done, p. 224.
They did not fight against God no more, p. 290.
Teach baptism unto they, p. 506.

Mormon scholars insist that new evidence corroborates the statements about the pre-Columbian history of this hemisphere, but non-Mormon archaeologists put no faith in the *Book of Mormon*. The Smithsonian Institution, an agency of the Federal Government, receives so many inquiries regarding the value of the *Book of Mormon* for archaeologists and anthropologists that it has prepared a form letter to send to inquirers:

SMITHSONIAN INSTITUTION
Bureau of American Ethnology
Washington 25, D.C.

STATEMENT REGARDING THE BOOK OF MORMON

The Smithsonian Institution has received hundreds of inquiries during the past several years regarding the use of the *Book of Mormon* as a guide to archeological researches. Answers to questions most commonly asked are as follows:

1. The Smithsonian Institution has never used the *Book of Mormon* in any way as a scientific guide. Smithsonian archeologists see no connection between the archeology of the New World and the subject matter of the book.

2. The physical type of the American Indian is basically Mongoloid, being most closely related to that of the peoples of eastern central, and northwestern Asia. It is believed that the ancestors of the present Indians came into the New World— probably over a land bridge known to have existed in the Bering Strait region during the last Ice Age—in a continuing series of small migrations beginning about 25,000 years ago.

3. Extensive archeological researches in southern Mexico and Central America clearly indicate that the civilizations of these regions developed locally from simple beginnings without the aid of outside stimulus.

4. Present evidence indicates that the first people to reach America from the East were the Norsemen who arrived in the northwestern part of North America about A.D. 1000. There is nothing to show that they reached Mexico or Central America. Some anthropologists think that there is evidence of voyages to America from the eastern Asiatic coast before the beginning of the Christian Era, but such evidence, based only on certain cultural parallels, is very inconclusive.

5. We know of no authentic cases of ancient Egyptian or Hebrew writing having been found in the New World. Reports of findings of Egyptian influence in the Mexican and Central American areas have been published in newspapers and magazines from time to time, but thus far no reputable Egyptologist has been able to discover any relationship between Mexican remains and those of Egypt.

6. There is one copy of the *Book of Mormon* in the United States National Museum; there is one copy and part of another in the Bureau of American Ethnology; and one copy was sent by the Smithsonian library to the Library of Congress for deposit. Two of these were gift copies, and one was received by transfer from another Government agency. One or two members of the staff have personal copies that were presented to them by Mormons.

SIL-76
11/56

The plain fact is that no non-Mormon anthropologists or archaeologists accept the thesis that the American Indians are of Jewish ancestry. They believe that the Indians are Mongoloids and not Mediterranean Caucasoids. Most scholars believe that they entered this continent across the Bering Straits and not by ships from Jerusalem.

Prof. James Griffin, curator of archaeology and director of the Museum of Anthropology at the University of Michigan, sums up the most widely held positions when he reports that the first Americans were peoples from northeast Asia who came to North America in at least three major prehistoric movements between 20,000 and 3,500 years ago. Some evidence even suggests that man appeared in the western part of North America as long ago as 28,000 B.C. "We are certain that the earliest American Indians were in the United States area by between 10,000 to 12,000 B.C.," declares Professor Griffin.

Although the theory of the Hebrew origin of the American Indians was the most prevalent theory at the time of the publication of the *Book of Mormon* and one well known to the Prophet Joseph Smith, the Mormons remain the only scholars to attempt to defend this theory in the twentieth century.

The *Book of Mormon* describes an extensive culture involving millions of people. The book lists thirty-eight specific cities but only one, the Hill Cumorah, has been discovered by archaeologists, and no artifacts which correspond to those described in Smith's book have turned up. The discovery of additional Inca, Aztec and Mayan ruins in South and Central America adds no corroborative proof to the authenticity of the *Book of Mormon*. Speculation about ancient civilizations in the Americas was so common in American literature in the early nineteenth century that any literate person who had not read such discussions would have been the exception instead of the rule in his community.

Smith's biographer, Fawn Brodie, comments on the *Book of Mormon:*

Its structure shows elaborate design, its narrative is spun coherently, and it demonstrates throughout a unity of purpose.

Its matter is drawn directly from the American frontier, from the impassioned revivalist sermons, the popular fallacies about Indian origin, and the current political crusades.[8]

Elsewhere she observes:

His [Smith's] talent, it is true, was not exceptional, for his book lacked subtlety, wit, and style. He was chiefly a tale-teller and preacher. His characters were pale, humorless stereotypes; the prophets were always holy, and in three thousand years of history not a single harlot was made to speak. But he began the book with a first-class murder, added assassinations, and piled up battles by the score. There was plenty of bloodshed and slaughter to make up for the lack of gaiety and the stuff of humanity.[9]

The religious ideal presented in the *Book of Mormon* is that of left-wing, sectarian Protestantism. The theology is Arminian rather than Calvinist and there is a strong emphasis on the belief that man is punished for his own, not Adam's, sins, and that he is saved by his works and not by faith alone.

Ye must stand before the judgment-seat of Christ, to be judged according to your works—Mormon 6:21.

Again and again the Nephites and other people of the *Book* enter the cycle of virtue to prosperity to pride to the fall to repentance and back to virtue.

Almost 50 years ago Walter F. Prince employed psychological tests to prove that the *Book of Mormon* could only have been written between 1826 and 1834. His study was published in the *American Journal of Psychology* and is considered conclusive by Whitney R. Cross,[10] author of *The Burned-over District*.

In general the non-Mormon has ignored the *Book of Mormon*. The judgment of the Reverend Leslie Rumble, M.S.C., is true as far as Gentile scholars are concerned:

There is not a single recognized authority in biblical studies, in history, archaeology, ethnology, philology, or any other field of science who takes the *Book of Mormon* seriously or regards it as having made a worthwhile contribution of any kind to the sum-total of human knowledge. It is simply ignored by reputable scholars, religious and non-religious alike.[11]

The Mormon archaeologist, Dr. Ross T. Christensen, admits that his fellow archaeologists ignore the *Book of Mormon*. In the Newsletter of the University Archaeological Society with headquarters at Brigham Young University he wrote:

With the exception of Latter-day Saint archaeologists, members of the archaeological profession do not, and never have, espoused the *Book of Mormon* in any sense of which I am aware. Non-Mormon archaeologists do not allow the *Book of Mormon* any place whatever in their reconstruction of the early history of the New World.[12]

Scholars seldom refer to it when discussing the great scriptures of mankind: the Bible, the Koran, the Vedas, etc. Many Gentiles have been content to dismiss the book without bothering to read it. Some seem to believe that it is a revision of the Bible. But after all is said and done, its production remains more or less a mystery to all but the devout Mormon. Hundreds of people have given their lives in testimony to its claims. Thousands left their homes in Europe and started a new life in Zion after accepting the authenticity of this volume. University presidents, governors, physicians, professors, senators, businessmen, scientists, accept it as a divine revelation along with the Bible and other writings of Joseph Smith, the Prophet.

Doubters can only conjecture how this remarkable book was written. The available evidence does not permit a flat assertion that it was plagiarized from a manuscript by Spaulding or Ethan Smith or Rigdon. There are too many missing links which will probably never be found. The non-Mormon can, however, examine the contents of the book, especially the contents of the original 1830 edition, and arrive at the conclusion that the *Book of Mormon* was clearly the product of a writer in early nineteenth-century America rather than a collection of ancient records miraculously translated from Reformed Egyptian.

4. *Kirtland, Missouri, and Nauvoo*

IN THE VILLAGE of Kirtland, Joseph Smith completed the organization of his church. Although he retained full control he ordained almost every male convert a priest and thus built a broad base of support. The frontier suspicion of clericalism was allayed by eliminating the distinction between clergy and laity. Campbellism tried to wipe out the distinction by making every believer a layman while Mormonism ordained almost every man a priest.

Smith established the United Order of Enoch which reflected Rigdon's scheme for a Christian communism. Converts were urged to turn over their property to the Church for the common good. The United Order never prospered but led to grumbling and defections. Eventually it would be supplanted by the revelation on tithing.

The appeal of Mormonism at this stage was basically intellectual. The prospective convert was asked to read the *Book of Mormon,* examine Smith's claims to prophethood, and make his decision for or against the restored gospel. However, the religious life of the Kirtland congregation resembled that of a modern Pentecostal sect. The Kirtlanders rolled on the floor during church services, claimed to speak in strange tongues, reported innumerable private revelations, engaged in faith healing. One of Smith's problems would be to control and channel these phenomena lest they destroy his church and turn it into simply another backwoods revivalist movement.

Oliver Cowdery brought back a glowing report from Mis-

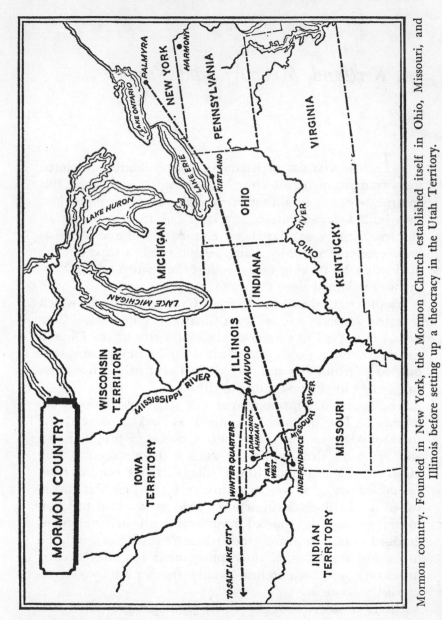

Mormon country. Founded in New York, the Mormon Church established itself in Ohio, Missouri, and Illinois before setting up a theocracy in the Utah Territory.

souri, where he had been attempting to convert the Lamanites. The Prophet made the 800-mile journey to Jackson County and helped establish the Mormon settlement at what is now Independence, Missouri. The infant church now had two centers: Kirtland and Independence. Smith would later reveal that Independence, the site of the original Garden of Eden, would become the central stake of Zion, the New Jerusalem of the millennium.

Back in Kirtland the Prophet turned his literary ability to the Bible itself. In Genesis he inserted a passage about himself: "Thus saith the Lord God of my fathers unto me, A choice seer will I raise up out of the fruit of thy loins, and he shall be esteemed highly among the fruit of thy loins . . . and his name shall be called Joseph, and it shall be after the name of his father. . . ." The Prophet changed a number of other passages but did not complete his revision. It was never published during his lifetime but Emma kept the manuscript and allowed the Reorganized Mormons to publish it in 1867.

The Prophet gained a reputation for healing and wonderworking. On one occasion a Campbellite preacher told Smith he would embrace Mormonism if he were convinced of its truth and would bring his entire congregation of several hundred into the new church. Smith started to expound his doctrines when the preacher interrupted: "Oh, this is not the evidence I want. I want a notable miracle. I want to see some powerful manifestation of the power of God."

"Well," asked the Prophet, "what will you have done? Will you be struck blind or dumb? Will you be paralyzed or will you have one hand withered? Take your choice and in the name of the Lord Jesus Christ it shall be done."

The preacher hastened to explain that he did not want that kind of a miracle.

"Then, sir, I can perform none. I am not going to bring any trouble upon anybody else, sir, to convince you," said Smith with a shrug.

Smith attracted enemies as well as followers in Kirtland. On the night of March 24, 1832, a band of Mormon-baiters captured the Prophet, beat and scratched him, and administered the frontier punishment of tarring and feathering. A doctor in the mob was urged to castrate the victim but refused. Emma and some disciples patiently scraped off the tar and bandaged his wounds so that he was able to mount the pulpit the next morning and deliver his usual Sunday sermon.

One November day in the same year, Smith was chopping wood near his house when he was greeted by an enthusiastic convert from his home state of Vermont. The convert, Brigham Young, would one day rally the dispirited Saints in Nauvoo and lead them to an intermountain sanctuary. The pair talked and prayed on the day of their first meeting and that evening Young attended a prayer meeting. Caught up in the excitement of the occasion Young began to babble strange sounds which the Prophet pronounced to be "the true Adamic language." This was the tongue spoken by Adam and Eve.

Brigham Young never publicly doubted the claims of Smith. On one occasion he would declare, "If he acts like a devil, he has brought forth a doctrine that will save us, if we abide by it. He may get drunk every day of his life, sleep with his neighbor's wife every night, run horses and gamble ... But the doctrine he has produced will save you and me and the whole world."

Through revelation Smith received instruction on the dimensions of a temple for his church. The fund-raising campaign was launched in 1833. A magnificent temple would distinguish his church from the dozens of sects competing for members.

Meanwhile, in the other Mormon settlement the Gentiles and the Saints began a feud which would lead to the expulsion of the latter. For one thing, Mormon claims that Zion would be established in and near Independence convinced many of the original settlers that they would soon be outnumbered and dispossessed by the Mormons. Furthermore, the fact that the Mormons did not own slaves antagonized the slaveholding Missourians. Mormon farms and villages were attacked. Through trickery the Saints were induced to surrender their weapons and thus were left helpless before the marauders.

To relieve the beleaguered Saints, Smith recruited a small army and marched to Missouri. He had hoped to enlist at least 500 volunteers in the force but settled for 130 after two months. The army was known as "Zion's Camp" and was led by a Saint carrying a banner on which was written the single word PEACE. The first contingent left Kirtland on May 1, 1834.

En route the members of Zion's Camp unearthed an Indian skeleton in a burial mound. Smith told the others: "This man in mortal life was a white Lamanite, a large, thickset man, and a man of God. His name was Zelph. He was a warrior and chieftain under the great prophet Onandagus, who was known from the eastern sea to the Rocky Mountains. The curse of the red skin was taken from him, or at least in part." The Prophet then described the battle in which Zelph was slain.

As the band neared its destination it became apparent that this military action only further infuriated the Gentile persecutors. The entry of Zion's Camp into the area would probably precipitate the massacre of the Missouri Saints. Smith realized the seriousness of the situation, thought over the consequences, saw some of his men come down with cholera, and decided to head back to Ohio.

Joseph installed many members of his family in high church positions. His father became patriarch, his older brother Hyrum was made second president, and another brother, Don Carlos, served as president of the high priests. Many of the Kirtland Saints grew angry when Joseph appointed his hot-tempered and unpopular brother William to be an apostle. William resigned the office but Joseph forced the Church hierarchy to take him back. The Smith brothers got into a fistfight when William branded Joseph a false prophet. He again resigned his apostleship but stayed in the Church to plague his brother to his dying day.

The abortive attempt to rescue the Missouri Saints was followed by three years of relative peace in Kirtland. The Prophet had revealed the Word of Wisdom in 1833, which was understood to forbid liquor, tobacco, tea and coffee. This was probably done at the suggestion of Rigdon, a temperance fanatic. Ceremonies of foot washing and anointing with oil were introduced into the Mormon ritual.

A traveling showman, Michael Chandler, toured the area with four Egyptian mummies and some papyri. He stopped at Kirtland in 1835 and allowed the Prophet to try his hand at translating the hieroglyphics. Smith examined the papyri and declared that one specimen contained the writing of Abraham and another was that of Joseph in Egypt. The attempted translation resembled the first two chapters of Genesis but established a doctrinal concept of God at variance with the monotheism of the *Book of Mormon*. Instead of reporting that God created the earth, the new translation revealed "The Gods organized the earth." Not one God but many gods, not creation but the organization of matter, were declared to be Mormon doctrine.

The Book of Abraham also revealed the spiritual inferiority of the Negroes which made them ineligible to receive ordination as Mormon priests. Fawn Brodie comments:

From the standpoint of the church which survived him, the Book of Abraham was the most unfortunate thing Joseph ever wrote. By outliving the Civil War, which forever banished slavery as an issue between Mormon and Gentile, its racial doctrine preserved the discrimination that is the ugliest thesis in existing Mormon theology.[1]

The papyri were purchased from Chandler by the Church and displayed at Kirtland and Nauvoo. Eventually the relics were burned in the Chicago fire, but three facsimiles were preserved which were published in 1842 with Smith's interpretations. Egyptologists have declared them to be garden variety funeral documents which have since been discovered in thousands of tombs and graves.

In the summer of 1836, Smith reverted to his earlier pastime of treasure hunting. He had heard that a large sum of money was buried in Salem, Massachusetts. He and some companions spent a month in Salem looking for the cache and preaching the gospel but gave up after the search proved fruitless. This trip provided the basis for Section III in *Doctrine and Covenants*. In part this section reads:

I, the Lord your God, am not displeased with your coming this journey, notwithstanding your follies.

I have much treasure in this city for you, for the benefit of Zion, and many people in this city, whom I will gather out in due time for the benefit of Zion, through your instrumentality.

And it shall come to pass in due time that I will give this city into your hands, that you shall have power over it, insomuch that they shall not discover your secret parts; and its wealth pertaining to gold and silver shall be yours.

Concern not yourselves about your debts, for I will give you power to pay them.

For there are more treasures than one for you in this city.

Many of Smith's revelations had been collected in a volume called the *Book of Commandments*. This was published at Independence in 1833 but most of the copies were destroyed when a mob destroyed the Mormon press. A revised edition appeared in August 1835 and was called the *Book of Doctrine and Covenants*. The present Utah edition includes 135 revelations given to Smith and a single revelation recorded by Brigham Young at Winter Quarters in 1847.

When Smith decided to dissolve the United Order in Kirtland he disguised the names of those receiving property. Thus

Sidney Rigdon became Pelagoram, Martin Harris was Mahemson, Smith himself became Gazelam, Oliver Cowdery was Olihah. Kirtland itself was called the City of Shinehah while New York was identified as Cainhannoch. The average Saint believed these to be biblical names when he read them in Section 104, *Doctrine and Covenants.*

The mounting debts which induced Smith to hunt for buried treasure in Salem remained unpaid. The Ohio legislature refused to allow the incorporation of a bank by Smith but the bank notes had already been engraved KIRTLAND SAFETY SOCIETY BANK. Smith simply imprinted the notes to read KIRTLAND SAFETY SOCIETY ANTI-BANKING COMPANY.

The Church paid off its debts with worthless bank notes issued by this wildcat bank. The bank collapsed and many depositors lost their life savings. Creditors descended on the city and hitherto loyal followers began to apostatize. Smith and Rigdon decided the best course would be to flee the city. They left by horseback in the middle of the night. Dissenters mounted the pulpit of the Kirtland temple and denounced the man they had once revered as a Prophet of God.

The pair headed for Missouri and were welcomed by 1,500 Saints in the Mormon city of Far West. After expulsion from Jackson and Clay counties the Mormons had received permission to organize Caldwell County with Far West as the main settlement. The 600 Saints who remained loyal to the Prophet in Kirtland left Ohio and joined their coreligionists in Far West, where they attempted to build a model city on a cooperative basis. The Saints founded another settlement which Smith called Adam-ondi-Ahman. This was described as the spot to which Adam retired after his expulsion from paradise.

Rumors began to circulate in the area about a secret society of Mormons variously called the Brothers of Gideon, the Daughters of Zion, Sons of Dan or simply the Danites. The Danites were said to have sworn complete loyalty to the Prophet. They protected Mormon settlers from attack and liquidated troublesome apostates and critics of the Church.

Peace between the Saints in Far West and the Missourians did not last long. The Missourians began to raid Mormon farms and harass the Saints. The Mormons retreated to their stronghold at Far West and built fortifications and forged swords.

In the most famous incident in the Mormon-Missouri clash about 200 Missourians descended on the isolated settlement at Haun's Mill. The Mormon men retreated into the blacksmith shop but the attackers shot through the cracks in the log walls and killed 17 Mormons, including two boys. The women and children ran into the woods when the shooting began. They returned after the massacre and lowered the dead bodies into a well and made their way to Far West, fifteen miles away.

The odds were heavily against the Saints in Far West and Adam-ondi-Ahman. Smith finally surrendered and saw 6,000 enraged Missourians pour into the city to rape the women, shoot the cattle and hogs, murder many of the leading elders of the Church. Joseph was taken prisoner and sent to the Liberty jail in Clay County while the Saints prepared to leave the state. Four months would pass before Smith was brought to trial and then his lawyer obtained a change of venue. The Prophet managed to bribe the sheriff holding him prisoner and escaped to rejoin his followers, who had been straggling across the state line into Illinois.

In a swampland on the Mississippi River the Saints tried for the third time to build Zion. They called their city Nauvoo which, Smith explained, was a Hebrew word meaning "beautiful plantation." With typical Mormon industry they drained swamps, laid out a model city with wide streets, built 250 houses during the first year, and dedicated the cornerstone for a new temple.

Missionaries in England directed converts to Nauvoo in increasing numbers. The population of the city would reach

20,000, which made it the largest city in the state at a time
when Chicago counted only 5,000 inhabitants. Smith continued to receive revelations including one which commanded the Saints to build a boardinghouse to be known
as Nauvoo House. Even the details of the stock arrangements
were not beneath the Lord's notice:

And they shall not receive less than fifty dollars for a share of
stock in that house, and they shall be permitted to receive fifteen
thousand dollars from any one man for stock in that house.

But they shall not be permitted to receive over fifteen thousand
dollars stock from any one man.

And they shall not be permitted to receive under fifty dollars
for a share of stock from any one man in that house.

Section 124, *Doctrine and Covenants* continues to elaborate the financial arrangements for the hotel.

One of the converts baptized by the Prophet was Dr. John
C. Bennett, an abortionist and opportunist who had become
quartermaster general of the Illinois militia. He had deserted
a wife and two children and pretended to accept Mormonism
in order to share in the prosperity of the booming city. He
fooled not only the Prophet but the Lord, for in Section 124,
Articles 16 and 17, *Doctrine and Covenants,* we read:

Again, let my servant John C. Bennett help you in your labor
in sending my word to the kings and people of the earth, and
stand by you, even you my servant Joseph Smith, in the hour of
affliction; and his reward shall not fail if he receive counsel.

And for his love he shall be great, for he shall be mine if he do
this, saith the Lord. I have seen the work which he hath done,
which I accept if he continue, and will crown him with blessings
and great glory.

The *LDS Reference Encyclopedia* calls Bennett an "un-
principled man" and a "moral leper." Like the organization
of Zion's Camp and the failure of the wildcat bank in Kirtland,

the Prophet's reliance on Dr. Bennett would be remembered as a major error.

Through Bennett's help the city of Nauvoo won an unusually liberal charter from the State of Illinois, which gave it almost the status of an independent city-state. Bennett became mayor and chancellor of the University of Nauvoo. He displaced Rigdon as second in command. The Prophet believed that Rigdon's inflammatory speeches in Missouri had contributed to the troubles in that state. Cowdery, John and David Whitmer had been excommunicated from the Church for alleged counterfeiting and misbehavior in Missouri.

Joseph Smith, Jr. headed a private army, the Nauvoo Legion. He received a commission as lieutenant general and both he and his followers regularly used the title "General." General Smith wore a blue uniform he had designed himself with gold braid, buff trousers, military boots and spurs, and a hat with ostrich feathers. He carried a sword and two pistols. The general rode a stallion called Charlie and frequently inspected his army. The Legion enrolled all able-bodied Saints between eighteen and forty-five and was supposed to forestall the attacks which drove the Saints out of Missouri.

Smith wrote his autobiography in 1842. He joined the Masonic Lodge and devised the secret temple rites which were obviously patterned after Masonic initiations. The Church of Jesus Christ of Latter-day Saints turned into a mystery religion. Brodie writes:

The secrecy, pageantry, and veiled phallicism appealed to very basic human instincts, and the fact that they seemed to be rooted in Old Testament tradition gave them an authenticity demanded by this Bible-reading people.[2]

Smith took the opportunity to enlighten the world on the origin of the word Mormon. In his newspaper *Times and Seasons,* he explained:

It has been stated that this word was derived from the Greek word *mormo*. This is not the case. There was no Greek or Latin upon the plates from which I, through the grace of God, translated the Book of Mormon. . . . We say from the Saxon, *good;* the Dane, *god;* the Goth, *goda;* the German, *gut;* the Dutch, *goed;* the Latin, *bonus;* the Greek, *kalos;* the Hebrew, *tob;* and the Egyptian *mon.* Hence, with the addition of *more,* or the contraction *mor,* we have the word Mormon; which means, literally, *more good.*[3]

Gentile visitors to Nauvoo were invited to see the exhibits in the museum. Two such gentlemen were given a personal tour by the general. At the museum he told them: "This is my mother, gentlemen. The curiosities we shall see belong to her. They were purchased with her own money at a cost of six thousand dollars." The visitors were expected to make a contribution to Mrs. Smith, the curator. He showed them four mummies and declared: "I want you to look at that little runt of a fellow over there. He was a great man in his day. Why, that was Pharaoh Necho, King of Egypt!" Some papyri were identified as the handwriting of Abraham, the autograph of Moses, and the writing of his brother Aaron.

The general's friendship with Dr. Bennett lasted for about a year and a half. Bennett was formally excommunicated on June 23, 1842. He then wrote a series of articles exposing the immoralities of Nauvoo. He presented titillating and fanciful stories about systematic prostitution in the city and outlined horrible crimes committed by the Danites. His generally unreliable observations were collected in a book entitled *The History of the Saints; or, An Exposé of Joe Smith and Mormonism.* The wily doctor insisted that he had joined the Mormons only to expose their nefarious carryings-on to the country. His charge that polygamy was being practiced in Nauvoo was indignantly denied by the Saints but it was one charge which history proved to be true.

Joseph Smith apparently toyed with the idea of introducing

polygamy into the Church as far back as his Kirtland days. Fawn Brodie indicates that the number of wives taken by the Prophet might have exceeded 50; the Utah Mormon church generally accepts 27 as the number of Smith's wives. In Mrs. Brodie's tabulation the wives range from fifteen to fifty-nine years of age and include five pairs of sisters and a mother and daughter set.

To the rank and file Saint, the charge of polygamy was vicious and ridiculous. It had been refuted by the Prophet and by Church publications for many years. They concluded it was Bennett's way of covering up his own seductions or else an abominable aberration he had tried to introduce into the Church. The Church hierarchy knew the truth of Bennett's charges and the Gentiles accepted the testimony of the former Nauvoo mayor and confidant of the Prophet.

Buoyed by his increasing influence in Illinois politics, Smith announced his candidacy for President of the United States with Rigdon as Vice-Presidential candidate. Mormon missionaries around the country became campaign workers. Smith drew up a political platform which advocated the purchase and freeing of slaves, prison reform, free trade, etc.

Many of the people of Illinois had welcomed the Mormons who had been driven from their homes in Missouri as they might any refugees. But the charges of Bennett, rumors of polygamy, growing fear of Mormon political power, and a common belief that the Mormons engaged in thievery stirred the Gentiles to opposition. A trusted Mormon elder, William Law, broke with the Prophet on the issue of polygamy and he and others remained in Nauvoo and began publication of a rival newspaper, the *Nauvoo Expositor*. Only one issue appeared, dated June 7, 1844. The paper confirmed the charges of polygamy and called for reform in the Church.

Smith believed he had to act against his critics. He could belittle the wild charges of Gentiles and disgruntled Saints outside of Nauvoo but he could not tolerate subversion within the holy city. He declared the paper to be a public nuisance and ordered his henchmen to destroy the press and pi the type.

This action touched off a new wave of anti-Mormonism in the area. Mobs formed in nearby Warsaw and Carthage with the avowed purpose of invading Nauvoo. In his last public appearance (June 18, 1844), General Smith told the assembled Saints:

"We have turned the barren, bleak prairies and swamps of this state into beautiful towns, farms and cities. . . . I call God, angels, and all men to witness that we are innocent of the charges. . . . All mob-men, priests, thieves, and bogus makers, apostates and adulterers, who combine to destroy this people, now raise the hue and cry throughout the state that we resist the law, in order to raise a pretext for calling together thousands more of infuriated mob-men to murder, destroy, plunder and ravish the innocent."

"Will you all stand by me to the death, and sustain at the peril of your lives, the laws of our country, and the liberties and privileges which our fathers have transmitted unto us, sealed with their sacred blood?"

"It is well. If you had not done so, I would have gone out there [pointing west] and raised up a mightier people."

"I call God and angels to witness that I have unsheathed my sword with a firm and unalterable determination that this people shall have their legal rights . . . or my blood shall be spilt upon the ground like water, and my body consigned to the silent tomb. . . . I would welcome death rather than submit to this oppression; and it would be sweet, oh sweet, to rest in the grave rather than to submit."

Governor Ford sent Smith a letter in which he said, "Your conduct in the destruction of the press was a very gross outrage upon the laws and liberties of the people. . . . I require any and all of you, who are or shall be accused, to submit yourselves to be arrested. . . ." To escape capture, Joseph and

Hyrum crossed the Mississippi in a small boat. The Prophet toyed with the idea of fleeing to the Rocky Mountains but word reached him that he was being branded a coward for deserting his people. He was sure he would be killed if he fell into the hands of his enemies but he told a friend, "If my life is of no value to my friends it is of none to myself." The pair returned to Nauvoo.

Joseph Smith hated to leave his wife and children, his followers, the city they had built. He sighed, "This is the loveliest place and the best people under the heavens. Little do they know the trials that await them."

They were promised safe conduct and protection in Carthage where they would be tried, but they knew it was a center of anti-Mormon agitation. On the way to Carthage the Prophet declared: "I am going like a lamb to the slaughter; but I am as calm as a summer morning. I have a conscience void of offense toward God and toward all men. I shall die innocent and it shall be said of me, 'He was murdered in cold blood.'"

In Carthage the brothers were charged with treason against the state for calling out the Nauvoo Legion. They were paraded like freaks before the townspeople whose hostility was all too clear.

The brothers, along with John Taylor and Willard Richards, were imprisoned on the second floor of the Carthage jail. After the governor left the city, a mob of men with blackened faces stormed the jail. The prisoners tried to hold off the attackers with smuggled pistols; Joseph fired six times and hit several of the assassins, but a bullet hit Hyrum in the face and he fell dead. Joseph tried to reach the window but a volley of shots ended his life and he fell into the courtyard below. Taylor was hit but slid under a bed in the cell while Richards hid behind a door. The date was June 27, 1844.

The mob scattered after the murders, as rumors circulated that the Mormons were on their way from Nauvoo to rescue the Prophet and his companions. Richards ventured out of the jail and dragged the Prophet's body back to the jail, laying it next to Hyrum's.

In his short life Joseph Smith, Jr. had written a book which thousands and eventually millions accepted as the word of God. His book and his doctrines inspired dozens of men and women to give their lives for his restored gospel. His message had induced thousands to leave their homes in England and Scandinavia to gather in Zion of the New World.

He had worn the rough clothes of a farm boy, the resplendent uniform of a general, the white temple garments of the endowment rites, the apron of Masonry. He once remarked: "Whenever I see a pretty woman I have to pray for grace"; and had introduced polygamy into a society dominated by Puritanism and dedicated to the ideal of monogamy.

Many would reject his claims and scoff at his pretensions, but few can review the final days of Joseph Smith without agreeing that these were his finest hours. The prophecies he uttered in his last days were soon fulfilled. Now his pen and voice were stilled. The grief-stricken Saints wondered what the morrow would bring. Would beautiful Nauvoo turn into a Haun's Mill on a gigantic scale? And who would lead them now that the Prophet of the Lord was slain?

5. *Brigham Young and His Successors*

Brigham young was seeking converts in Boston when the Prophet was shot to death in the Carthage jail. Along with most of the apostles and church authorities he had been stumping the country for votes for candidate Smith as well as for souls. It was two weeks before he heard the news of the murder.

In the meantime the bodies of Joseph and Hyrum were brought back to a mourning Nauvoo. After the funeral the bodies were first interred in the basement of Nauvoo House and then reburied in a secret grave to prevent desecration.

Young hurried back to the city of the Saints but Sidney Rigdon got there first. Rigdon had had a falling-out with the Prophet and had moved back to Pittsburgh. Now he appeared again in Nauvoo and tried to win the allegiance of the leaderless Saints. He called for a conference on August 6 but it was postponed for a few days. The fate of the Mormon people was shaped by that postponement, because Brigham Young reached the city on the evening of the 6th and was able to frustrate Rigdon's plans.

At the outdoor assembly next to the unfinished temple Rigdon presented his credentials to succeed Smith as head of the Church and claimed the authority by divine revelation. He had talked for more than an hour and a half when Young arose and asked to speak. Some witnesses said that Brigham Young seemed to take on the appearance of the dead Prophet and his words seemed to be the words of Joseph Smith. He chided the people for unseemly haste in looking for a new president. Rather they should have been in mourning for their slain Prophet. He pleaded with them to place their confidence in the Council of the Twelve Apostles. By this stratagem he pitted the newly arrived Rigdon against the twelve apostles appointed by Smith. A vote showed overwhelming support for Young. The apostles finally excommunicated Sidney Rigdon, who returned to the East and obscurity. As president of the Council, Brigham Young assumed charge of the Church; three years later he would be sustained as Prophet, Seer, and Revelator.

Like Smith, Brigham Young was born in Vermont. The date was June 1, 1801. His father had served as a soldier under General Washington in the Revolutionary War. When he was only fourteen his mother died. Years later Young would describe the stern discipline of his youth: "It was a word and a blow with my father, but the blow came first."

Brigham became an apprentice carpenter and painter and by the time he was sixteen he was earning his living at these trades. His formal schooling was limited to 11 days, but his mother had taught him how to read and write before she died.

He sampled the theological wares of many churches before joining the Methodists at the age of twenty-two. The next year he married Miriam Works, who bore him two daughters; she became an invalid. Young obtained a copy of the new *Book of Mormon* a few weeks after its publication but mulled over the doctrines and remarkable claims of the new church before asking for baptism on April 15, 1832. Not long after his baptism his wife died.

Young went to Kirtland and began to work as a carpenter on the temple as well as a number of homes in the village. To further his sketchy education he attended classes at the School of the Prophets which Smith had established. He married again and this time the bride was a convert from New England who had also come to Kirtland: Mary Ann Angell. Like every committed Mormon he served as a missionary, fulfilling assignments in Canada and the eastern states. When Smith appointed the original band of twelve apostles, Brigham Young was among them and he also was chosen to accompany the Prophet in the abortive effort to rescue the Missouri Saints.

Young left Kirtland on December 22, 1837, and later wrote that he left

... in consequence of the fury of the mob and the spirit that prevailed in the apostates, who had threatened to destroy me because I would proclaim, publicly and privately, that I knew, by the power of the Holy Ghost, that Joseph Smith was a Prophet of the Most High God, and had not transgressed and fallen as apostates declared.

When the authorities arrested the leading Mormons in Missouri, Young was the only high-ranking official to escape capture. The president of the Twelve, Thomas B. Marsh, left the Church, and the second in line died—leaving Brigham Young the ranking member of the Council. Governor Boggs of Missouri declared that "the Mormons must be treated as enemies and must be exterminated or driven from the State," and it was Young who directed the exodus of the Saints to neighboring Illinois.

Once his own family was settled in Nauvoo, Young left for another mission in England. He sailed for Liverpool on March 7, 1840. He spent a little over a year in England and supervised the baptism of between 8,000 and 9,000 converts.

By the time he returned to the United States he saw that the same antagonisms which had aroused the Gentiles in Ohio and Missouri had followed the Saints to Nauvoo. And now the Prophet had secretly introduced the principle of celestial marriage, which was sure to provide ammunition to the Mormon-baiters. Young accepted the new doctrine and married eight women in Nauvoo.

Now that the Prophet was dead, Gentile harassment of the city intensified. Raids on Mormon farms in the vicinity and attacks on Mormons themselves were common. The Saints took defensive measures. Strangers who visited the Mormon city were subjected to the subtle intimidation of the whittling deacons. Shortly after their arrival, the visitors would discover that wherever they went in the city they were followed by a silent knot of young men whittling on sticks with bowie knives. Most visitors took the hint.

On August 6, 1842, the Prophet had predicted "that the Saints would continue to suffer much affliction and would be driven to the Rocky Mountains. Many would apostatize; others would be put to death or lose their lives in consequence of exposure and disease. Some would live to go and assist in making settlements and building cities and see the Saints become a mighty people in the midst of the Rocky Mountains."

Brigham Young realized that once more the Saints would have to leave their lands and homes. He agreed to evacuate the city by the spring of 1846. Plans were made for the trek West, and almost every house and shop was converted into a workshop to build wagons. Although they knew their days in Nauvoo were numbered, the Saints rushed to complete their temple. By October 1845, it was almost finished and during the next two months 1,000 people received their endowments. Teams of Mormon priests labored day and night to initiate the brothers and sisters in the esoteric rites of the Church.

Young and 2,000 others crossed the frozen Mississippi River in February 1846 and camped on the Iowa side. The rest of the inhabitants followed although the final thousand were attacked by Gentile mobs. Nauvoo, the beautiful city, was all but deserted. In his last official entry in the Nauvoo record, Young wrote:

Our homes, gardens, orchards, farms, streets, bridges, mills, public halls, magnificent temple and other public improvements, we leave as a monument of our patriotism, industry, economy, uprightness of purpose and integrity of heart, and as a living testimony of the falsehood and wickedness of those who charge us with idleness, dishonesty, disloyalty to the Constitution of our country.

Although Smith had talked about resettling in the Rocky Mountains, no definite site had been selected. When the Mormons left Nauvoo they believed they were leaving the United States, since the area toward which they were heading was claimed by Mexico. Nine months after they reached their destination this area became a possession of the United States by means of the treaty of Guadalupe Hidalgo.

The temperature at the Sugar Creek camp in Iowa reached 20 below zero on February 15, 1846, but nine babies were delivered in the camp. To keep up their spirits the dispossessed Saints prayed and sang and danced to the tunes of Captain William Pitt's brass band. Captain Pitt and his entire ensemble had joined the Church in England and emigrated to Nauvoo.

During the summer of '46, between 12,000 and 15,000 Mormons made camp at Winter Quarters near what is now Omaha, Nebraska. They built a thousand log cabins and prepared to spend the winter there and continue their journey in the spring.

While at Winter Quarters, Young received a request from President Polk for 500 Mormon men to serve in the war against Mexico. The Saints were astounded: the Government, which had refused them aid in their plight in Missouri and Illinois, now asked for their help in war. But although the loss of 500 able-bodied Saints would be a hardship, it was also seen as a blessing. Young realized that by enlisting in the army the men could get free passage to the West and could send home their salaries which their families could use to buy food and supplies. The Government provided an enlistment allowance of $48 a man, which came to a welcome $21,000. Young consented to the request and the volunteers of the Mormon battalion marched off on the 2,000-mile hike to San Diego. Their job was not to fight the Mexicans but to guard California. Most of the men in the battalion would later rejoin their families in Utah, but a few stayed on and were numbered among the first to discover gold in California.

Finally the snows melted and spring came. Brigham Young left Winter Quarters on April 7, 1847, with an advance party of 143 men, 3 women and 2 children. Father DeSmet, the French missionary and explorer, had met the Mormon Moses in Winter Quarters and described the Great Salt Lake Valley.

As usual Young insisted that strict discipline in the wagon-train be continued. On July 24, 1847, the wagon in which he was riding came into view of the valley. "This is the right place. Drive on," Young told his companions.

The valley as the Mormon pioneers saw it was bleak and desolate. It was treeless and the soil was sandy and dry. But two hours after reaching the valley the Mormons had begun to plow the land and plant seeds. They discovered the mountain streams which would provide water for a vast irrigation system. In a few days Brigham Young laid out the contours of a model city and determined the site for the new temple.

After spending barely a month in the valley Young and a small party returned to Winter Quarters, 1,000 miles away, to guide other settlers who had been awaiting his orders. On December 27, 1847, Brigham Young was sustained as president of the Church and the next month delivered his one and only published revelation, which appears as Section 136 in the Utah *Doctrine and Covenants*. He organized a second party of 2,400 Saints which left at the end of May, 1848.

The settlers were appalled the next summer when clouds of crickets swarmed into the valley and began to devour all the crops and vegetation. The Saints fought the insects with fire, brooms and prayers. They had almost despaired of saving anything when flocks of sea gulls descended and started to gorge themselves on the crickets. The birds ate all they could, disgorged themselves, and went back to the feast. To the Mormons the timely arrival of the sea gulls was nothing short of a miracle; they erected a monument to the bird which stands in Salt Lake City.

Other parties completed the hazardous journey from Winter Quarters to the new Zion. Converts from England and Scandinavia, especially Denmark, helped swell the population of the area. President Young inaugurated the Perpetual Emigration Fund which paid for the passage of foreign converts. Once in Zion, the converts were expected to pay back what they had drawn from the fund.

In colonizing the area, the Mormons adopted the farm-village pattern of land settlement instead of the more familiar isolated farm pattern. The Saints lived in small villages separated from their farmland as in many European cultures. This living arrangement helped solidify religious, social and political ties.

The California gold rush proved to be a bonanza for the Saints. Thousands of 49ers left equipment and goods in Salt Lake City as they made their way to the gold fields and what they thought would be their fortunes. Traders laden with merchandise for the gold fields unloaded at bargain prices when they found out they had been beaten by their competitors, who reached California by ship. Young continually warned his people against the lure of gold and against fraternizing with the Gentiles passing through Zion. He wanted to build his society on a basis of agriculture, not mining.

The Mormons petitioned Congress to recognize the State of Deseret. "Deseret" was a name which appears in the *Book of Mormon* and was said to mean "honey bee." The boundaries of the proposed state extended from Mexico to the Snake River; San Diego was designated as its gateway to the sea. Congress had a different idea, however, and the area which finally became the territory of Utah was limited to what is now Utah and Nevada. Instead of adopting the Mormon name "Deseret," Congress called the territory Utah after the Ute Indians. Young became the first territorial governor. The population would grow from 11,354 in 1850 to more than 120,000 in 1880.

Not all of President Young's ideas worked out. In an economy drive Young proposed that emigrants forego expensive wagons and oxen and instead pull handcarts from the end of the railroad line in Iowa City to Salt Lake City, a distance of about 1,300 miles. The handcarts could carry a minimum of food and essential items. Some of the handcart expeditions made the trip successfully but the last two to leave ran into snow and freezing weather in 1855. One company of 500 counted 77 dead of freezing, disease and starvation, and another company of 575 lost 140 men and women.

Young wielded almost absolute power as president of the Church, territorial governor, and superintendent of Indian Affairs. He preached thrift, industry, and isolation from the Gentiles. With only modest success he tried to preserve Utah for the Latter-day Saints. In a sermon on March 28, 1858 he lashed out at Gentile merchants:

"Let the calicoes lie on the shelves and rot. I would rather build buildings every day and burn them down at night, than have traders here communing with our enemies outside, and keeping up a hell all the time, and raising devils to keep it going. They brought their hell with them. We can have enough of our own without their help."

The Church organized a spy system to see which Mormons were trading with Protestant, Catholic, Jewish and apostate merchants. The four Walker brothers were converted to the Church in England but lost their enthusiasm when they reached Zion. They set up a department store which was boycotted by loyal Mormons for many years. In 1868 President Young asked all Latter-day Saints to put the motto HOLINESS TO THE LORD and the all-seeing eye symbol over their shops to distinguish them from the Gentiles.

Brigham Young could never understand the demands of

his wives and other Mormon ladies for fashionable clothes. During the 1850's he designed a simple "Deseret Costume" with bloomers, full skirt, cape and sunbonnet, but the costume never received popular acceptance. A sermon he delivered in September 1861 reveals his attitude toward fashion as well as his earthy vocabulary:

"The women say, let us wear hoops, because the whores wear them. I believe if they were to come with a cob stuck in their behind, you would want to do the same. I despise their damnable fashions, their lying and whoring; and God being my helper, I'll live to see every one of those cussed fools off the earth, saint or sinner.... Who cares about these infernal Gentiles? If they were to wear a piss pot on their head, must I do so? I know, I ought to be ashamed, but when you show your t'other end I have a right to talk about t'other end.... There are those fornication pantaloons, made on purpose for whores to button up in front. My pantaloons button up here where they belong, that my secrets, that God has given me, should not be exposed."
(*Mormon Expositor*, Vol. 1, No. 1)

The men did not escape his anathemas. He thundered against the new "fornication pants" which buttoned up the front:

"The Church is against these pants ... they're an invention of the devil. They make things too easy; it's a temptation, and takes your mind off your work. I heard of a case in San Francisco where a man's hardly had his buttoned up since he got them. If I can help it, the Latter-day Saints of the Church of Jesus Christ will wear pants that open on the sides; they're plenty good enough, and speedy enough, for us in Salt Lake City. And I hope the women don't encourage things to the contrary."

Language serves as an effective social barrier, which may be why the Mormons experimented with the Deseret Alphabet, a semiphonetic method of writing English. It used 38 symbols. The Utah legislature appropriated $2,500 to prepare the type font in 1855, but the new system never gained acceptance. A school primer was printed in the Deseret Alphabet and then the entire *Book of Mormon,* but the movement died out after Young's death.

After 1852 the Church openly taught the doctrine of celestial marriage or polygamy. We will discuss this aspect of Mormonism at greater length in Chapter 8. Not all the Saints approved of polygamy; a number of the converts from England left the Church when they reached Zion and saw that what was vehemently denied by the missionaries who baptized them was wholeheartedly accepted in Utah.

Tom Thumb, the famous midget from Barnum's circus, once visited Salt Lake City and confessed to Brigham Young that he did not understand the principles of polygamy. Brigham roared with laughter and told Tom not to worry because when he was his size he did not understand it either.

One revolt was led by Gladden Bishop, who could hardly be called a model Mormon since he had been excommunicated and received back into the Church thirteen times. He denounced polygamy and the Church hierarchy and gathered a few followers who were known as Gladdenites. Their meetings were broken up by other Latter-day Saints, and Brigham Young called the schismatic Bishop "a poor, dirty curse." Most of the Gladdenites went on to California, or repented and rejoined the Church.

The blackest mark against the Mormon Church was the Mountain Meadows Massacre although Young was probably innocent of the crime. In the fall of 1857 a wagon train of 136 men, women and children on their way from Arkansas to California passed through Utah. Rumors circulated among the Saints that the expedition included members of the mob which had stormed the Carthage jail. Mormons refused any assistance to the travelers.

On September 3, 1857, the party reached the grassy area known as Mountain Meadows and was attacked by Indians and white men dressed like Indians. After four days of fighting, the emigrants were approached by John D. Lee, the adopted son of Brigham Young, an Indian agent and Mormon bishop. Lee offered the besieged party protection if they would surrender their arms. The Arkansas travelers believed his word and gave up their weapons. They formed a column with a Mormon assigned to each Gentile. At a signal each Mormon turned and shot his counterpart. Other Mormons fired into the wagons carrying the wounded and children. One of Lee's lieutenants exclaimed as he shot the defenseless victims: "O Lord, my God, receive their spirits. It is for Thy kingdom that I do this."

The Mormons spared only 17 small children. After breakfast they returned to the scene of the carnage and discovered that the Indians had scalped the dead and bashed in their skulls.

Before the massacre other Mormons had asked President Young what attitude they should take toward the emigrants and he had told them to let them pass through unmolested. His instructions came too late. If he had anything to do with the massacre it was indirect, in that he had continually preached vengeance against those who had persecuted the Saints in Missouri and slain the Prophet in Carthage. This theme combined with the speculations on blood atonement apparently led the culprits to believe they were serving God by killing the travelers.

Lee wrote that he informed Young in person of the affair and Young wept when he heard the details. He commanded Lee to keep it secret and the other participants were sworn to secrecy. As superintendent of Indian Affairs for the territory, Young sent a false report to Washington on January 6, 1858, pinning the entire blame on the Indians.

Young and Lee remained friends for many years but suddenly, about 17 years after the crime, Lee was excommunicated from the Church. President Young stipulated that "under no circumstances should he ever be admitted as a member again." Shortly afterwards Lee was arrested and tried for murder. Young informed Lee's wives that they could feel free to leave him since he no longer belonged to the Church; eleven Mrs. Lees left him. John D. Lee was sentenced to be shot at the scene of the massacre.

As Brigham Young betrayed Lee, so Lee turned on Young and penned an exposé entitled *Mormonism Unveiled* while in prison awaiting execution. It was published many years later. The jail was closely guarded since there were reports that Lee's 64 children might try to storm the jail and rescue their father.

Lee did not escape his sentence. He sat on his own coffin and chatted with the executioners and onlookers. The ex-Mormon bishop professed his belief in Joseph Smith but denounced Young. He was blindfolded and asked the guards to aim for his heart. (On April 20, 1961, the First Presidency of the Church authorized that Lee be reinstated to "member-ship and former blessings." The proper ordinances were per-formed in the Salt Lake City temple on May 8 and 9.) [1]

Part of the antagonism of the Mormons toward the Gentiles at this time was attributed to the so-called Mormon War. Reports were received in Washington that the Mormons planned to secede from the Union, were disloyal, refused to provide justice for Gentiles as well as Mormons.

Some of these impressions were reinforced by unwise com-ments by Mormon leaders. At a Pioneer Day celebration Daniel H. Wells told the Saints that "the United States were a stink in our nostrils." After the death of Zachary Taylor in 1850, Young snorted: "Zachary Taylor is dead and gone to hell and I am glad of it! I prophesy, in the name of Jesus Christ, and by the power of the priesthood that is upon me, that any other President of the United States who shall lift his finger against this people, will die an untimely death, and go to hell."

When James Buchanan entered the White House he decided to send an expedition against the Mormons to quell any rebellion. He said: "This is the first rebellion which has existed in our Territories, and humanity itself requires that we should put it down in such a manner that it shall be the last."

Buchanan sent 2,500 troops to Utah along with a new governor to take Young's job, and new judges. As they neared Zion, Young announced a scorched-earth policy. More than 30,000 Mormons left for the southern part of Utah. Brigham Young warned that he would burn every house, workshop and public building in Salt Lake City if the army entered the city.

After lengthy negotiations Young agreed to receive the new governor. He was given a Mormon militia escort which stopped several times during the night. When they stopped, most of the escort would dash ahead so that the governor got the impression that the mountains were saturated with Saints under arms.

Finally, to save face, President Buchanan sent a peace emissary and offered to pardon Young and the Mormons for their alleged crimes. By this time the Mormon War was generally known as "Buchanan's Folly." Young accepted the pardon and allowed the federal troops to march through the city without stopping in order to reach their new encampment in Cedar Valley, 44 miles away. The soldiers tramped through the deserted streets; the only faces they saw were those of the handful of Mormons left behind with flints and steel to set fire to the shavings and kindling in the houses.

The Mormon War cost the Federal Government about $15 million and accomplished nothing which reasonable negotiation could not have achieved. The commander of the forces, General Albert Sidney Johnston, who fulminated against the rebels of Utah, became a Confederate hero and died in the battle of Shiloh.

After his visit to Salt Lake City in 1860 Burton wrote:

But they [the Latter-day Saints] make scant pretension of patriotism. They regard the States pretty much as the States regarded England after the War of Independence, and hate them as the Mexican Criollo does the Gachupin—very much also for the same reason. Theirs is a deep and abiding resentment, which time will strengthen, not efface: the deeds of Missouri and Illinois will bear fruit for many and many a generation.[2]

During the Civil War the Mormons sided with the North. President Lincoln followed a policy of live and let live but the campaign against Mormon polygamy was resumed after the end of the war.

A far more serious threat to the Church than the Gladdenites was the so-called "New Movement" which began with the founding of the *Utah Magazine* by W. S. Godbe and E. L. T. Harrison. The pair traveled to New York in 1868 and compared notes on the train and in their hotel rooms. They expressed their dissatisfaction at the totalitarian rule of Brigham Young. In particular they objected to the Church's economic policies and refusal to encourage mining in Utah. They won several educated Latter-day Saints to their side and all were excommunicated. Godbe himself drifted into spiritualism. The schismatics founded the *Salt Lake Tribune,* which then passed into Gentile control and became the anti-Church newspaper.

President Young survived these schisms and heresies with no great inconvenience to himself. His position was never seriously threatened.

He encouraged dancing, the theatre, music and education, although he probably never read a book himself which was not a Mormon text. In his later years he spent the winter at St. George in the warmer, southern part of the state. He engaged in numerous business ventures so that he was able to leave an estate of $2 million to his heirs.

Brigham Young died August 29, 1877, at the age of seventy-seven. His last words were said to be "Joseph! Joseph! Joseph!" His funeral was held in the Tabernacle and he was buried in a plain pine coffin.

His statue stands in the Hall of Fame in the nation's

capital and no one would dispute his achievements as a colonizer, statesman, religious leader and husband. Had Sidney Rigdon won the support of the Mormons in Nauvoo or had a lesser man stepped into the role of leader of the Church, we doubt if the Church of Jesus Christ of Latter-day Saints would today claim the allegiance of 2 million souls. With a martyr and a dynamic leader, the Saints were able to establish a separate community in the Rocky Mountains which could withstand Gentile infiltration, the condemnation of an indignant public opinion, and even a federal army.

Of him Richard Burton wrote:

He is the St. Paul of the New Dispensation: true and sincere, he gave point, and energy, and consistency to the somewhat disjointed, turbulent, and unforeseeing fanaticism of Mr. Joseph Smith; and if he has not been able to create, he has shown himself great in controlling, circumstances.[3]

Two of Young's sons, Brigham, Jr. and John W. Young, wanted to inherit their father's religious authority but the principle of succession he himself had established in Nauvoo was maintained. The president of the Council of the Twelve, John Taylor, became the new "Seer, Revelator, Translator and Prophet."

Born an Anglican and converted to Methodism at the age of fifteen, Taylor left his native England for Canada, where he was introduced to Mormonism by Parley Pratt. He and his wife were baptized in 1836. He became an apostle in Far West. When Joseph Smith was ordered to Carthage, Elder Taylor accompanied him and witnessed the murder. Later Taylor returned to England on a mission and spent some time in France. In Utah he served in the legislature and as a probate judge.

John Taylor was sustained president on October 10, 1880. He did his best to withstand the increasing federal pressure against polygamy. On October 5, 1885, the First Presidency declared:

We did not reveal celestial marriage. We cannot withdraw or renounce it. God revealed it, and he has promised to maintain it and to bless those who obey it. Whatever fate, then, may threaten us, there is but one course for men of God to take; that is, to keep inviolate the holy covenants they have made in the presence of God and angels.

The Edmunds Act of 1882 had tightened the vise on polygamists, and many Saints with their wives and children fled to Canada and Mexico. Then in 1887 the Federal Government seized all Church property except that used for worship, and disfranchised the polygamists. President Taylor went underground and died in hiding in 1887.

An eighty-two-year-old Mormon elder was chosen to succeed Taylor in 1889. Wilford Woodruff was born in Connecticut in 1807 and baptized in 1833. The Church was in a shambles when he took office. It faced bankruptcy and its leaders were either dead or in hiding. Finally President Woodruff wrote the Manifesto of 1890 by which the Church agreed to discontinue the practice of plural marriage. He told the Saints that both Smith and Young had visited him in his dreams and approved the change of Church policy. He dedicated the Salt Lake City temple in 1893; he had driven a stake to mark its location 46 years before. Woodruff lived to see Utah achieve statehood in 1896. He died in 1898.

The Church did not consider the laws against polygamy to be retroactive. A polygamist was not required to break up his home to satisfy the law. The Church only refused to authorize future plural marriages. Even so, a number of high-ranking Latter-day Saints were excommunicated for contracting plural marriages long after the publication of the Manifesto.

Lorenzo Snow served only three years as president, from 1898 to 1901. He emphasized tithing as a means to recoup Church losses; the Church's indebtednesss was finally paid off in 1907. His successor was Joseph F. Smith, a son of

Hyrum Smith. He was a lad of five when his father and uncle were killed. A veteran of the Hawaiian and English missions, he served as president of the Church until his death in 1918. His son, Joseph Fielding Smith, is the current president of the Council of the Twelve Apostles and a popular Mormon author. He will become president if President McKay dies before he does, but McKay is only three years older than Smith.

The next president, Heber J. Grant, had served as a missionary to Japan and had been appointed an apostle at the age of twenty-six. His father was Jedediah M. Grant, the zealous Mormon who inspired the Mormon Reformation of the early 1850's. Jedediah was so busy rebaptizing sinners that he spent many of his waking hours in cold water and died of pneumonia in 1856. President Grant dedicated temples in Hawaii, Alberta, and Arizona. He emphasized strict adherence to the Word of Wisdom and organized the Welfare Plan in 1936 which has become an important feature of Mormon life. He urged the Church to develop the sugar-beet industry.

George Albert Smith, another relative of the Prophet and a leader in the Boy Scout movement, served as president from 1945 to 1951 when the present incumbent, David O. McKay, took office.

6. *Mormon Theology*

To UNDERSTAND THE THEOLOGY of Mormonism we must first examine in some detail the distinctive Mormon concepts of the nature of God and man. These concepts as developed by Joseph Smith and Brigham Young stand in radical contrast to those of traditional Christianity. They are not simply modifications of older beliefs but absolute contradictions of the doctrines of God and man in other denominations.

Smith advanced from the monotheism or unitarianism of the *Book of Mormon* to tritheism and the doctrine of the plurality of Gods, which is fundamental to Mormon theology today. At Kirtland the Prophet began to study Hebrew and noticed that the word Elohim in Genesis was plural rather than singular. He concluded that the Bible had been carelessly translated and that it revealed the existence of not one God but of many Gods.

These Gods may assemble to decide actions of momentous importance but for the individual human being the God of this world is the only God he need worship and serve. The plan of salvation for the inhabitants of this planet is undoubtedly duplicated many times for the children of other Gods on other planets. Whether these Gods acknowledge a chief God is left to speculation, and such theological speculation is discouraged in contemporary Mormonism.

The Prophet declared: "I want to set forth in a plain and simple manner: ... to us there is but one God—that is pertaining to us; and he is all and through all." [1]

Brigham Young confessed: "How many Gods there are, I do

not know. But there never was a time when there were not Gods and worlds, and when men were not passing through the same ordeals that we are passing through. That course has been from all eternity, and it is and will be to all eternity."

Prof. Sterling M. McMurrin, former U. S. Commissioner of Education, and author of *The Philosophical Foundations of Mormon Theology,* discussed metaphysical monism in contrast to Mormon pluralism. He wrote:

Nowhere is this pluralism more evident than in the doctrine of God, for instance, where not only is the Godhead defined as three independently real persons, in contrast to the common Christian notion of the Trinity, that the Father, Son, and Holy Ghost are one in substance, but where there is the idea that for the total universe there is a multiplicity of personal deities who are genuinely real as individuals.[2]

The God of this world is powerful and the literal father of all human beings who have or will live on this earth but He is not the one, almighty God of orthodox Christianity or Judaism. Orson Pratt, the Mormon theologian, explained:

In the heaven where our spirits were born, there are many gods, each of whom has his own wife or wives which were given to him previous to his redemption while yet in his mortal state.[3]

God is not an immaterial Being. He has a body of flesh and bones but not of blood. Smith declared:

God Himself was once as we are now, and is an exalted man, and sits enthroned in yonder heavens ... if you were to see him today you would see him like a man in form—like yourself in all the person, image, and very form as man; for Adam was created in the very fashion, image and likeness of God, and received instruction from and walked, talked and conversed with him, as one man talks and communes with another.[4]

Talmage dismissed all those who believed in God to be im-material as atheists.

> We affirm that to deny the materiality of God's person is to deny God; for a thing without parts has no whole, and an im-material body cannot exist.[5]

No religion teaches a more anthropomorphic concept of God than Mormonism. The God (s) of Mormonism was once a man dwelling on a planet. He has a body. The references in the Old Testament in which man is pictured as conversing with God, seeing God, hearing God, are accepted in a purely literal sense by Mormons.

God was not always as He is today and will not always be what He is today. He is a self-made deity who did not realize His full potential until He was exalted to the status of a God. John A. Widtsoe explained:

> As already said, God is the supreme intelligent Being in the universe, who has the greatest knowledge and the most perfected will, and who, therefore, possesses infinite power over the forces of the universe. However, if the great law of progression is ac-cepted, God must have been engaged from the beginning, and must now be engaged in progressive development, and infinite as God is, he must have been less powerful in the past than he is today.... It is clear also that, as with every other being, the progress of God began with exercise of his will ... until he at-tained at last a conquest over the universe which to our finite understanding seems absolutely complete....
>
> We may be certain that, through self-effort, the inherent and innate powers of God have been developed to a God-like degree. Thus he has become God.[6]

The contrast of this current Mormon belief with that ex-pressed in the *Book of Mormon* is striking:

> For I know that God is not a partial God, neither a changeable being; but He is unchangeable from all eternity to all eternity (Moroni, 8:18).

Likewise *Doctrine and Covenants* makes references to the unchangeableness of God:

By these things we know that there is a God in heaven, who is infinite and eternal, from everlasting to everlasting the same unchangeable God, the framer of heaven and earth and all things which are in them (20:17).

The contemporary view is that the God of this world seems to be infinite and all powerful from the standpoint of man but that He is actually in the process of development. He is a man who has achieved divinity. He is still progressing and giving His own spirit-creatures the opportunity to become Gods themselves as some other God gave Him the same opportunity. (The theological ideas in this chapter are those held by the Utah Mormons and not by the Reorganized Church or smaller LDS bodies.)

No aphorism in Mormonism is as widely known as that first penned by Lorenzo Snow: "As man is, God once was, and as God is, man may become." In a nutshell it expresses the Mormon view of a progressive divinity. Young repeated the same idea in many passages:

The Lord created us for the purpose of our becoming Gods like Himself when we have been proved in our present capacity —growing up from the low estate of manhood to become Gods until we can create worlds on worlds.[7]

Young further stated:

The God that I serve is progressing eternally, and so are his children: they will increase to all eternity, if they are faithful.[8]

A Mormon writing in 1961 elaborates the same thought:

The truth we have found to be that gods, angels, devils, and men are of a common parentage. They are the same in physical appearance and original potentiality. Gods are those members of the divine race who have reached the status that might be called perfect maturation, or realization of the maximum potential.[9]

The difference between the members of the divine race is that the Gods have achieved their full potential, angels have elected to become servants of the Gods, men are in the process of deciding their final status, and the devils have lost all happiness through rebellion.

God physically begat all the spirits in His world, those who have chosen to undergo the experience of mortality as well as those who rebelled and have become devils. God is married to one or more female deities. The familiar hymn by Eliza R. Snow, a widow of the Prophet, expressed this common Mormon belief in a heavenly Mother:

> In the heavens are parents single?
>   No; the thought makes reason stare!
> Truth is reason, truth eternal tells
>   me I've a mother there.
>
> Father, Mother, may I meet you in
>   your royal courts on high?
> Then at length, when I've completed
>   all you sent me forth to do,
> With your mutual approbation let me
>   come and dwell with you.

God did not create the matter which makes up the physical world. God, gross matter and intelligence existed from eternity. God only "organized" matter. Just as in Mormon terminology God is called infinite and almighty although He is neither, so He is called the Creator although He did not create. Professor McMurrin explains:

New Mormon theology denies the doctrine of creation, holding that the world in its ultimate parts is uncreated, and that the divine creative activity is exhausted in the structuring and transformation of self-existent ingredients.[10]

He adds:

For in the Mormon concept of reality, whatever may be said of the divine creative activity, it is firmly established that God is not the ultimate ground of all being, and that the human spirit has the foundations of its existence within itself.[11]

Three separate personages organized this world. Young stated:

It is true that the earth was organized by three distinct characters, namely, Elohim, Jehovah, and Michael, these three forming a quorum, as in all heavenly bodies and in organizing element, perfectly represented in the Deity, as Father, Son and Holy Ghost.[12]

The Christian doctrine of the Trinity that God is three distinct Persons in one nature is understood in a radically different sense by the Mormons. God the Father and God the Son are not only distinct in Mormon theology but are also separate personages with separate bodies of flesh and bones. The Holy Ghost is a personage of spirit without a body. Talmage explains that the three are "as distinct in their persons and individualities as are any three personages in mortality." [13]

After the God of this world had procreated the billions of spirit creatures who were his sons and daughters, He proposed His plan of salvation and exaltation. He presented His plan at a great council and asked for volunteers to execute the details. One of His sons, Lucifer, proposed a plan which would have abrogated man's free will while Jehovah (Jesus), the firstborn son of the Father and Mother, proposed an alternate plan which would have accepted the risk of free will. The Father favored Jehovah and designated him to be the creator of this earth. Lucifer and about one-third of the spirits rebelled and tried to overthrow the Father. They were defeated and punished by being denied the possibility of ever obtaining a human body and therefore of becoming Gods.

Jehovah organized this world in six days of 1,000 years each and two of the Father's choicest spirit creatures, Adam and Eve, were given bodies and established in the Garden of Eden, near Independence, Missouri. They were not how-ever mortal beings and were not subject to death. Blood did not run in their veins.

They were given commandments by God, including the commandment to refrain from eating of the Tree of Knowl-edge and to increase and multiply. Eve succumbed to the temptation of Satan and ate of the forbidden fruit which meant that she was to be banished from paradise. If she were banished, however, the two could not have sexual intercourse and would have to disobey the command of God to beget children. Adam was faced with the choice of disobeying one of the two commandments; he chose to eat of the fruit with Eve and to be banished with her to a spot outside of the Garden, near the town of Adam-ondi-Ahman in Missouri.

Mormons therefore revere Adam and Eve as the two who made possible the plan of salvation rather than as sinners. Had Adam chosen the other course, he and Eve would have remained childless. But his action brought sickness and death on his children. God promised a redeemer—Jehovah—who would one day lift the penalty of death from the sons of Adam and Eve.

Adam left the Garden and was baptized by immersion. He and his children built temples where they baptized, washed, anointed and laid hands on each other. They wore sacred undergarments identical with those now worn in the Mor-mon endowment rites. Adam instructed his children in the secret passwords, signs and tokens needed to get by the sen-tinels of heaven.

Three years before he died Adam called the human family together to a council at Adam-ondi-Ahman. He ordained Seth and others to the Melchizedek priesthood. The true religion was practiced by Adam and his descendants, but Satan visited humans and began to turn them away from the truth. He founded the evil Mahanic (Masonic) lodge which initiated Cain as its first member.

A few faithful men tried to preserve the true religion. Enoch and Noah were baptized and ordained Mormon priests. The 10,000 residents of the city of Enoch were taken up in a body and transplanted to another planet. A Mormon tradition suggests that this planet was scooped up out of the Gulf of Mexico.

After the flood, Noah's ark landed not in the Western Hemisphere but in Asia. The families described in the *Book of Mormon* repopulated this hemisphere. The Lord again and again restored the true religion and priesthood after it had been lost through apostasy.

Finally the time for the redemption arrived. Mormonism identifies Jehovah or Yahweh of the Old Testament as Jesus rather than as God the Father. God had marital relations with Mary to beget Jesus in the flesh. The Mormons reject the doctrine that the Son was begotten by the Holy Ghost.

Talmage writes: "We believe April 6th to be the birthday of Jesus Christ . . . We believe that Jesus Christ was born in Bethlehem of Judea, April 6, 1 B.C." [14]

Brigham Young emphasized the denial that Jesus was begotten by the Holy Ghost by writing: "If the son was begotten by the Holy Ghost, it would be very dangerous to baptize and confirm females, and give the Holy Ghost to them lest he should beget children, to be palmed upon the elders by the people, bringing the elders into great difficulties." [15]

Mormonism accepts the account of Jesus' miracles, teachings, and death given by the four Evangelists in the New Testament. To this account some Mormons add their own belief that Jesus was not a celibate but a married man, probably a polygamist. Some Mormon writers believe that He must have had children by his wives; they explain that Jesus' marital status was too personal a thing to be mentioned in the Gospels.

The death of Christ accomplished two chief purposes: it redeemed all men from death and from the consequences of personal sins. The penalty for Adam's disobedience was death, not original sin. Jesus assumed the responsibility for Adam's sin and served as the vicarious sacrifice for all men.

After His crucifixion and resurrection, Jesus appeared to His disciples and established His church. This was another of the many restorations of the true Mormon religion. This religion is the religion proclaimed in heaven, revealed to Adam, restored to Abraham, Moses, Jesus, and Joseph Smith, Jr.

Jesus also appeared to the Nephites in America and established a church for them as well. He appointed another set of 12 apostles for the Nephite Church: Nephi, Timothy, Jonas, Mathoni, Mathonihah, Kumen, Kumenonni, Jeremiah, Shemnon, a second Jonas, Zedekiah, and Isaiah. The Church established in Jerusalem fell into apostasy shortly after the disappearance of the last apostle; it lost its priesthood and teaching authority and began to offer the people a corrupt gospel. The Nephite Church also fell into a state of apostasy so that for many centuries the true Church was no longer to be found on earth. It was restored by Joseph Smith and today the Church of Jesus Christ is the only church pleasing to God. All others lack authority to baptize, preach, or ordain priests.

To realize his full potential, a spirit creature must have agreed to accept a human body and risk the temptations, sickness, and perils of humanity. Although every human being has lived for eons as a spirit creature with his father and mother in heaven he has consented to allow his memory of this pre-existence to be darkened.

If he has been fortunate enough to have entered mortality since the restoration of the true Church by Smith and has heard the Mormon gospel, his salvation lies in his accepting this gospel and obeying the priesthood. The Mormon formula of salvation is identical to that proclaimed by the Campbellites: faith, repentance, baptism by immersion and laying on of hands by the elders, and reception of the gift of the Holy Ghost. To qualify not only for salvation but for the highest glory—exaltation (Godhood)—a man must comply with this formula of salvation, be ordained a Mormon priest, receive his temple endowments, marry, observe the Word of Wisdom, tithe his income, attend church regularly. If he lives and dies a faithful Mormon he may enter the highest of the three degrees of glory, the celestial.

The Mormon belief in a graded heaven was taken from an interpretation of St. Paul's First Letter to the Corinthians. Here St. Paul reports:

And there are bodies celestial and bodies terrestrial: but, one is the glory of the celestial, and another of the terrestrial.

One is the glory of the sun, another the glory of the moon, and another the glory of the stars. For star differeth from star in glory (I Cor. 15:40–41).

Smith's interpretation of these passages appears in *Doctrine and Covenants* as Section 76, familiarly known as "The Vision." He describes three degrees of glory as the celestial, terrestrial, and the telestial (a name invented by Smith to identify the third heaven).

God Himself dwells in the celestial heaven. God's own planet is near the body Kolob. Men who have lived and died as faithful Mormons may hope to enter the celestial domain which is essential for further advancement in divinity. The residents of the celestial kingdom will be able to beget spiritual children who will stand in the same relationship to them as humans do to the God of this world. Widtsoe describes the cycle:

If sex is eternal, it follows of necessity, that the marriage contract may also be eternal. It is not a far step to the doctrine that after the earth work has been completed, and exaltation in the next estate has been attained, one of the chief duties of men and women will be to beget spirit children. These spirits, in turn, in the process of time, will come down upon an earth, there to obtain an acquaintance with gross matter, and through the possession of earthly bodies to control more fully, and forever, the manifold forces surrounding them. It is one of the rewards of intelligent development, that we may be to other spiritual beings, what our God has been to us.[16]

President Brigham Young declared:

I expect, if I am faithful, with yourselves, that I shall see the time, with yourselves, that we shall know how to prepare to organize an earth like this—know how to people that earth, how to redeem it, how to sanctify it, and how to glorify it, with those who live upon it who hearken to our counsels.[17]

Contemporary Mormons quote scientific articles which suggest life on other planets as confirmation of the Mormon cosmology. If life does exist elsewhere it is probably in the kingdoms of Mormons who have reached Godhood. Among those who have already achieved Godhood are Abraham, Isaac and Jacob (D & C, 132:37). Most Mormons assume that Joseph Smith has also progressed to this stage of development and reigns as a God over his own realm.

Mormons who fall below the standards expected of a devout Mormon and exceptionally good Protestants and Catholics may aspire to a lesser degree of glory, the terrestrial. God does not dwell in the terrestrial kingdom but Jesus Christ will visit the terrestrial heaven.

Finally, the average person will spend eternity in the telestial heaven which can claim the presence of neither God nor Jesus Christ. The Holy Ghost and angels will minister to those in this heaven. Within the telestial heaven as in the former two are numerous stages of glory depending on the works performed by the man during mortality. Mormonism believes that man is saved by grace but exalted by works.

Parley Pratt explained that the heathen will not be damned:

The heathen nations, also, will then be redeemed, and will be exalted to the privilege of serving the Saints of the Most High. They will be the vine-dressers, the gardeners, builders, etc. But the Saints will be the owners of the soil, the proprietors of all real estate and other precious things, and the kings, governors and judges of the earth.[18]

Only a handful of murderers, adulterers and apostates will be damned as "sons of perdition." They will join the hosts of Satan. Mormonism preaches a practical universalism which provides salvation for almost all and exaltation for faithful Mormon priests and their wives.

No other religion except perhaps spiritualism concerns itself more with the dead than Mormonism. Those who died before the restoration of the Church in the early nineteenth century or those who never had an opportunity to embrace Mormonism must also be baptized if they would attain celestial glory. Living Mormons undergo baptism for the dead by proxy in Mormon temples and participate in the other rites necessary for the highest glory. The dead are free to accept or reject these ministrations in the afterlife. If they accept them they too can begin the progression toward divinity.

Knowledge gained in this mortal life will be useful to those who progress toward godhead in the next. This gives an extra impetus to the Mormon emphasis on education.

The marriage relationship also continues throughout eternity if the man and his wife or wives are joined in matrimony in a Mormon temple. Those so married will continue to beget spirit children for their own domain and the process of salvation will continue with the celestialized Mormon taking his place as God the Father of his own world. Those not married in these rites are ineligible to reach the celestial state.

The Bible is accepted as the word of God "insofar as it is correctly translated." Utah Mormons generally accept the King James version as the most nearly correct although the Reorganized Mormons also use the version attempted by Smith in Kirtland. In addition to these, Mormons accept three other books as standard works. They are the *Book of Mormon, Doctrine and Covenants,* and the *Pearl of Great Price.* The last contains the Book of Moses revealed to Smith in 1830, the translation of the Chandler papyri called the Book of Abraham, and the Writings of Joseph Smith which include his version of the 24th Chapter of Matthew and an account of his receipt of the golden plates, their translation, and the conferring of the priesthood.

The *Pearl of Great Price* is also printed with the 13 Articles of Faith. These Articles were prepared in Nauvoo and have been used over the years by Mormon missionaries to summarize the Mormon theological positions. Actually they differ only slightly from creeds of Protestant bodies and give no hint of distinctive Mormon beliefs regarding the plurality of Gods, pre-existence, baptism of the dead, the endowment ceremony, eternal marriage. They tend to minimize the differences between the Church of Jesus Christ of Latter-day Saints and other denominations on the American frontier. The Articles are as follows:

1. We believe in God, the Eternal Father, and in His son, Jesus Christ, and in the Holy Ghost.

2. We believe that men will be punished for their own sins, and not for Adam's transgression.

3. We believe that through the Atonement of Christ, all mankind may be saved, by obedience to the laws and ordinances of the Gospel.

4. We believe that the first principles and ordinances of the Gospel are: first, Faith in the Lord Jesus Christ; second, Repentance; third, Baptism by immersion for the remission of sins; fourth, Laying on of hands for the gift of the Holy Ghost.

5. We believe that a man must be called of God, by prophecy, and by the laying on of hands, by those who are in authority to preach the Gospel and administer in the ordinances thereof.

6. We believe in the same organization that existed in the Primitive Church, viz., apostles, prophets, pastors, teachers, evangelists, etc.

7. We believe in the gift of tongues, prophecy, revelation, visions, healing, interpretation of tongues, etc.

8. We believe the Bible to be the word of God as far as it is translated correctly; we also believe the Book of Mormon to be the word of God.

9. We believe all that God has revealed, all that He does now reveal, and we believe that He will yet reveal many great and important things pertaining to the Kingdom of God.

10. We believe in the literal gathering of Israel and in the restoration of the Ten Tribes; that Zion will be built upon this [the American] continent; that Christ will reign personally upon the earth; and, that the earth will be renewed and receive its paradisiacal glory.

11. We claim the privilege of worshiping Almighty God according to the dictates of our own conscience, and allow all men the same privilege, let them worship how, where, or what they may.

12. We believe in being subject to kings, presidents, rulers, and magistrates, in obeying, honoring, and sustaining the law.

13. We believe in being honest, true, chaste, benevolent, virtuous, and in doing good to all men; indeed, we may say that we follow the admonition of Paul—We believe all things, we hope all things, we have endured many things, and hope to be able to endure all things. If there is anything virtuous, lovely, or of good report or praiseworthy, we seek after these things.

In 1962, President Hugh B. Brown told the General Conference:

That these articles are not, and were not intended to be, a complete and final exposition of beliefs is evidenced by the fact that we receive and expect continued revelation.... These articles are authoritative; however, they form but an outline for the study of the theology of the Church.[19]

Mormonism affirms the existence of angels (such as the Angel Moroni). They are of three types: spirits who have not yet become men, people who have lived on earth but have not been resurrected with bodies of flesh and bones; and those who have been resurrected but must be content with a lower glory because they led average or evil lives or failed to embrace Mormonism. These angels will minister to those who are eventually raised to Godhood.

Likewise, the spirit creatures who followed Lucifer have become devils. They will never receive human bodies, which is their greatest punishment. They seek to destroy the Mormon Church, subvert the priesthood, tempt men and women to lose their faith. President Woodruff estimated there were 100 evil spirits for every man, woman and child living on earth at any one time, which makes the earthly journey a perilous one for those trying to serve God. The relatively few sons of perdition join the ranks of the devils. Orson F. Whitney wrote:

Satan and his legions, those cast out of heaven, are all wicked spirits, and they wander up and down the world, endeavouring to lead mortals astray. Whenever possible, they take possession of the bodies of men and even of lower animals. Therefore is power given to the Priesthood to cast out devils. Against these fallen spirits, mortals must be ever on the defensive, lest their souls be ensnared.[20]

Joseph Smith provided a simple test by which men could detect good and evil spirits:

When a messenger comes saying he has a message from God, offer him your hand and request him to shake hands with you.

If he be an angel he will do so, and you will feel his hand.

If he be the spirit of a just man made perfect he will come in his glory; for that is the only way he can appear—

Ask him to shake hands with you, but he will not move, because it is contrary to the order of heaven for a just man to deceive, but he will still deliver his message.

If it be the devil as an angel of light, when you ask him to shake hands he will offer you his hand, and you will not feel anything; you may therefore detect him.

These are three grand keys whereby you may know whether any administration is from God.

(D & C, 129:4–9)

Four personages who appear again and again in Mormon folklore are known as the Nephite brothers or the peripatetic immortals. Three of the 12 apostles of the Nephite Church along with the Apostle John declined to die and agreed to stay on earth to go about doing good. At the Second Coming they will be changed immediately into immortality. They appear suddenly and are described as of medium height with flowing white hair and beards. They perform their good deeds and disappear as suddenly as they appear.[21]

Mormonism administers only one sacrament, the Lord's Supper. Baptism and marriage are considered ordinances, not sacraments. The communion service is held each Sunday as in Campbellite churches. Mormonism understands the communion as a memorial service. The officiating priest blesses the bread:

"O God, the Eternal Father, we ask thee in the name of thy Son, Jesus Christ, to bless and sanctify this bread to the souls of all those who partake of it, that they may eat in remembrance of the body of thy Son, and witness unto thee, O God, the Eternal Father, that they are willing to take upon them the name of thy Son, and always remember him and keep his commandments which he has given them; that they may always have his Spirit to be with them. Amen."

A similar prayer of consecration is said over the water which is used instead of wine or grapejuice in the Mormon communion.

The *Book of Mormon* declares, "It is a solemn mockery before God that ye should baptize little children." Children are baptized when they reach the age of accountability, reckoned at eight. Only baptism by immersion by an authorized Mormon priest is considered to be an authentic Christian baptism. A brief confirmation service follows the baptism.

The very name of the Church indicates that Mormonism was early concerned about the Second Coming. The first Mormons just as the first Christians were certain they were living in the latter-days and that they would live to establish Zion and to see the Lord return in all power and majesty. Today the millennial aspect in Mormonism is much less evident than in early Mormonism or in contemporary Seventh-day Adventism or Jehovah's Witnesses.

Just before the Second Coming a great council will be held at Adam-ondi-Ahman where Adam will present the keys to Jesus Christ. At the start of the millennium the tribe of Judah will be gathered at Jerusalem and the tribes of Israel will gather in Zion in the New World. The Ten Lost Tribes of Israel will return from the polar regions where they have lived for centuries, shut off from the rest of the world by ice barriers. They will bring treasures with them and share these riches with the Latter-day Saints. The city of Enoch will descend from its planetary home. Except in Jerusalem and the New Jerusalem the world will be witnessing tremendous slaughter and destruction. Jesus will reign in person for 1,000 years and supervise the construction of hundreds of Mormon temples in which to carry out baptisms and other ordinances for the dead.

What we have been saying about Mormon theology is, we believe, what a Mormon missionary would believe and teach today. Several other doctrines were certainly taught at one time or another but are not considered binding on the faith-

ful nor essential to Mormonism. For example, Brigham
Young speculated that the God of this world was none other
than Adam:

Now hear it, O inhabitants of the earth, Jew and Gentile,
saint and sinner. When our Father Adam came into the Garden
of Eden, he came into it with a celestial body and brought Eve,
one of his wives, with him. He helped to make and organize this
world.... He is our Father and our God and the only God with
whom we have to do.[22]

Pratt disagreed with Young in this interpretation and it
was quietly forgotten. Modern Mormon theological works
make no reference to the possibility that Adam was also God.

Brigham Young also taught the doctrine of blood atonement which meant that certain horrendous crimes such as
adultery and apostasy could be forgiven only by the shedding
of the sinner's own blood. He wrote:

Suppose you found your brother in bed with your wife, and put
a javelin through both of them, you would be justified, and they
would atone for their sins and be received into the kingdom
of God....[23]

In another sermon President Young asked:

Now take a person in this congregation who has knowledge
with regard to his being saved in the kingdom of God and our
Father, and being exalted, one who knows and understands the
principles of eternal life ... and suppose that he is overtaken
with a fault, that he has committed a sin that he knows will
deprive him of that exaltation which he desires, and that he
cannot attain to it without the shedding of his blood, and also
knows that by having his blood shed he will atone for that sin,
and be saved, and exalted with the Gods, is there a man or
woman in this house but what would say: "Shed my blood that
I may be saved and exalted with the Gods"? Will you love your
brothers and sisters likewise, when they have committed a sin

that cannot be atoned for without the shedding of their blood? Will you love that man or woman well enough to shed their blood? [24]

Another leading Mormon, Jedediah Grant, exclaimed:

Brethren and sisters, we want you to repent and forsake your sins, and you who have committed sins that cannot be forgiven through baptism, let your blood be shed, and let the smoke ascend, that the incense thereof may come up before God as an atonement for your sins, and that the sinners in Zion may be afraid.[25]

Some of the crimes attributed to the Danites were said to have been executed out of a spirit of love to enable the victims to obtain such forgiveness. A relic of this doctrine of blood atonement—no longer preached or believed by very many Mormons—is the firing squad method of execution still used in capital punishment by the State of Utah. All other states with the death penalty use the noose, electric chair or gas chamber but these do not involve the shedding of blood. Utah provides the option of death by bullets and many convicts choose this method if they are believing Mormons.

In view of the Mormon belief in continuous revelation, these doctrines proclaimed by President Young become something of an embarrassment since they are now disowned. The Mormon will probably suggest that the president of the Church was simply engaged in speculation and was not speaking ex cathedra.

Many questions in Mormon theology remain unanswered and delving into these mysteries is officially discouraged. Without a professional clergy Mormonism is content to expound the theological system worked out by Smith in his *Doctrine and Covenants* and *Pearl of Great Price* without the systematic study of theology found in Catholic and Protestant churches.

In a society dominated by the idea of original sin Mormonism proclaimed that man was accountable only for his own sins. While other sects harped on man's depravity Mormonism told its followers that they might evolve into Gods. Mormon theology nourished the virtues of self-confidence, optimism, family solidarity, industry which helped it survive the persecutions in Missouri and Illinois and to build an empire in the desert.

7. Are Mormons Protestants?

M OST PEOPLE classify Mormonism as a Protestant denomination albeit one which stands near the outer limits of orthodoxy. For that matter the average American calls anyone a Protestant who is not a Roman Catholic or Jew. Is Mormonism simply another Protestant denomination or is it distinct from Protestantism?

Mormon writers themselves unanimously deny that Mormonism is a Protestant church. They assert that the Church of Jesus Christ of Latter-day Saints is a restoration, not a reformation. Catholic and Protestant theologians differ on whether Mormonism is a Protestant church or even a Christian one.

Although the Church of Jesus Christ of Latter-day Saints belongs to neither the National Council of Churches of Christ nor the World Council of Churches, officials of the National Council evidently consider it a Protestant church. The *Yearbook of American Churches* published annually by the Council includes the various Latter-day Saints bodies as Protestant churches and includes their membership in the Protestant total. And yet the editor carefully segregates the membership totals of the Armenian Church of North America, the Old Catholic Church, and the Polish National Catholic Church. Any student of comparative religion would consider the theological differences between the separately listed Eastern Orthodox and the Roman Catholic churches as relatively insignificant compared to the differences between Mormonism and mainline Protestantism.

Several years ago when the same National Council prepared a map of the United States, indicating by color the states with Catholic or Protestant majorities, it identified Utah as a predominantly Protestant state. At least, for purposes of tabulation the National Council lumps Mormonism, Christian Science, Jehovah's Witnesses, Spiritualism, Unitarianism and Ethical Culture as "Protestant" churches.

Yet when we study the writings of Protestant students of American cults such as Horton Davies, Walter Martin, George B. Arbaugh, J. K. VanBaalen, we find that they refuse to extend the term "Protestant" to Mormonism. Protestants—Presbyterians, Methodists, Baptists and the like—in Utah and the intermountain states never consider Mormons as fellow Protestants. They try to proselytize among the Mormons in the belief that by leaving Mormonism, a Saint can discover genuine Christianity.

Mormons have no objection to their exclusion from the Protestant category since this is their basic position. They would and do object to anyone's suggesting that their church is not a Christian church, since they maintain that it is the one and only Christian church on earth today. Some Mormon apologists point out that Mormonism is as close to Roman Catholicism as to Protestantism; some features of Mormonism bear this out. The nature of teaching authority in religion and the emphasis on a properly ordained priesthood in Mormonism find parallels in Catholicism. Minor positions such as the discouragement of lodge membership and contraception are shared by Catholicism and Mormonism. On the other hand, the idea of theocracy and the practice of polygamy find counterparts in Old Testament Judaism more than in Christianity.

To determine whether Mormonism can logically be classed as a Protestant church we must define what we mean by Protestant. If we accept the popular definition by elimination that anyone who is not a Catholic or Jew must be a Protestant we will, of course, call Mormons Protestants. Popular opinion is an untrustworthy guide to theological distinctions because the same simple tri-faith definition also eliminates the Eastern Orthodox, Secular Humanists, Buddhists, Moslems and other commitments shared by other Americans. We must go beyond the preconceptions of the theologically uninformed.

First of all we must define Protestantism as a branch of Christianity. Those who consider Mormonism a Protestant church cannot then refuse to admit that it is also a Christian church. What constitutes a Christian church is disputable. Some would say that a Christian church must acknowledge at the very least that Jesus Christ was divine, the Second Person of the Trinity. The World Council of Churches calls itself a "fellowship of churches which accept our Lord Jesus Christ as God and Saviour." The mere recognition of Jesus as a historical personage or even a great teacher does not make a theological system Christian. Jesus appears in such clearly non-Christian cults as Theosophy, Baha'i, I Am, and Rosicrucianism. Islam recognizes the prophetic role of Jesus but calls Mohammed its prophet. Even though the World Council of Churches has not defined such terms as "God" and "Saviour," we have every reason to believe that they would reject the application of the Church of Jesus Christ of Latter-day Saints in the unlikely event that the LDS would attempt to join the Council. The Mormon conception of Jesus clearly differs from the historic Christian understanding of his nature and work.

Horton Davies, professor of the history of Christianity at Princeton, maintains:

Their [the Mormons'] faith is not Christo-centric, for Christ is to them merely a forerunner of Joseph Smith and they have dared even to falsify the Gospel records in order to make the Messiah fit in with their preconceptions. A faith cannot be called "Christian" with any justice, if it judges Christ instead of submitting itself to His authority, and if it replaces the "obedience of faith" by obedience to the dictates of the Mormon hierarchy as the condition of salvation.[1]

Those who would accept the minimal definition of the World Council as normative for a Christian body would have to deny that the Mormons, along with Jehovah's Witnesses, Christian Scientists and Unitarians, are Christians. If they also accept the proposition that not all Christians are Protestants but all Protestants are Christians, they would have to answer the question of whether Mormons are Protestants in the negative.

If some would feel that the acceptance of Jesus as God and Saviour is too restrictive a definition of Christian, they would want to continue the examination of whether Mormons are somehow Protestants. If by Protestant we mean followers of the Protestant Reformers of the sixteenth century, we will have little difficulty admitting the Mormon affirmation that Mormons emphatically reject the principles of the Reformation.

Those Christian churches which developed during and after the Protestant Reformation were distinguished by two chief principles: the sole sufficiency of the scriptures and justification by faith alone. If we accept these as two basic criteria of Protestantism we will have little difficulty placing Mormonism outside of the Protestant community of churches.

By recognizing the normative value of supplementary scriptures—the *Book of Mormon, Doctrine and Covenants,* and the *Pearl of Great Price*—Mormonism obviously denies the Protestant doctrine of the sole sufficiency of the scriptures, i.e., the Old and New Testaments. As a matter of fact the Mormon Standard Works are far more evident in Mormon theological writings than the Christian Bible. We probably do not need to labor this point.

Mormons frankly deny the material principle of Protestantism as well. The popular Mormon theologian James E.

Talmadge declares: "The sectarian dogma of justification by faith alone has exercised an influence for evil." [2] He continues to criticize the statement of this doctrine by Martin Luther and the proposition that man is saved by faith without works. The Christian concept of grace simply finds no place in Mormon theology.

Even a cursory examination of Mormonism reveals the discrepancies between traditional Protestantism and Mormonism. Instead of a priesthood of all believers, Mormonism posits the necessity of an elaborate Aaronic and Melchizedek priesthood. Instead of private interpretation of the scriptures, Mormonism expects its adherents to accept the official interpretation by the Church hierarchy and the acquiescence to any additional revelations which may come to the presidents of the Church as Prophets, Seers, Revelators, etc. Basic to Mormonism is the belief in continuous revelation, whereas both Protestants and Catholics believe that divine revelation ended with the death of the last Apostle.

Several Roman Catholic scholars classify Mormonism as a Protestant denomination on the basis that private interpretation as a Reformation principle characterizes Mormonism. For example, Fr. John A. Hardon, S.J., author of *The Protestant Churches of America,* writes:

Mormons deny they are Protestants because their founder belonged to no other sect and admitted no succession from another church society. The fact is that Mormonism is derived from the Reformation principle of religious freedom carried to the extreme of not only appealing to the inner voice of God for private interpretation of the Bible, but elucubrating a whole body of new revelation alien to the Scriptures of traditional Christianity.[3]

Another Jesuit student of comparative religion, Fr. Gustave Weigel, S.J., extends the term Protestant to Mormonism but adds:

What does distinguish Mormons from Protestants in general is their great insistence on the notion of the Church of Christ. Protestant churches do not believe that any one of them is the Church of Christ, but rather that all these churches belong to the Church of Christ. The Mormons insist that they and they alone are the Church for our time.[4]

Father Weigel understands the Mormons' refusal to accept the designation "Protestant":

Protestantism is rooted in Catholicism and only by that reason can it claim continuity with the first Christian community.... In their own way the Mormons see this. They justify their existence by an entirely new revelation made in our time, uncontained either in Protestantism or Catholicism. As the Mormon sees it, Protestantism derives from Catholicism which had already lost all authority at the moment of the separation. For the Mormon then, Protestantism could not be a channel to the revelation of Christ. Nor can Catholicism, but with this difference; Catholicism did have the authority up to the fourth century and then it became apostate. But the Mormon sees that the Protestant claim to possess Christian revelation must be derived from the Catholic Church.[5]

Other Catholics put Mormonism outside the pale of both Protestantism and Christianity. Fr. George Tavard, A.A., the ecumenical scholar, brands Mormonism a Gnostic sect:

The Gnostic sects have the common characteristic that they have renounced Christianity and substituted or added a further dogmatic. The Jehovah's Witnesses, the Church of Christ, Scientist, and the Church of Jesus Christ of the Latter-day Saints (Mormons) represent three varieties of "improvement" on the teaching of Christ. They would have no title to be listed here were they not too often mistaken for genuine Protestant Churches. But there is nothing in common between a Protestant Christian and an initiate of these movements. It is important to distinguish between an imperfect Christianity, like that of the separated Churches, and, at a further stage of decay, of the sects, and a non-Christian religion such as may be found in the Gnostic sects of our day.[6]

Professor Konrad Algermissen, author of the monumental *Christian Denominations,* writes:

Mormonism is a mixture of Gnostic and ancient pagan teachings about the gods, Mohammedan polygamy, Jewish theocracy, rationalist Protestant biblical interpretation, and a polity inclined to Catholic practice, with an addition of American nationalism and Anglo-Saxon tenacity.[7]

Mormon writers are unanimous in rejecting a Protestant identification. All Protestant churches are apostate as is the Catholic Church and all lack authority to teach or baptize. The Church of Jesus Christ of Latter-day Saints is the only true Christian church in the world.

Certainly Brigham Young had no doubt that the Mormon Church was the true church while all other denominations were apostate:

I will now say to my friends—and I call you all, and all mankind, friends, until you have proved yourself enemies—you who do not belong to this Church, that we have got the Gospel of life and salvation. I do not say that we have a Gospel, but I say that we have the definite and only Gospel that ever was or ever will be that will save the children of men.[8]

Again Young declared:

When I first came into the Church it was a subject of considerable thought to me why people whom I knew to be as good and moral as they could be, should have to repent. But I could see afterwards that if they had nothing else to repent of they could and ought to repent of their false religions, of their narrow, contracted creeds in which they were bound, of their ordinances of men, and get something better. These narrow, contracted religions have spread infidelity in the world.[9]

He presented his indictment of other Christian bodies in a few words:

What is the sin of the ministry and people of the present Christian denominations? It is that light has come to them and they reject it.[10]

The same desire to disassociate themselves from Protestantism is evident in the writings of contemporary Mormons such as Gordon B. Hinckley:

They [the Mormons] are generally classed as Protestants, since they are not Catholics. Actually they are no closer to Protestantism than they are to Catholicism. Neither historically, nor on the basis of modern association, theology, or practice can they be grouped with either.[11]

LeGrand Richards classifies Christian churches as Catholic, Protestant or Latter-day Saint. The third category includes

Those who believe that the Church established by Jesus Christ while upon earth, fell into an apostate condition as predicted by the Apostles, and that the Church could not be reestablished upon the earth merely through a reformation but only through a restoration.[12]

Again and again Mormon writers emphasize that their church is not a reformed church but a restored church. In this they find kinship with Campbellism, which exercised a considerable influence on early Mormonism, especially through Sidney Rigdon, the former Campbellite preacher.

Mormon criticisms of other so-called Christian bodies are severe. These churches are impostors, unauthorized. They lack even the authority to baptize. As the *Book of Mormon* states:

Behold there are save two churches only; the one is the church of the Lamb of God, and the other is the church of the devil; wherefore, whoso belongeth not to the church of the Lamb of

God belongeth to that great church, which is the mother of abominations; and she is the whore of all the earth (1 Nephi 14:10).

A contemporary Mormon apologist brands all Christians idolaters if they believe God to be a spirit rather than a material body:

Therefore, the Christians who believe that God is a spirit, not only are idolaters (and who would say that an idolater has faith in the true God?), but they have denied the Christ—in ignorance, perhaps, but a denial just the same. When they believe Christ is a spirit, they are believing in error, not in Christ.[13]

The same author states flatly "... every person who believes in Christ will accept the *Book of Mormon*." [14] The implication is that the hundreds of millions of Christians who reject the Mormon scriptures as spurious do not really believe in Christ.

Gradually the Latter-day Saints are succeeding in establishing their claim to a separate religious category. Mormon servicemen can obtain LDS "dog tags." National politicians are beginning to invite Mormon preachers to offer the invocations at party conventions along with representatives of the other major religious traditions.

The scholar who maintains that Mormonism belongs in the Protestant category must be prepared to maintain also that a Protestant can believe in polytheism, in the pre-existence of souls, in polygamy as the divine pattern of marriage, in the materiality of God, in the existence of supplementary scriptures to the Bible, in the absolute necessity of secret temple rites for admission to the highest estate of the after-life, etc.

Those who attempt to classify Mormonism as Protestant on the basis of private interpretation of the scriptures and freedom of religious thought must ask themselves if there are no limits whatsoever to Christian orthodoxy. Mormonism aside, could a church which believed that Jesus was a fictitious person or a woman or a demon claim the title "Christian" on the basis of private interpretation? If we set no limits to the application of "Protestant" then we must distinguish between mainstream or historic Protestantism and quasi-Protestantism.

Some Mormons seem to claim a closer kinship with Judaism than with Protestantism. In 1959 Harry Howard, a Mormon convert of Jewish ancestry, filed an appeal against his expulsion as president of the San Gabriel Valley Lodge of B'nai B'rith, the Jewish benevolent association. Said Howard:

My tribe, the tribe of Judah, is so fraught with internal disorder that I merely decided to walk across the street and live with my in-laws—the tribe of Joseph. Mormonism is a continuation of Judaism; all Jews are Israelites, but not all Israelites are Jews. Mormons are Israelites, too.[15]

The author believes that the time will come when even the general public will distinguish between Protestantism and the various LDS bodies. The continued exclusion of Mormonism from the widening Protestant fellowship of ecumenical agencies and local cooperation will point up the basic differences between the Mormon and the Protestant positions. The Latter-day Saints themselves should welcome this distinction since they have no desire to align themselves with the apostate churches of Christendom: Catholic or Protestant.

8. *Polygamy*

For nearly ten years in secret and forty years in public the Mormon Church preached and practiced polygamy. Mormondom remained a monogamous society but a significant percentage of its hierarchy and wealthy members took additional wives with the full blessing of the Church. One Mormon patriarch, Heber C. Kimball, held the record with 45 wives and 65 children.

By espousing polygamy the Mormon Church aroused the antagonism of Protestant ministers, reformers, Utah Gentiles, and politicians. Once slavery was settled by the Civil War, these forces turned to attack that "twin relic of barbarism"—polygamy.

The Mormons appealed to the example of the Old Testament prophets and patriarchs as polygamists revered by the Bible-reading Christians of the nineteenth century, but their arguments fell on deaf ears. They pointed out that all human societies save those of Europe and the United States sanctioned polygamy. They insisted that their doctrine of plural marriage was a purely religious issue protected by the First Amendment, which guaranteed freedom of religion, but the rest of the nation refused to tolerate the new marriage patterns. Polygamy would have to go and the effort to dislodge this practice almost wrecked the Mormon Church.

Long before the official acknowledgment of the revelation authorizing plural marriage in 1852, long before the first secret polygamous marriages in Nauvoo, the Mormon

Church was rumored to have preached the doctrine of polygamy. In Kirtland and Missouri, these rumors as much as anything contributed to the Mormons' troubles with the Gentiles. The Church itself at this time indignantly denied the charge and could point to at least five separate denunciations of polygamy in the *Book of Mormon*. Among these passages were the following:

Behold, David and Solomon truly had many wives and concubines, which thing was abominable before me, Saith the Lord ... Hearken to the word of the Lord: For there shall not any man among you have save it be one wife; and concubines he shall have none (Jacob 2:24, 27).

And it came to pass that Riplakish did not do that which was right in the sight of the Lord, for he did have many wives and concubines (Ether 10:5).

Behold, the Lamanites, ... they have not forgotten the commandment of the Lord, which was given unto our fathers—that they should have save it were one wife, and concubines they should have none, and there should not be whoredoms committed among them (Jacob 3:5).

Likewise in *Doctrine and Covenants,* the Mormons could silence their critics by quoting these passages relating to marriage:

Thou shalt love thy wife with all thy heart, and shalt cleave unto her and none else (42:22).

Marriage is ordained of God unto man; wherefore it is lawful that he should have one wife, and they twain shall be one flesh (49:15, 16).

Until 1866 the following revelation appeared as Section 109:4, but after this date it was deleted. (It continues to be published in the *Doctrine and Covenants* of the Reorganized Church as Section 111:4.)

We believe that one man should have one wife; and one woman but one husband, except in case of death, when either is at liberty to marry again.

Perhaps Joseph Smith thought he might as well introduce polygamy into his church since he was being accused of it anyway. Apparently the Prophet worked out the theory of plurality of wives in 1839 and 1840, but this new doctrine was kept secret from the ordinary Saint. In the *Millennial Star*, Smith denied that the Latter-day Saints believed in a "community of wives" and called this "an abomination in the sight of the Lord." In 1842, a Saint by the name of Udney Hay Jacob published a defense of polygamy as an Old Testament form of marriage. His pamphlet was printed on Smith's press and the Prophet could hardly have been unaware of its publication. It did serve as a trial balloon. The reaction from the average Mormon was unfavorable and Smith realized that this drastic affront to Puritan morals would have to be introduced slowly and secretly lest it disrupt the church.

Fawn McKay Brodie, a niece of the president of the Mormon Church, has written the most comprehensive life of the Prophet. She lists a Miss Fanny Alger, a seventeen-year-old orphan taken into the Smith home in Kirtland, as Smith's first plural wife. Mrs. Brodie says that Smith was said to have seduced the young girl who was forced to leave the Smith home by Emma even though she was pregnant at the time.

Mrs. Brodie lists 26 women married to Smith between 1840 and the summer of 1843. He married an additional 18 women between July 12, 1843, when the revelation was given, and the day of his death.

At times Smith's marital adventures led to consequences he had not foreseen. For example, both Smith and John C. Bennett sought the hand of Nancy Rigdon, Sidney's daughter. Neither managed to woo the lady but this rivalry helped turn Bennett into an enemy and also infuriated the elderly Ridgon.

William Clayton, the Prophet's private secretary, related the story of the revelation on plural marriage, in an affadavit signed February 16, 1874. He said that he and Smith took a walk one day in February of 1843. Smith said that he knew that Clayton had his eye on a woman convert in England and asked why he did not send for her to come to Nauvoo. Smith promised to give him the authority to take her as another wife and explained his new doctrine. He concluded, "It is your privilege to have all the wives you want."

Hyrum Smith asked his brother to write up the doctrine. He promised to show it to Emma and placate her feelings but she was understandably resentful and bitter. At Emma's insistence, Smith destroyed the original revelation but in the meantime another copy had been made for Bishop Newell K. Whitney. The existence of this second copy was not generally known until 1846 and its contents were not revealed to the general public until the Mormons were entrenched in their Rocky Mountain sanctuary.

As it appears in the current Utah edition of *Doctrine and Covenants,* the significant part of Section 132 reads:

> ... if any man espouse a virgin, and desire to espouse another, and the first give her consent, and if he espouse the second, and they are virgins, and have vowed to no other man, then he is justified; he cannot commit adultery for they are given unto him; for he cannot commit adultery with that that belongeth unto him and to no one else.
>
> And if he have ten virgins given unto him by this law, he cannot commit adultery, for they belong to him, and they are given unto him; therefore he is justified (132: 61, 62).

This new revelation was prefaced by the statement:

> For behold, I reveal unto you a new and an everlasting covenant; and if ye abide not that covenant, then ye are damned;

for no one can reject this covenant and be permitted to enter into my glory (132:4).

Put in these terms, the Mormon Church could do nothing but fight to the end to preserve its system of plural marriage until the full weight of the Federal Government seemed to threaten the existence of the Church. This is also why the so-called Fundamentalists continue to practice polygamy even though it means sure excommunication from the Church if discovered.

Polygamy fitted into Smith's evolving theology, a remarkably original theology which displayed the qualities admired on the American frontier in the early nineteenth century. The God of the Christian Trinity he understood to be only the god for this world. Other gods ruled other worlds and the head God Elohim had organized millions of worlds and billions of spirits. A man who was baptized, accepted the restored gospel, and was married for time and eternity in the temple could hope to achieve godhead himself. And every woman's salvation was dependent on her marriage to a man holding the Mormon priesthood.

The more wives a man had, the better his chance of attaining a superior divine status and the more glorious his life as a god. A woman unmarried in this life might achieve her salvation by undergoing a proxy marriage in the temple to a deceased Mormon priest; she thereby shared in his glory after death. A woman contemplating marriage would do better marrying an already married apostle or bishop than a bachelor who held an inferior grade of the priesthood.

Thus in Mormonism two living persons may be sealed to each other for time and eternity. A living man may be sealed to a dead woman, which gives him an additional wife in the next world. A living woman may be sealed to a dead man, allowing her to achieve salvation. At one time the Church also allowed two living people to be sealed for eternity only— even though they were married for time to other mates. In

Nauvoo, for example, a married woman might get permission to spend eternity with another man than her husband.

Kimball Young, a grandson of Brigham Young and head of the sociology department at Northwestern University, has observed:

The plurality idea was likewise applied to the whole doctrine of the godhead ... Smith was elaborate in his fantasies and the notion of eons of time and endless numbers of worlds and universes in which human beings would in time emerge as gods provided at least some rationalization for the return to the patriarchal order of marriage.[1]

Mormon concern for sexuality extended to the most sacred spiritual personages. The God of this world was himself married and actually begat the billions of spirit creatures. His wife was probably Mary, to whom he had been married for time and eternity.

Even Jesus Christ Himself was thought to be not only married but married to more than one woman. Mormons speculated that Jesus was married to Mary and Martha and Mary Magdalen. Orson Pratt declared: "It is necessary that he [Jesus] should have had one or more wives by whom he could multiply his seed, not for any limited period of time, but for ever and ever; thus he truly would be a father everlastingly, according to the name which was to be given him."

Orson Pratt suggested that the wedding feast at Cana was an occasion of one of Jesus' own weddings. When Jesus showed himself to the women after his resurrection Pratt observed: "Now, it would be very natural for a husband in the resurrection to appear first to his own dear wives, and afterwards show himself to his other friends."

Mormons delighted in taunting their Protestant critics, who devoured the lives of the Old Testament prophets and patriarchs, with the question of why they considered polygamy such a horrible crime while honoring these ancient polygamists. Even Martin Luther approved the plural marriage of Philip, the Landgrave of Hesse.

Most Mormons accepted the Principle, as the teaching of polygamy was known, only for religious reasons. This practice went against their Puritan grain; the personal, economic and social problems it entailed more than overshadowed the attraction of sexual variationism. The very idea that a man would enter the Principle for reasons of lust or would indulge in sexual intercourse for the pleasure it afforded was abhorrent. The Mormon took additional wives because God through his Prophet commanded it and because it enhanced his opportunities for a higher state in the next life.

At Nauvoo only the highest-ranking Mormons knew of the new doctrine revealed to Joseph Smith. The rank-and-file members continued to suffer excommunication and denunciations for suggesting polygamy as a possible marital arrangement. *Times and Seasons* for February 1, 1844, reports the excommunication of Elder Hiram Brown for "preaching polygamy . . . in the county of Lapeer, State of Michigan."

Those who objected to polygamy formed the nucleus of Smith's opposition in Nauvoo. They included William Law and his brother Wilson, who began the *Nauvoo Expositor* whose destruction led to the Prophet's arrest and murder. The first and only issue of the *Nauvoo Expositor* charged:

Inasmuch as they have introduced false and damnable doctrines into the Church such as the plurality of gods above the God of this universe, and his liability to fall with all his creation; the plurality of wives, for time and eternity; the doctrine of unconditional sealing up to eternal life, against all crimes except that of shedding of innocent blood by a perversion of their priestly authority . . . we therefore are constrained to denounce them as apostates from the pure and holy doctrines of Jesus Christ.

In the same month the Prophet's brother Hyrum was denying the teaching of polygamy:

Whereas Brother Richard Hewitt has called on me today, to know my views concerning some doctrines ... that a man having a certain priesthood, may have as many wives as he pleases, and that doctrine is taught here ... there is no such doctrine taught here; neither is any such thing practiced here. And any man that is found teaching privately or publicly any such doctrine is culpable, and will stand a chance to be brought before the High Council, and lose his license and his membership also.[2]

Bennett, the former mayor of Nauvoo and once the second most powerful man in the Church, was excommunicated and published an imaginative exposé of polygamy which went far beyond the facts. Before his defection he had used the new doctrine to seduce a number of Nauvoo ladies.

In Bennett's exposé, which was reprinted around the country, he described the Danites and Avenging Angels but spent most of his time outlining an elaborate secret society of women in Nauvoo. Like the Masonic lodge, this society included three degrees. The first order, the Cyprian Sisters, granted their sexual favors to all the elders of the Church; the Chambered Sisters of Charity limited their favors to certain members of the hierarchy; and the third order, the Cloistered Saints or Saints of the Black Veil, were married in secret ceremonies to polygamists. These disclosures were snapped up by editors who had no way of verifying the facts. Actually only the third order bore much resemblance to the marital activities in Nauvoo.

A contemporary Mormon apologist insists that Gentile critics were invariably motivated by prurient passions when discussing polygamy:

The writers worked from the original assumption that polygamy was wrong and un-Christian. The attitude of their readers thus assured, it remained only for the scribes to point the finger of scorn and to fill in all the lurid sexy details. This was done, evidently, by drawing heavily upon their imaginations, their intimate knowledge of erotic literature, and the ordinarily suppressed pornographic tendencies of their own self-righteous minds.[3]

When all is said and done, however, the Utah Mormons must admit that the Gentile writers were correct in maintaining that polygamy was taught and practiced in Nauvoo and the Church was practicing not only polygamy but duplicity during the years 1843 to 1852 in denying the revelation authorizing plural marriage.

The Prophet's widow never admitted that he had taken other wives. Shortly before her death she declared: "No such thing as polygamy, or spiritual wifery, was taught publicly or privately, before my husband's death. . . . He had no other wife but me; nor did he to my knowledge ever have." Smith's direct descendants, members of the Reorganized Church of Jesus Christ of Latter Day Saints, continue to deny that the Prophet taught or practiced polygamy. They maintain that this heresy was introduced by Brigham Young, who also usurped the leadership of the Saints which should have gone to Smith's eldest so .

For years after leaving Nauvoo, the Church stoutly denied the doctrine of plural marriage. Gentiles who brought up the subject were 'accused of trying to libel the Church. Finally at a routine conference of about 100 Mormon missionaries on August 29, 1852, Brigham Young dropped the bombshell and admitted the truth of the long-standing charge.

Early in the morning Orson Pratt, the husband of ten wives himself and a leading apostle, told the assembled missionaries: "It is well known . . . to the congregation before me that the Latter-day Saints have embraced the doctrine of plurality of wives as part of their religious faith." He said that its practice is "necessary for our exaltation to the fullness of the Lord's glory in the eternal world." Those who rejected the doctrine would be damned, saith the Lord. He anticipated some difficulty with the Federal Government but predicted that any laws restricting the religious practice of polygamy would be declared unconstitutional.

That afternoon Brigham Young took the rostrum. He continued the discourse and announced:

"The Revelation will be read to you. The principle spoken upon by Brother Pratt this morning we believe in. And I tell you—for I know it—it will sail over and ride triumphantly above all the prejudice and priestcraft of the day; it will be fostered and believed in by the more intelligent portions of the world as one of the best doctrines ever proclaimed to any people."

Young then read the new revelation which, he said, was locked in his desk for many years. Of course, travelers to Utah had known about polygamy for years. The Mormon harems could not be hidden from the journalists, federal officers, 49ers, and explorers who invaded the intermountain sanctuary.

Polygamy, as openly advocated in Utah, followed a few rules of thumb but the social relations were diverse. Plural families played it by ear, since polygamy was introduced with no preparation into a society dominated by Puritanism. The polygamy of African, Moslem, or Chinese society drew on the accumulated wisdom of generations. The Mormon polygamists had little to go by but the brief revelation by Smith and the day-by-day counsel of the Church leaders.

Each husband who wished to take an additional wife had to first get the approval of his first wife as well as his bishop. Sometimes the first wife accompanied the bride and groom to the temple for the ceremony. Many Mormon wives rebelled at the idea of a second woman in the house but a few welcomed a younger woman to help with the chores.

One Mormon polygamist married four sisters and another married two sisters and their widowed mother. A few men married older women with no intention of indulging in sex relations, but ordinarily plural marriage carried the usual marital privileges. It was not unusual for Mormon patriarchs to take young wives after they themselves had passed their sixtieth or seventieth birthdays. Married men often competed for the hand of eligible brides with the bachelors of the community; the higher-ranking Mormon priest was likely to win since he could provide a higher standard of living and promise a happier afterlife.

Living arrangements varied. Some polygamists housed their wives and children under one roof while others maintained separate houses in the same or neighboring towns. Especially after 1880, when the Federal Government began an active prosecution of polygamists or "cohabs," the wives were scattered in various communities.

One wife readily agreed to her husband's suggestion that he take a second wife, accompanied the pair to the temple, and broke down only when she heard her husband's boots drop on the floor of the second wife's bedroom.

Artemus Ward related the tale of one unusual marital arrangement:

I had a man pointed out to me who married an entire family. He had originally intended to marry Jane, but Jane did not want to leave her widowed mother. The other three sisters were not in the matrimonial market for the same reason; so this gallant man married the whole crowd, including the girl's grandmother, who had lost all her teeth, and had to be fed with a spoon. The family were in indigent circumstances, and they could not but congratulate themselves on securing a wealthy husband. It seemed to affect the grandmother deeply, for the first words she said on reaching her new home were: "Now, thank God, I shall have my gruel reg'lar."

Apostle Parley Pratt married as his 12th wife, the estranged wife of Hector McLean of San Francisco. Mrs. McLean had joined the Mormon Church before she met the Apostle. She moved to Utah and was sealed to Pratt, but she and her new husband were arrested by McLean. When the Apostle was released from jail he was stabbed and shot to death by

McLean. The case became a *cause célèbre* in the nation, with the Mormons considering Pratt a martyr and the Gentiles concluding that he got just what he deserved as a wife stealer.

Exactly what percentage of Mormons lived in polygamy is not known. At one time the Church estimated that only 2 or 3 percent of the Mormon men were polygamous, but now the most quoted figures are much higher. Senator Wallace F. Bennett, in his book *Why I Am a Mormon,* uses the estimate of 8 to 10 percent; other writers, Mormon and non-Mormon, agree that the number of polygamous men was several times more than 2 or 3 percent. The preference for polygamy increased with the higher ranks of the hierarchy since this was considered a religious practice, and also since wealth enabled a man to support multiple families and also to advance in the priesthood. Gentile visitors sometimes estimated that half the Mormon families in Utah were polygamous, a figure that was certainly too high. As in most western communities, men outnumbered women and the spread of polygamy was limited by the number of available women Saints. Some passive resistance to polygamy was evident, especially among bachelors, and wives who could not bring themselves to welcome a second wife in their homes.

Sometimes apologists for polygamy suggest that it was adopted by the Mormon Church in order to provide husbands for a surplus of women converts. But the U. S. census records from 1850 to 1940 as well as all available Church records show a preponderance of males in Utah and in the Church. Another explanation for polygamy is that the Church encouraged this system of marriage in order to bring about a phenomenal increase in membership. Actually the husbands in polygamous unions had many more children than the monogamous husbands but the wives had fewer children on an average than if they had each been married to one man.

Brigham Young practiced what he preached. He denied

that sexual variationism had anything to do with the adoption of polygamy. "God never introduced the patriarchal order of marriage with a view to please man in his carnal desires but He introduced it for the express purpose of raising up to His name a royal priesthood," he declared.

A year before Smith dictated his revelation on plural marriage, Young had taken a second bride at Nauvoo who later bore him 7 children. By the time he announced the official revelation in 1852, he was living in a household which included 19 wives.

On January 21, 1846, Brigham Young married four women. Some of his wives were divorcees and some were widows. (Although Section 132 of *Doctrine and Covenants* speaks only of virgins, the Mormons married many widows and divorcees under its authorization.) Two of his wives were only sixteen when he took them in marriage and one was forty-five. The great love of his later years was Amelia Folsom, whom he married when he was sixty-one. She refused to live in the main house with the other women and persuaded him to build a separate house for her which the Saints called "Amelia's Palace." She became queen of the harem. Brigham Young sired a total of 31 daughters and 25 sons. In 1849 alone he became a father five times.

The president of the Church apparently believed that polygamy would eliminate many of the evils of society: prostitution, adultery, social disease, spinstership. He grew furious at Gentiles who dared to criticize Mormon marital arrangements. On one occasion in 1850 a federal judge addressed an assembly of Mormons in the Bowery, a temporary tabernacle in Salt Lake City. The Mormons had offered to send a block of marble to the Washington Monument and after questioning the loyalty of the Saints and in particular that of President Young, the judge added: "In order to make this presentation acceptable you must become virtuous, and teach your daughters to become virtuous, or your offering had better remain in the bosom of your native mountains."

The Mormon audience rose to its feet in anger and Young tore into the outspoken judge, calling him an "illiterate ranter" and a "coward." At a signal from the president of the Church the judge would have been a dead man, but the reprisals from the Government would have destroyed the Church.

Brigham Young should have stopped adding wives when his total reached 26. Wife 27 proved to be more troublesome than the rest of the wives combined. She had been born Ann Eliza Webb at Nauvoo the year that the Prophet was assassinated and Young assumed the leadership. Her parents took her to Utah where she eventually married an immigrant from England, James Leech Dee. The ceremony for time and eternity was performed in 1863 in the Endowment House in Salt Lake City with President Young presiding.

As Mrs. Dee she bore two sons but claimed that her husband abused and struck her. She obtained a divorce in 1865. The president had had his eyes on her for some years and encouraged her in a career as an actress. In 1869, when she was twenty-four and Young was sixty-eight, they were married and she became his 27th and last wife.

Life in polygamy did not satisfy Ann Eliza and she startled the Mormon and Gentile worlds by filing suit for divorce in 1873. This put the state in a dilemma since the state did not recognize polygamy, but the federal authorities relished the idea of forcing Brigham Young to pay a substantial alimony to the disgruntled wife.

Befriended by Gentiles, Ann Eliza began a new career as a lecturer and author of exposés of Mormon polygamy. She spoke to standing room only audiences in the east and often under Protestant Church auspices. Her remarks were designed to arouse Christian womankind against the practice of polygamy and few dry eyes could be seen in the crowds as she repeated the plaintive words of a little Mormon girl: "Mama, I do wish God had made men enough so that every little girl could have a father to love her." Ann Eliza was billed as the Rebel of the Harem. President Grant attended one of her lectures in Washington, D. C., and met her after the program. Her crusade influenced a stronger legal course against polygamy.

Ann Eliza also wrote a best-selling book which she called *Wife No. 19,* although no one has been able to figure out how she arrived at the number 19. Historians list her as No. 27.

Back in Utah, Young went into court and swore that he had but one wife, Mary Ann Angell. He reported that his monthly income was only $6,000 while ex-wife Ann Eliza claimed that it was closer to $40,000. The court found Young guilty and ordered him to pay $3,000 court costs and $9,500 alimony. He refused to pay the alimony and was found in contempt of court. The judge sentenced the Mormon president to one year in jail and fined him $25. He spent the night of March 11, 1875, in jail. Eventually the sum was reduced and Brigham ended up paying court costs. In 1877 another court decided that Ann Eliza could not claim alimony, since her marriage to Young was null and void. This meant that in the eyes of U. S. courts the plural wives except for the one legal wife were considered concubines. Later in the year, Young died. Ann Eliza disappeared from public eye after 1909 and no one seems to know where or when she died.

Ann Eliza's lectures and writings contributed to a flood of material about Mormon polygamy avidly followed by reformers and roués. In the Preface to an exposé of polygamy by Fanny Stenhouse, Harriet Beecher Stowe wrote:

> May we not then hope that the hour is come to loose the bonds of cruel slavery whose chains have cut into the very hearts of thousands of our sisters—a slavery which debases and degrades womanhood, motherhood, and the family?

Novels depicted lecherous Mormon missionaries luring innocent foreign girls to America where they became prisoners in Utah harems. Funds were raised to open an Industrial House in Salt Lake City where refugees from polygamy might find help; seldom did the project house more than a dozen such women.

Mark Twain visited Mormon country and penned the following tongue-in-cheek observation of polygamy as he saw it:

...With the gushing self-sufficiency of youth I was feverish to plunge headlong and achieve a great reform here until I saw the Mormon women. Then I was touched. My heart was wiser than my head. It warmed me toward these poor, ungainly, and pathetically "homely" creatures, and as I turned to hide the generous moisture in my eyes, I said, "No—the man that marries one of them has done an act of Christian charity which entitled him to the kindly applause of mankind, not their hard censure—and the man that marries sixty of them has done a deed of open-handed generosity so sublime that the nation should stand uncovered in his presence and worship in silence." [4]

Orson Pratt came to the defense of the Mormon experiment:

The peculiar custom of plurality, practiced by some in Utah, in no way interferes with the rights of anyone; it is in no way immoral; it in no way injures the parties themselves, or anyone else; it is in no way unscriptural; it is in no way conflicting with the Constitution; it is in no way violating any of the laws of Utah, or any other laws to which the citizens of that territory are amenable. Therefore, there is no reason whatever for calling it a crime, or for passing legislative enactments against it.

As early as 1856 the Republican Presidential nominee John Charles Frémont blasted "those twin relics of barbarism— polygamy and slavery." The party platform declared it was the "right and duty of Congress" to abate both evils. The Democrats preferred to attack Mormon polygamy rather than to stir up the issue of slavery which could split their party.

Justin Morrill, later to achieve fame as author of the Land-Grant Acts, introduced a bill "to punish and prevent the practice of polygamy in the territories of the United States." It died in committee. Although President Lincoln was inclined to let the Mormons alone, he finally signed a similar bill by Morrill in July 1862.

President Grant in his message to Congress in December 1871 said:

"In Utah there still remains a remnant of barbarism, repugnant to civilization, decency, and to the law of the United States. . . . Neither polygamy nor any other violation of existing statutes will be permitted in the territory of the United States. It is not with the religion of self-styled saints that we are now dealing, but their practices. They will be protected in the worship of God according to the dictates of their consciences, but they will not be permitted to violate laws under the cloak of religion. . . ."

An amendment to strengthen the anti-polygamy bill of 1862 was introduced in 1882 by Senator George F. Edmunds. It defined polygamy as a crime and defined "unlawful cohabitation" as living with more than one wife. If convicted, polygamists could be excluded from voting or holding public office. The Edmunds bill was declared constitutional by the Supreme Court and the Mormon Church faced a showdown with the Federal Government.

An even stronger Edmunds-Tucker bill passed in 1887 confiscated the property of the Mormon Church which was disincorporated. This too was held constitutional in 1890.

The Church began to waver. The Edmunds-Tucker bill hit the Church in the pocketbook. Church leaders knew that their cherished dream of a state would never come about if they persisted in supporting polygamy. Some of the Saints themselves were less enchanted by polygamy, particularly the many single men who were unable to find one wife while Church leaders corralled harems.

For years a hide-and-seek game was played in Utah and neighboring states by the "cohabs" and the "deps" or federal officers. Plural families were dispersed. Some polygamists constructed secret rooms and trapdoors to escape the prying federal investigators. A few fled to Mexico and Canada, where they continued polygamy without governmental interference. In 1887 alone, 200 Saints from Utah and Idaho were sent to jail as cohabs.

Mormon leaders tried to sustain morale in the community by elevating polygamy to an essential Church doctrine—to the embarrassment of later generations of Mormons. For example, Young himself declared:

It is the word of the Lord, and I wish to say to you, and all the world, that if you desire with all your hearts to obtain the blessings which Abraham obtained, you will be polygamists.... This is as true as that God lives.[5]

Heber C. Kimball, the polygamist par excellence and counselor to Young, predicted:

It would be as easy for the United States to build a tower to remove the sun, as to remove polygamy, or the church and kingdom of God.[6]

A similar prediction was made by Lorenzo Snow, fourth president of the Church who went to jail for practicing polygamy:

Tho I go to prison, God will not change His law of celestial marriage. But the man, the people, the nation, that oppose and fight this doctrine and the Church of God, will be overthrown.[7]

Finally, the elderly president of the Church, Wilford Woodruff, issued a declaration suspending the practice of polygamy on September 24, 1890. He wrote in part:

Inasmuch as laws have been enacted by Congress forbidding plural marriages, which laws have been pronounced constitutional by the court of last resort, I hereby declare my intention to submit to those laws, and to use my influence with the members of the Church over which I preside to have them do likewise.

And I now publicly declare that my advice to the Latter-day Saints is to refrain from contracting any marriage forbidden by the law of the land.

This declaration or manifesto is included at the end of the revelations in the Utah edition of *Doctrine and Covenants* but apparently does not have the same standing as an official revelation. This capitulation by the Church brought about an amnesty for the cohab prisoners and a return of Church property in 1893.

A practice going back almost 60 years in the Church could not be stopped without some lapses. Sporadic plural marriages brought forth a "Second Manifesto" in 1904 by President Joseph F. Smith. Some apostles continued to promote polygamy outside of the United States and two such apostles were forced to resign in 1906.

In 1898 Brigham H. Roberts was refused a seat in Congress because he was a polygamist, and in a special election a Mormon with one wife was elected to serve. The seating of Senator Reed Smoot was later questioned but he was finally confirmed.

Although the Church now refused to solemnize plural marriages it sympathized with members involved in plural marriages. It did not wish to break up polygamous families if it could be helped. The Mormon community tried to protect plural families from further harassment by the federal authorities.

Not all Mormons accepted Woodruff's Manifesto. What was commanded by the Lord could not be abandoned for the sake of expediency. This belief was put into practice by the Fundamentalists in the 1920's and thousands continue to practice the marriage pattern outlined by Joseph Smith. We will discuss the Fundamentalists in Chapter 18.

George Bernard Shaw had his own explanation for the demise of Mormon polygamy. He wrote: "Polygamy when tried under modern democratic conditions, as by the Mormons, is wrecked by the revolt of the mass of inferior men who are condemned to celibacy by it; for the maternal instinct leads a woman to prefer a tenth share in a first-rate man to the exclusive possession of a third-rate."

Polygamy was not denied by the 1890 Manifesto. It remains a divine revelation even though its practice has been suspended in obedience to the laws of the state. Kimball Young observes:

It must be remembered that theologically speaking, plurality of wives is still a principle of Mormonism and this at least is one way of providing for future happiness and glory.[8]

He adds:

There is evidence that polygamy is being practiced in Mormon settlements in Canada and Mexico. Moreover, there is more than mere rumor to the stories that the system is secretly in operation even in Salt Lake City and other cities in Utah.[9]

O'Dea also points out:

Yet the official doctrine of the Mormon Church still holds that in some sense polygamy is the divinely preferred form of matrimony.[10]

For ten years the Mormon Church denied that polygamy was practiced by members of the Church. During all these years Brigham Young declared that he had kept the 1843 revelation in his locked desk drawer, even though he and leading Mormons had taken multiple wives. Most historians agree that Joseph Smith, Young and other Mormon officials married second and subsequent wives before the revelation was supposed to have been received in Nauvoo. Again vehement denials were issued by the Church when rumors of polygamy were published.

Today Mormons prefer not to discuss polygamy. Mormon missionaries are instructed to avoid the subject. The average Mormon would rather not dwell on this aspect of Church history. He seeks respectability and accommodation to American society even though his father or grandfather may have lived as an outlaw to practice plural marriage.

Whatever attitude a Mormon in the 1960's may take, polygamy was presented to the Church as a divine revelation. It was practiced by the Prophet and by Brigham Young and most of the presidents of the Church. The leading families in the Church today come from polygamous households of the late nineteenth century. And the doctrine itself has never been denied. Only the practice has been suspended for political reasons.

A contemporary Mormon author, John J. Stewart, who is editor of publications at Utah State University affirms:

The Church has never, and certainly will never, renounce this doctrine. The revelation on plural marriage is still an integral part of LDS scripture, and always will be.[11]

He adds:

As well might the Church relinquish its claim to the Priesthood as the doctrine of plural marriage.[12]

The chief reason why the Mormon Church, "though forced by evil circumstances to suspend its practice here upon earth," will never deny the doctrine of plural marriage is that "plural marriage is the patriarchal order of marriage lived by God and others who reign in the Celestial Kingdom." [13]

Stewart's book, *Brigham Young and His Wives,* carries a 1961 copyright date.

9. *Church Organization and the Priesthood*

MARK TWAIN once remarked that the only rival to the Mormon Church in the area of organization was the Prussian Army. More recently *The New York Times* observed, "The Church of Jesus Christ of Latter-day Saints must be the most elaborately organized and disciplined religious structure of modern times." [1] Both Mark Twain and the *Times* were probably correct.

Even the well-organized Roman Catholic and Methodist churches take on the character of rather loose fellowships compared to the meticulously organized Church of Jesus Christ of Latter-day Saints. Practically every "worthy" adult male in the Mormon Church holds some rank in the priesthood and undertakes corresponding obligations. Holders of the priesthood now number more than 450,000, about the same number as the world total of Catholic priests. Mormon wives participate in a network of auxiliary organizations as do girls and boys.

Each group of priests is organized in small units known as quorums. This term carries a technical meaning in Mormonism which has nothing to do with parliamentary voting majorities.

At the top of this huge priestly structure is the president of the Church, who is believed to have inherited the mantle of authority of Joseph Smith, Jr. as Prophet, Seer, and Revelator. He holds office for life and his power rivals that of the Pope; his decisions are accepted as the will of God.

Mormons claim that their Church organization parallels that of the Apostolic Church although the positions of the president and assistant presidents who together form the First Presidency do not seem to be spelled out in the New Testament. Mormon apologists insist that only a church with 12 apostles can lay any claim to being the one true Church of Jesus Christ.

Mormondom's autocratic form of church government contrasts with the generally democratic polity of the frontier Baptists, Disciples of Christ, and Congregationalists. Mormon officials submit to votes of confidence in these "sustainings" but rarely does anyone cast a negative vote.

When founded in 1830 the Church was ruled by only two officers: Smith as First Elder and Oliver Cowdery as Second Elder. Sidney Rigdon later replaced Cowdery as second in command and the Prophet received a revelation that henceforth he was to be the only one to receive and announce revelations for the entire Church. A multiplicity of prophets would have fragmented the early Church.

In 1832 Smith assumed the office of president of the High Priesthood and in March 1833 he established the First Presidency. The Church became concerned to reestablish the ancient offices of the Christian Church such as deacon, priest, and apostle. A Mormon advances from one rank to the next in the priesthood as a Mason might advance from the Entered Apprentice degree to the 33rd degree of the Scottish rite.

Smith consolidated his position as head of the Church in Kirtland and Missouri so that by the time the Saints fled to Illinois he was unquestionably in command. At his death, Brigham Young assumed the leadership of most of the Saints in virtue of his position as head of the Council of the Twelve.

The theocratic structure of Mormonism is built around the priesthood. Smith and Cowdery claimed to have received the keys of the Aaronic or lesser priesthood from John the Baptist in 1829. Later, at an unspecified time, they received the keys of the Melchizedek priesthood from the Apostles

Peter, James and John. This event is thought to have taken place while the two were translating the *Book of Mormon* in Harmony, Pennsylvania.

In Mormon belief their priesthood is the only valid priesthood on earth today. All other Christian ministries, Catholic and Protestant, lack authority. Their baptisms are not accepted by God and their churches do not qualify as Christian churches. Mormons believe that Adam, Noah, Abraham and Moses all held the same Mormon priesthood. The Christians of the first and second centuries held an identical priesthood but the keys of this priesthood were lost by apostasy soon after the death of the Apostles.

Joseph Weston, a Mormon, asserts: "The priesthood is the directing agency between God and man. It is the government of God, whether on earth or in the heavens. It governs all things, directs all things, sustains all things, and deals with all things associated with God and truth." [2] The same author declares: "To put it baldly, Mormons appropriate for their priesthood all good abilities ever hinted, revealed or made available to humankind." [3]

Among the powers of the Mormon priests are those of healing. A Mormon who is sick will probably call in the priests to anoint his head and pray for his recovery. At one time belief in faith healing tended to disparage reliance on medicine but this is no longer true of younger Mormons.

The gift of speaking in tongues is also claimed for the priest which means that the Mormon Church could properly be classified as a Pentecostal church. Cases of glossolalia in the pioneer Mormon Church, especially in Kirtland, are common. Prominent Mormons not only spoke in unknown tongues but translated the babblings of others. Today the gift is usually acknowledged in a more symbolic way as an aid to young missionaries preaching in foreign countries.

Weston observes that the priesthood also possesses the power of discernment: "Possessors of the priesthood through the ages have been able to detect the power of magicians and sorcerers, and thus be able to frustrate them." [4] The Prophet himself, as you will recall, gave detailed instructions on how to detect a good angel from a devil by shaking hands with the personage.

Priests can receive private revelations from God but may not publish these for the entire Church. A church which bases its claim on a continuous revelation could not afford to give free rein to private revelations unless it wished to risk disintegration and continuous schism.

Only the Mormon priest can baptize for the living and the dead; Mormons refuse to acknowledge the validity of baptisms administered by Catholic priests or Protestant ministers. All converts must be baptized or rebaptized by immersion by a Mormon priest. Clergymen from other denominations must enter the Mormon Church at the lowest rung of the ladder as deacons. Likewise a Mormon who is stripped of the priesthood and repents must start over again as a deacon. In recent years one of the apostles was so disciplined; he returned to his ward and started the climb again.

Only the Mormon priest can seal contracts for time and eternity in the temple or administer the Sacrament in the ward chapel. He is also privileged to receive special revelations from heavenly beings to guide him in the conduct of his private life or in the carrying out of Church duties.

A Mormon lad begins his advance in the priesthood by being ordained a deacon at the age of twelve. This is the lowest office of the Aaronic priesthood and is usually conferred about four years after baptism. His duties as deacon are to assist the teachers in their work and to collect fast offerings from families in the ward. After three years as a deacon he becomes a teacher himself and two or three years later he is ordained a priest.

At the age of eighteen or nineteen the young man is ordained an elder, which is the lowest rank in the Melchizedek priesthood. Those who leave for a mission assignment receive this ordination before starting their journey; those who return from a mission usually become "seventies," which is the next higher office in the Melchizedek priesthood. The highest office in this Mormon priesthood is that of high priest. All major Church offices are held by high priests. Holders of the Melchizedek priesthood are assigned to spiritual tasks, while the Aaronic priests are supposed to take care of the material needs of the Church.

The office of patriarch to the Church is a hereditary one held by some member of the Smith family. Since all of the direct descendants of the Prophet belong to the Reorganized Church, the holders of this office in Utah trace their ancestry to his brother, Hyrum. The patriarch dispenses special blessings to faithful Church members; it is a full-time job and the holder of the office receives a salary.

Joseph Smith, Sr. was appointed first patriarch by his son in 1833. When he died in 1840 the office was assumed by Hyrum. An uncle, John Smith, succeeded Hyrum, and the office has since been filled by a son or brother of the deceased patriarch. The incumbent is Eldred Gee Smith who took office in 1947.

The mature, experienced Mormon aspires to the office of high priest. High priests are looked upon as model Mormons. Adults who fail to meet one or another of the Church's qualifications for full membership remain in the lesser priesthood and are known as adult Aaronics.

The office of bishop is actually assigned to the Aaronic priesthood but it can be filled only by a Mormon who holds the rank of high priest. The Church also allows anyone to hold this office who can prove he is a lineal descendant of Aaron, the first high priest of the Jews; such a person may hold the office without counselors. So far the extensive genealogical records in Salt Lake City have not turned up anyone with this pedigree.

Explained Brigham Young: "The Bishopric by right belongs to the literal descendants of Aaron, but we shall have to ordain from the other tribes, men who hold the High Priesthood, to act in the Lesser, until we find a literal descendant of Aaron, who is prepared to receive it." [5]

Each rank of the priesthood is organized in quorums with the following memberships:

deacons, 12
teachers, 24
priests, 48
elders, 96
seventies, 70
high priests, no limit

These quorums hold regular meetings. Instruction in the duties of each stage of the priesthood forms a large part of the meeting agendas.

At the top of the hierarchy is the Presidency and the Council of Twelve Apostles. On the death of the President of the Church the apostles choose one of their number to succeed to the office. The new president in turn picks assistants as his counselors; all men carry the title "President." The president fills any subsequent vacancies in the Council of the Twelve arising from death, retirement, or excommunication. In 1965 President McKay enlarged the Presidency by appointing two additional counselors for a total of four.

Decisions of the Presidency are not doubted by the rank and file or the lower hierarchy. Twice a year, in spring and fall, the Church calls a general conference which is held in the Salt Lake City Tabernacle. All church officials and most bishops are expected to attend. The top officers are routinely sustained by a conference vote.

The apostles resemble the College of Cardinals in the Roman Catholic Church. They visit missions and stakes, write many of the Church's theological tracts and Sunday school lessons. They are often elderly gentlemen and success-

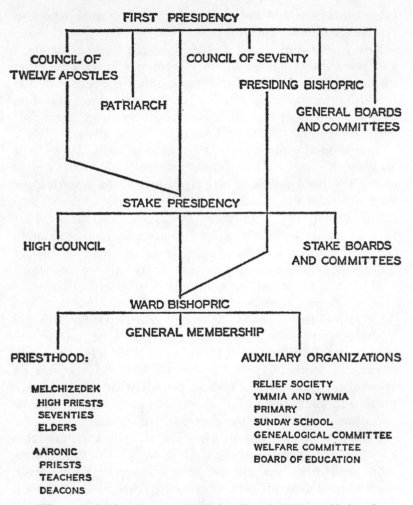

The organizational structure of the Church of Jesus Christ of Latter-day Saints.

ful businessmen and are assisted by younger men who also receive an annual stipend.

The First Council of Seventy consists of seven members and takes direct charge of the Mormon Church's far-flung missionary effort. The Presiding Bishopric consists of the presiding bishop and his two counselors. The presiding bishop receives all the tithes and donations from the wards and handles many of the Church's business affairs.

The 40 men who comprise the General Authorities of the Mormon Church are the First Presidency (5), the Council of the Twelve Apostles, twelve Assistants to the Apostles, the Patriarch, the First Council of Seventies (7), and the Presiding Bishopric (3). In recent years the assistants to the apostles have grown in prestige and are now counted among the General Authorities. The holders of these offices are ordinarily full-time employees and receive allowances which enable them to maintain a comfortable standard of living.

The current President, Prophet, Seer, Revelator and Trustee-in-Trust is David O. McKay, ninety. Of Scottish and Welsh ancestry, he was born in Huntsville, Utah, and graduated from the University of Utah in 1897. He served as a missionary in Scotland from 1897 to 1899. McKay became an apostle in 1906 and was chosen president of the European mission in 1922. Before his selection as president in 1951 he had been counselor to two previous presidents.

President McKay gets to his office at 5:30 A.M. but takes a long nap after lunch. He spends his weekends at his Huntsville farm where he keeps five horses; however, he has given up riding. During his term of office he has seen the Mormon Church experience its most dramatic growth. The annual harvest of converts has grown from 17,000 to more than 100,000 and the Church has never been more prosperous.

Some Mormon writers continue to maintain that only a handful of men and women receive a salary from the Church. Actually the Mormon Church employs hundreds of people in administrative as well as clerical positions. It does not pay local bishops who serve as pastors but it could not operate its vast business and missionary enterprises without a full-time bureaucracy. The General Authorities and their assistants, office workers, professors and staff members at Brigham Young University, editors of the *Deseret News,* temple doorkeepers, administrators of Mormon hospitals, and hundreds of others work for the Church and receive their salaries from Church funds.

The 3,897 wards of the Mormon Church correspond to the Catholic parish or Protestant congregation. About 400 ward branch organizations serve Mormons in areas where the membership is too small to support a regular ward. In addition, there are nearly 2,000 mission branches. Ward membership averages between 200 and 500 people and the tendency is to break up the larger wards into smaller units.

The bishop is the senior church officer in the ward. He usually holds down a secular job but devotes as much as 40 hours a week to church work. The bishop receives the tithes of ward members, baptizes and confirms, conducts funerals, signs recommendations for members who wish to do temple work, counsels his flock, and organizes the spiritual program for the ward. For this he receives about $10 a month for stationery and supplies. Among Mormon bishops we find college professors, corporation presidents, physicians, farmers, teachers, and lawyers.

The bishop meets every week with his two counselors and the ward clerk. He must keep detailed records of all baptisms, blessings, confirmations, ordinations, marriages (for time, not for time and eternity), divorces, excommunications, and deaths. Every five years he must take a complete census and forward the data to Salt Lake City headquarters. The bishop accepts the position when asked to do so by Church authorities and continues until he is relieved or dies.

If large enough the ward will have a quorum of 48 priests with the bishop as president. The well-run Mormon ward will also support auxiliary organizations such as the Relief

Society, Sunday School, Mutual Improvement Association for young people, Primary Association for children, and Genealogical Class. These organizations involve every member of a Mormon family except babes in arms.

Every Mormon family in the ward is visited once a month by the teachers, often accompanied by one or two deacons. Through this "teaching" the Church provides instruction on points of doctrine and also discovers any evidence of spiritual or material needs which may be remedied by the bishop or other members of the ward. For example, a family hit by sickness or unemployment should be able to draw upon the bishop's storehouse for food and other necessities.

Five to ten wards are organized into larger units known as stakes of Zion (dioceses). There are now 379 such stakes around the globe. The General Authorities select the stake presidents. In typical Mormon organizational pattern he is assisted by two counselors. For many years before his election as governor of Michigan, George Romney headed the Detroit stake of the Church. The stake holds a conference every three months; these weekend meetings are often visited by a representative of the General Authorities.

Like the patriarch to the Church, the various stake patriarchs dispense blessings to devout Latter-day Saints. The larger stakes may have more than one patriarch. In order to obtain such a blessing the applicant must obtain a "recommend" from his bishop.

With this extensive division of responsibility the Mormon Church can offer any man or woman as much opportunity for church service as the individual wishes to accept. O'Dea estimates that from one-third to one-half of all Mormons are active in their church, which is a remarkable achievement which puts most Catholic and Protestant churches in the shade.

Although it goes through the motions of sustaining all its officers at conferences, the Mormon Church makes little pretense of democracy in its government. The president of the Church holds more power than any other church head with the possible exception of the Pope and the president of the Watchtower Bible and Tract Society (Jehovah's Witnesses). He is believed to hold the keys of the only valid priesthood on earth. He is the only man alive who can receive revelations from God, Jesus, the original Apostles and angels which apply to the entire Church. He holds office until death and appoints all the other major members of the hierarchy.

The tight, disciplined organization of the Church enabled it to survive the exoduses from Ohio, Missouri and Nauvoo, to undertake the march to the Rocky Mountains, to bring thousands of immigrants from the British Isles and Scandinavia to Utah, to survive years of harassment and legal persecution over the doctrine of plural marriage. It provides almost every member with a sense of personal involvement. While the Campbellite movement abolished the distinction between clergy and laity by trying to abolish the office of priest, the Mormons blurred the distinction by making it possible for every male member to become a holder of the priesthood.

The organization is not perfect. It tends to favor the elderly businessmen and contributes to the ultraconservative theological stance which is estranging some of the younger Saints from their heritage.

Kimball Young also points out "... the Mormon Church is dominated by a few more or less select families. New families may move into this elite, but the essential control for many decades now has remained in the hands of not more than 15 or 20 families." [6] These pioneer families—the Bensons, Romneys, Smiths, Kimballs, Cannons, Richards, et al.— provide a disproportionately large percentage of the top officials of the Church. Their prestige, wealth, and family connections and the oligarchic structure of the Church polity guarantee that they will continue to direct the destiny of the Church of Jesus Christ of Latter-day Saints for many years to come.

10. *Wealth of the Mormon Church*

With an estimated daily income of more than $1 million the Mormon Church is the dominant financial institution in the Rocky Mountain area and the wealthiest church per capita in the world.[1] Mormon wealth comes from the tithes of 2,400,000 members, profits from commercial enterprises owned and operated by the Church, and dividends and capital gains from common stock in corporations in which the Church has an interest.

Details of the Mormon financial empire are not published. Only the highest Church officials know how much comes from which sources; they do not issue an annual report or reveal this information to ordinary Latter-day Saints, much less to Gentiles. At one time the Church did report annual disbursements but this figure soared to $55 million and the Church discontinued this practice. Perhaps only President McKay and President Nathan Eldon Tanner, the financial expert of the Church, know the full extent of Mormon wealth.

Each active member of the Church of Jesus Christ of Latter-day Saints is expected to contribute 10 percent of his gross income to the Church. This is computed before taxes. Some Saints who give only 5 percent are still considered in good standing. Each member makes his contribution to the bishop of his ward who issues a receipt and forwards the money to the Presiding Bishop. No one but the bishop in the ward knows how much an individual contributes; he is therefore the only person who can provide a "recommend" admitting the qualified Latter-day Saint to one of the temples. Only tithers can pass its portals.

No one is excused from the obligation of tithing: bread-winners, newsboys, students, servicemen, widows, etc. Utah is not a particularly wealthy state. In 1958 it ranked 30th among the states in per capita income. Nevertheless many Mormons have achieved success in business and the professions in Utah and other western states. The Church enrolls at least 300 millionaires.[2] The tithes of all these hundreds of thousands of faithful Mormons provide the Church with an enormous financial resource.

Tithing has been prescribed for all Saints since 1841. In a sense it supplanted the cooperative United Order whereby converts would simply turn over all their property to the Church. The only other church which has had a similar success with tithing has been the Seventh-day Adventists. Many Adventists offer a double tithe: 10 percent to the local congregation and another 10 percent to the larger Church.

In addition to this tithe the average Mormon contributes another 2 percent of his income for the upkeep of the local ward. By comparison we might note that in 1960 the average contribution of a member of the Protestant Episcopal Church was $64.51 plus an extra $1.53 for the missions. The average contribution of a member of a Protestant or Eastern Orthodox church belonging to the National Council of Churches of Christ was only $66.76 plus $2.04 for missions for the same year.

On the first Sunday of each month Mormon families give up two meals and donate the equivalent money to the Church welfare program. This money is used to buy food, clothing and other items for the bishops' storehouses from which unemployed or sick Mormons can draw provisions.

With the tithes of Mormons, the Church has been able to purchase and develop all types of properties, mostly in the Rocky Mountain states. These pioneer investments in western real estate, manufacturing, finance, and natural resources have grown as the West has grown. The continued movement of population from East to West can only benefit the Church from a financial standpoint.

To provide accommodations for visitors to Salt Lake City the Church opened a small hotel. Today the Mormon Church owns the Hotel Utah, the Hotel Temple Square, and a motel. None of these hostelries includes a cocktail lounge but all serve a good cup of coffee to Gentile guests.

The oldest department store in the United States, Zion's Cooperative Mercantile Institution or ZCMI, was founded in 1868. At that time the Church urged its members to boycott Gentile and apostate merchants. Brigham Young obtained 772 of the original 1,990 shares of ZCMI which also supplied 150 cooperative stores through the territory. Actually ZCMI is not a true cooperative in the Rochdale sense since it distributes profits according to shares owned rather than purchases. Recently the Church opened a $3,500,000 suburban branch of ZCMI about a dozen miles from the downtown store. The Mormon Church also owns the Deseret Book Store, with annual sales exceeding $1,500,000 in Mormon and secular books. Employees of these stores may designate the tithe as a payroll deduction.

The Church owns radio station KSL and KSL–TV, the CBS outlets in Salt Lake City. KSL began broadcasting in 1922 to become the first radio station between the Mississippi and the Pacific Coast. For many years the station has carried the concerts of the Tabernacle Choir and the weekly sermonettes of Richard L. Evans, one of the apostles. Like other Church-owned businesses it is non-union and resists any attempts to organize the employees.

In 1962 the Mormons bought the short-wave radio station WRUL for $1,750,000. This is the only commercial station in the United States with an overseas audience. From its studios in New York City it beams programs in English and Spanish to Europe and Latin America. Its current schedule includes three religious programs each week in English and three more in Spanish.

One of Salt Lake City's two daily newspapers is the *Deseret News*. The only other church-owned daily in the nation is the respected *Christian Science Monitor*. A comparison of the two newspapers puts the *Monitor* far ahead in almost every department. Although the *Deseret News* is the official organ of a church many times the size of the Church of Christ, Scientist, it has a circulation of only 88,000, which is about half the *Monitor*'s paid circulation. The Mormon paper has never garnered the prizes for reporting, editorials or typography which have come to the Boston paper. It is dominated by the extremely conservative wing of the Mormon Church. During the Roosevelt years the *Deseret News* was outspokenly anti-New Deal and pro-Republican.

Two insurance companies—Beneficial Life Insurance and Home Insurance—are owned by the Church and sell policies mainly to Latter-day Saints. Tenants in about 70 of Salt Lake City's leading business buildings pay rent to the Mormon Church. The Church even operates a funeral home, the Deseret Mortuary. To handle its vast real estate interests the Church has organized the Zion's Securities Corporation, a management firm.

Throughout the United States and the world the Mormon Church owns 600 farms, 30 canneries, 40 mills, factories and salvage stores. It has a 48 percent interest in the Utah-Idaho Sugar Company with assets of close to $60 million. Its holdings of Florida cattle land have reached 360,000 acres so that the Church has become one of the largest landholders in Florida. The Mormon temple in Hawaii is built on a 6,500-acre sugar plantation owned by the Church for almost a century.

The Church has recently invested $1.5 million in Kaie Village in Hawaii. It seeks to attract tourists to its exhibits of Polynesian life and the nightly variety show which features Samoan fire dances and a Tongan ballet.

Brigham Young urged Mormons to cultivate sugar beets as an exportable cash crop. Today the Church controls the sugar beet industry in this country. Critics of Ezra Taft Benson, President Eisenhower's Secretary of Agriculture, asked how he could make decisions affecting the sugar beet industry since he was also an apostle (corresponding to a Roman Catholic cardinal) of the church which controlled the industry.

Under construction in New York City is a 30-story skyscraper which will serve as eastern headquarters for the Mormon Church. The Church will use about 25 percent of the space and rent the rest of the building for commercial uses. The area occupied by the Church itself will be used for a chapel, information center, missionary center, and administrative offices. The Church paid about $100 a square foot for the land on 57th and 58th streets near Fifth Avenue. The entrance to the Mormon chapel will be directly across from the Plaza Hotel.

An 18-story multimillion-dollar office building in Salt Lake City was expected to be completed in 1965. The builder is Zion's Securities Corporation. The Zion's First National Bank will occupy the first floor and the Kennecott Copper Corporation will take over the top five floors. Brigham Young, archfoe of all mining enterprises, would be surprised to find that the Church was now going to be landlord to a mining company. Several years ago the Church sold its controlling interest in Zion's First National Bank for a reported $10 million. Young founded the bank in 1873.

Church investment in real estate is so extensive that some have said there is no such thing as a two-way property transaction in Salt Lake City. The Mormon Church is a third party to every large transaction.

The full extent of Mormon ownership of stock in other American corporations is difficult to determine. It is commonly believed, for example, that the Church owns substantial shares in an airline, a food store chain, and a bus company. Former President Heber J. Grant sat on the Union Pacific board for 20 years. Elder Harold B. Lee now sits on the Union Pacific board as well as on the boards of the Equitable Life Assurance Co., American Red Cross, and Zion's First National Bank. Representatives of the Church sit on boards of other western corporations to vote Church stock. Few major financial decisions are made in the Rocky Mountains or on the West Coast without consulting the business officials of the Church of Jesus Christ of Latter-day Saints.

During the Reed Smoot case the sixth president of the Church, Joseph F. Smith, testified that he served as president of at least 12 companies. The involvement of the president of the Church in business affairs continues to this day. No one knows the full remuneration Church officials receive from these many Church-owned businesses; however, the State of Utah does require an accounting of all salaries received by officers of its insurance companies. This information is available to the public. In 1961 these records indicated that the following LDS Church officials received remuneration from the Church-owned Beneficial Life Insurance Co.:

David O. McKay	$12,950
Henry D. Moyle	8,750
Joseph Fielding Smith	5,750
Hugh B. Brown	2,250 [3]

Unlike most other churches the Mormon Church need not devote its income to paying salaries of local ministers. Only a handful of top Church authorities draw on the Church treasury. The president receives about $12,000 a year and the apostles get about $400 a month; they are usually men who can live comfortably on income from property and investments. The man who succeeded the late President Henry D. Moyle in 1963—Nathan Eldon Tanner—became a millionaire through his Canadian oil and mining holdings.

The Mormon Church has no paid ministry; all pastors (bishops) are volunteers. They need no long and expensive seminary training to fill their posts. The 12,000 young men and women serving as missionaries are supported by their families not by the Church. The Mormon Church operates no parochial school system such as that maintained by the Roman Catholics, Lutherans, and Adventists. The huge income it receives can be channeled into church building, welfare programs, Brigham Young University, investments.

During the 1880's the Mormon Church was stripped of almost all of its property in its conflict with the Federal Government over polygamy. The decision seems to have been made by the Church, perhaps subconsciously, that money talks in this country and that wealth would bring the Church the protection and respectability it was unable to win by flight, prayer, Freemasonry or subterfuge. Since then the Church has favored the appointment of the successful businessman to the Church hierarchy. Most of the apostles are men who have distinguished themselves in the business world. Indeed, only shrewd businessmen could manage the worldwide investments of the Church, and only committed believers would undertake this management for the pittance offered by the Church in lieu of salaries.

We do not expect the Church ever to open its books to the public. As reporter Neil Morgan observes:

The reticence of the Mormon Church to discuss its wealth is understandable. Most Mormons are people of modest income, whose rigid 10 percent tithe is not the end of their financial obligation to the Church. They give heavily of their time and remaining funds to the construction of temples and churches, and to the Church welfare program. A poor Mormon farmer near the hamlets of Moroni, Ephraim or Manti—educated to the high standards of his Church—might occasionally bristle at some family sacrifice necessary to meet his tithe if the extent of Church wealth were known to him.[4]

The average Mormon seems content to believe that this wealth is used only to aid needy Mormons and that there is nothing incompatible between spiritual values and success in the business world. He glories in the temples being built around the world and takes satisfaction in the reports of record conversions. Perhaps this feeling is well worth the tithe he has paid all his life and expects to pay until he is clothed in his LDS Approved Garments and laid to rest from the Deseret Mortuary.

11. *Temple Rites*

In ELEVEN TEMPLES around the world Mormons in good standing perform secret rites for the salvation and exaltation of the living and the dead. Gentiles may not enter a Mormon temple after its dedication and Mormons who do not tithe their incomes, observe the Word of Wisdom and attend church regularly are also barred from the temples.

Lewis Browne once visited Salt Lake City on a lecture tour and called on President McKay. He expressed regret that he could not see the interior of the temple and asked McKay if it could not be arranged.

"Certainly," replied the elderly president.

"Now?" asked the author excitedly.

"All you will have to do is to adhere to the faith, give up alcohol and tobacco, and donate to the Church one-tenth of your income in perpetuity."

Ceremonial work in the temples is performed mainly for the dead by living proxies. The living too will go to a temple to enter a marriage for time and eternity or to receive certain higher ordination to the priesthood. Talmage comments, "The temples of today are maintained largely for the benefit and salvation of the uncounted dead."[1] During 1965 the Church recorded 71,579 ordinances performed for the living in the 11 operating temples and 3,607,962 ordinances performed for the dead.

A Mormon may be baptized in a ward chapel or in a local YMCA swimming pool, but when he seeks baptism for his dead ancestors he must go to a temple. Mormons may be married for time in a ceremony in a ward chapel but they must later undergo the full marriage ceremony in a temple if they wish to be married for time and eternity, which is basic to the Mormon scheme of salvation.

At the present time the main temple ordinances are baptism, specifically baptism for the dead; ordination and endowments of the priesthood; marriage and other sealing ceremonies, such as the sealing of children to parents. As we shall see, Joseph Smith drew largely on the Masonic ritual to construct his temple ritual.

Every Mormon is expected to perform vicarious work for the dead so that they may get the opportunity to accept the gospel. As a result, Mormons have become diligent genealogists. A Mormon will try to trace his family tree as far back as possible. Literally millions of hours have been spent in such searches.

A Mormon named Frank Pomeroy claimed to trace his ancestry back to Antenor, the King of the Cimmarians, who died in 443 B.C. The king was baptized by proxy in the Salt Lake City temple on April 9, 1927. Pomeroy became doorkeeper of the Arizona temple and he and his family kept busy undergoing baptisms and ordinances for the 83 generations from the parents of Antenor to the present day.

The Church urges Mormons in the vicinity to visit the temple at least once a month for such vicarious work. Retired Mormons sometimes move to a temple city and spend all their spare time in the temple.

Any baptized Mormon may be baptized for a dead relative even though the proxy himself has not yet received his endowment in the temple. These baptisms are separate from the secret endowment rites and are conducted in the basement of the temples. For each such baptism the Church asks a record of information on the deceased including his name, his relationship to the proxy, his birth date, date of marriage, and death. Present besides the proxy must be a recorder, the baptizing elder, and two witnesses.

Baptism for the dead is only the first of a series of rites which must be performed. The dead must also be confirmed, given their endowments, married and sealed to their children if they would be enabled to reach the highest degree of glory in the next life. As spirits they are free to accept or reject these ministrations. A Mormon may spend many hours going through these rites for his dead grandfather, although Grandpa may prefer to remain a Methodist or Baptist in the spirit world.

No such baptisms or secret rites were practiced in the first Mormon temple, dedicated in 1836 at Kirtland. Anyone, Mormon or not, could enter this temple and observe what was going on inside. It resembled the Salt Lake City Tabernacle or a ward chapel more than a present-day Mormon temple. Public worship services were conducted on the main floor while the upper floor was used as a classroom for missionaries and Church officials.

Extraordinary spiritual phenomena were reported by the early Saints in the Kirtland temple. At various times the congregation began to prophesy and speak in tongues, to see angels, to witness heavenly visions. Eliza R. Snow wrote:

There we had the gift of prophecy—the gift of tongues—the interpretation of tongues—visions and marvelous dreams were related—the singing of heavenly choirs was heard, and wonderful manifestations of the healing power, through the administration of the Elders, were witnessed. The sick were healed—the deaf made to hear, the blind to see, and the lame to walk, in very many instances.[2]

Orson F. Whitney wrote that during the dedication ceremony an angel appeared and sat down on the rostrum. He said he was "a very tall personage, black eyes, white hair, and stoop-shouldered." He wore a garment which extended to his ankles and had sandals on his feet. Whitney also reported that the Apostle John was seen by many in the congregation as were cloven tongues of fire.

When the Kirtland Saints either fled the village or left the Church, the temple was abandoned. The building was used to house cattle, to provide an auditorium for traveling shows and a floor for community dances. James A. Garfield learned his three R's in the Kirtland temple when it was being used as a schoolhouse.

Today the Kirtland temple is owned by the Reorganized Church, which has restored it and opened it to the public. Talmadge remarks, "The building is yet standing, and serves the purposes of an ordinary meeting-house for an obscure sect that manifests no visible activity in temple building, nor apparent belief in the sacred ordinances for which temples are erected." [3]

In Independence the Prophet dedicated the plot on which the great temple would be built but the Church did not own this real estate. No progress had been made in building this temple by the time the Latter-day Saints were driven out of the state. Later the Church of Christ (Temple Lot) bought the ground and has refused all financial offers from the Utah church. Plans to build this temple have been shelved although the Utah church has always insisted that the greatest of its temples will be built in this Kansas City suburb and not in Utah.

When Smith dedicated the temple plot on August 3, 1831, he revealed: "For verily, this generation shall not all pass away until an house shall be built unto the Lord, and a cloud shall rest upon it, which cloud shall be even the glory of the Lord, which shall fill the house" (*Doctrine and Covenants,* Sec. 84:4). This prophecy is expected to be fulfilled although each passing year makes it less likely that anyone alive in 1831 is still alive today. Brigham Young emphasized his belief that the temple would be built in "this generation."

Here then we see a prediction, and we believe it. Yes! The Latter-day Saints have as firm faith and rely upon this promise as much as they rely on the promise of forgiveness of sins when they comply with the first principles of the Gospel. We just as much expect that a city will be built, called Zion, in the place and on the land which has been appointed by the Lord our God, and that a temple will be reared on the spot that has been selected, and the cornerstone of which has been laid, in the generation when this revelation was given; we just as much expect this as we expect the sun to rise in the morning and set in the evening; or as much as we expect to see the fulfillment of any of the purposes of the Lord our God, pertaining to the work of His hands. But, says the objector, "thirty-nine years have passed away." What of that? The generation has not passed away; all the people that were living thirty-nine years ago, have not passed away; but before they do pass away this will be fulfilled.[4]

To reassure Saints who might question this prophecy, the 13th printing of *Temples of the Most High* by N. B. Lundwall, released in 1962, adds two footnotes about a Siberian peasant who claimed to be 142 years old in 1940 and an Armenian who died at the age of 115.[5]

According to revelation, the Independence temple will dwarf all the other Mormon temples. It will accommodate from 12,000 to 15,000 people. The names of its 24 rooms were also revealed to Smith. These rooms will be used by the different quorums of the priesthood. The temple and the city of New Jerusalem will be built with materials which will never decay. President Lorenzo Snow told an assembly of Saints on June 12, 1901:

"Many of you will be living in Jackson County and there you will be assisting in building the Temple; and if you will not have seen the Lord Jesus at that time you may expect Him very soon, to see Him, to eat and drink with Him, to shake hands with Him and to invite Him to your houses as He was invited when He was here before." [6]

At Nauvoo the Saints began to build a second temple. This temple was never fully completed and was not dedicated until two years after Smith's death. Since Kirtland, the Prophet's theological system had evolved and the Nauvoo temple was built for additional purposes such as baptism for the dead.

Smith had begun to baptize his followers for their dead in the Mississippi River but he received an additional revelation that this rite could be performed only in the temple. As soon as the basement of the temple was completed and the baptismal font installed, the Prophet inaugurated a program of mass baptism for the dead. Like all Mormon fonts for this ordinance, this one rested on the backs of twelve brass or bronze oxen.

Meanwhile Smith had followed his brother Hyrum, Brigham Young and Heber Kimball into the Masonic Lodge. Smith's own background was nonliturgical and as he elaborated his temple ritual he borrowed freely from the Masonic initiations. The Prophet began to introduce certain of the Saints to the secret rites in the room above his store. Eventually the attic of the Nauvoo temple was set apart for the administration of the new sacred endowments; Brigham Young himself took the part of Elohim in the sacred play. Thousands of Saints clamored to receive their endowments in the temple even as Nauvoo was harassed by the neighboring Gentiles.

Within a year after Young had led the first contingent of Saints out of the city the temple was in enemy hands. An arsonist set the torch to the structure in 1848 and a tornado in 1850 leveled its remaining walls. The stones were hauled away for building purposes and some of these now buttress the walls of a Catholic convent in Nauvoo.

A few Mormons received their endowments in makeshift quarters in Utah, but it was nearly ten years after the end of temple work at Nauvoo that the Old Endowment House was dedicated in Salt Lake City in 1855. These rites differed little from those exemplified in the attic of the Nauvoo temple. Young continued to take the role of Elohim. Heber

Kimball was Jehovah; Eliza R. Snow, the plural wife of both Smith and Young, played Eve; and W. W. Phelps took the part of the devil. The references to polygamy were clear and the candidates were instructed in the doctrine of blood atonement should they fall into apostasy or serious sin. The oath of vengeance against the State and Federal governments which had failed to protect the Saints in Missouri and Illinois was certainly administered during 1856 and 1857.

The first temple built after Nauvoo was in St. George, an almost completely Mormon community about 350 miles southwest of Salt Lake City. Baptisms for the dead were performed here in 1877 and the next year Brigham Young and most of the Church officials presided at the inauguration of the new endowments for the dead. The form of these endowments has not changed substantially since that date.

President Woodruff reported at the General Conference on April 10, 1898, that he had been visited by George Washington and all the signers of the Declaration of Independence in the St. George temple and had arranged for their proxy baptisms:

"Every one of those men that signed the Declaration of Independence with General Washington called upon me, as an Apostle of the Lord Jesus Christ, in the Temple at St. George two consecutive nights, and demanded at my hands that I should go forth and attend to the ordinances of the house of God for them ... Brother McAllister baptized me for all these men, and I told these brethren that it was their duty to go into the Temple and labor until they got their endowments for all of them. They did it." [7]

At an earlier General Conference on September 16, 1877, Woodruff explained that he had been baptized not only for the signers but for 50 other "eminent men, making 100 in all, including John Wesley, Columbus, and others. I then baptized him [McAllister] for every President of the United

States except three; and when their cause is just, somebody will do the work for them."

What we will present in this chapter is an abbreviated description of the endowment ceremonies which ordinarily take about three hours. Mormons, like Freemasons, do not discuss the secret rites under penalty of horrendous tortures, now understood in a symbolic sense. Our information has come from various sources including former Mormons. It is believed to be in substantial agreement with the ritual as it is now performed in Mormon temples.

We do not present this description of the endowment merely to satisfy the curiosity of non-Mormons. We believe that to try to understand Mormonism without knowing what goes on in the sanctums of the temples is like trying to understand Roman Catholicism without examining the Mass.

In order to enter a temple for any purpose a Mormon must obtain a "recommend" from his local bishop. The bishop knows if the applicant pays his tithe, follows the Word of Wisdom, and is faithful to his other religious duties. Lax Mormons, even parents of the bride or groom in a temple marriage, may be denied a "recommend" if they fail to meet these standards. Six months of good behavior before the marriage will usually enable a Mormon to qualify for a "recommend."

The candidate must then assemble his or her temple garments. The man's garments include a special undergarment, a shirt and pair of white pants, a robe and girdle, a cloth cap like a baker's cap, cloth moccasins, and a green silk apron upon which are embroidered nine fig leaves. The woman assembles the same garments substituting a white blouse and skirt for the shirt and pants. Garments may be rented.

With his "recommend" and temple garments in hand the candidate goes to the temple and enters through an attached building known as the "annex." He presents his credentials to the doorkeeper. A few days before his visit he has sub-

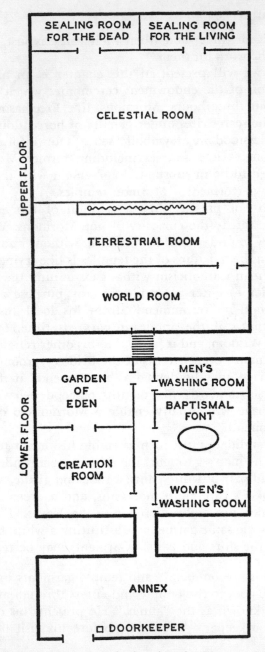

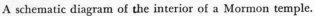

A schematic diagram of the interior of a Mormon temple.

mitted necessary genealogical information such as the time and place of his birth, that of his parents, etc. If he is taking his endowments for some deceased relative he has presented these vital statistics. Years ago this information was given to the recorder when the patron came to the temple, but the numbers now going through require advance registration.

The candidate proceeds to a chapel in the annex and waits while the others going through the temple that day complete the preliminary procedures. When all are assembled, the group sings a hymn, recites a prayer, hears a short address, and sings another hymn.

Those men taking endowments for the dead retire to an alcove where they are ordained elders on behalf of the dead. No one can take these endowments except those who hold the Melchizedek priesthood. One of the temple workers lays hands on the candidate and says:

"Brother—In the name of the Lord Jesus Christ and by the authority of the holy Melchizedek Priesthood, I ordain you an elder of the Church of Jesus Christ of Latter-day Saints for and in behalf of ____, who is dead."

The candidate now rejoins the men who already possess the Melchizedek priesthood and the women. They enter the lower level of the temple and the men and women enter separate washing rooms. These rooms used to contain a number of bathtubs with hot and cold water. The regulations of several boards of health now rule out tubs. The candidate undresses, sits on a stool and waits for an attendant to wash him with a spray nozzle. The following prayer is recited during the washing:

Brother, having authority, I wash you that you may be clean from the blood and sins of this generation. I wash your head that your brain may work clearly and be quick of discernment; your eyes that you may see clearly and discern the things of God; your ears that you may hear the word of the Lord; your mouth and lips that they speak no guile; your arms that they may be strong to wield the sword in defense of truth and virtue; your breast and vitals that their function may be strengthened; your loins and reins that you may be fruitful in the propagating of a goodly seed; your legs and feet that you may run and not be weary, walk and not faint.

After being dried with a towel, the candidate is anointed with oil by another attendant. The olive oil is applied to the various organs of the body including the procreative and a similar prayer is recited. Men and women go through the washing and anointing in separate quarters, and candidates and attendants are of the same sex.

The candidates are now allowed to put on their endowment garments. These garments, known in the trade as LDS Approved Garments, are now manufactured exclusively by the Relief Society. Originally the garment was a long union suit of muslin or linen with the specified cabalistic marks. It has been abbreviated in recent years especially in the interests of feminine fashions. The full-length garment is still worn in the temple. The Masonic square is embroidered on one breast and the compass on the other. Stories of the protection given Mormons wearing their temple garments on the battlefield or in accidents are common in Mormon folklore. A faithful Mormon is buried in his full temple garments including the undergarments, robe, cloth cap, moccasins, and apron. As he is given permission to wear the undergarment an official says:

"Brother, I now give you these garments, which are patterned after those given to our father Adam when he was found naked in the Garden of Eden. They are called the garments of the holy priesthood, and will provide a shield and protection to you till you have finished your work in righteousness upon the earth. They are never to be removed except for purposes of cleanliness, and then for no longer than necessary. With these garments I give you a new name which is never to be divulged to anyone. It is a key word and will be required of you at a certain part of these proceedings this day. The name I shall give you is _____."

The official whispers the secret name to the candidate. Usually the name is taken from the *Book of Mormon* or the Bible. It might be Enoch or Lehi or Abraham or some other scriptural name.

A Mormon in full temple garments. A faithful Mormon will be buried in these garments and will wear the sacred underwear throughout his life.

The candidate retires to the dressing room where he puts on a shirt and white trousers and stockings. In the early days a long white smock was the only garment men and women wore over their undergarments. The Mormon enters the first room of the temple itself in much the same garb as a candidate for the first or Entered Apprentice degree of the

Masonic lodge. The Masonic initiate also wears a white shirt, white pants, a slipper on one foot. He wears a cable tow around his neck which does not find a parallel in the Mormon rites. Both the Masonic and Mormon candidates carry their aprons and the Mormon also includes his robe, cap and sandals in his bundle.

The older Mormon temples including all the temples in Utah contain five main rooms: the Creation Room, Garden of Eden, World Room, Terrestrial Room, and Celestial Room. Candidates pass from one room to the other to watch playlets illustrating the Mormon view of creation, the fall, the atonement, and salvation. In the new Mormon temples in London and Bern, a slide projector beams various scenes on the walls of one large room; those going through the rites in these temples stay in the main assembly room.

The candidate waits at the door to the first or Creation Room. He wears his undergarments, shirt and pants and carries his bundle with his other temple garments. An attendant gives him a ticket of admission; if he is doing vicarious work the name of the dead person is written on the ticket. He waits in the room until all have completed their washings and anointings.

This room is also known as "Chaos or the Lower Instruction Room." It is supposed to represent the state of affairs before the world was organized. It has no ornamentation except a painting of two hands clasped over a doorway, concealed by a curtain. This doorway leads to the next room, the Garden of Eden. Men sit on the right of the aisles and women on the left in theatre-type seats. The temple worker representing Elohim steps in front of the curtain; he is dressed in white flannels:

"Brethren, you have been washed and pronounced clean, that is, clean from the blood and sins of this generation. You have been anointed that you may become kings and priests to our God and His Christ; not that you have been anointed kings and priests, but that you may become such. This will depend on your faithfulness.

"Sisters, you have been washed and anointed that you may become queens and priestesses unto your lords, that is, your husbands. You also have had garments given you and with those garments, a new name which you were told never to divulge to anyone; it is, however, a key word and will be required of you at a certain place in going through these endowments this day.

"And here I would ask if any of you desire to retire at this stage of the proceedings. If so, you have now an opportunity to do so by raising the right hand. [*No one accepts the offer.*]

"You will now hear three voices—the voices of Elohim, Jehovah and Michael. Elohim will command. Now give your attention and hear what you shall hear."

He retires behind the curtain and in a few minutes voices are heard. Elohim calls, "Jehovah! Michael! See, there is matter unorganized. Let us go down and form a world like unto other worlds which we have formed, where the spirits who are awaiting bodies may tabernacle." Jehovah and Michael respond, "We will go down."

Jehovah and Michael appear and enact the creation of the world according to the account in Genesis. At the end of each phase the pair say, "We will now go and report this our labor of the first [second, third, etc.] day." On receiving further instructions from Elohim, they answer again: "We will go down." Elohim replies: "It is well." On the fourth day, when Elohim gives the order to place lights in the firmament, the lights of the chandelier are switched on. At the end of the fifth day Michael speaks: "Jehovah, see the earth which we have formed and plentifully supplied with animals and vegetable life; it looks glorious and beautiful." Jehovah agrees and adds, "It does, Michael. We will return and report this our labor of the fifth day."

Now all three characters appear. Michael seats himself in a chair facing the audience, and Elohim and Jehovah stand on either side. Elohim declares, "We will make man in our own image." Elohim and Jehovah stand in front of Michael, make passes over him, breathe on him. He appears to fall asleep. Elohim tells the spectators, "This man who is now being operated upon is Michael who helped form the world. When he awakes he will have forgotten everything, will have become as a little child, and will be known as Adam."

Elohim calls in a loud voice: "Adam, awake!" He awakes and looks around startled. Elohim says, "It is not good for men to be alone." Jehovah agrees: "It is not, Elohim, for we are not alone."

Elohim explains, "We will cause a deep sleep to fall upon Adam and make for him a woman to be with him." Adam again falls asleep and Elohim tells the men in the audience, "The brethren will close their eyes as if they were asleep." While Adam slumbers Eve enters and stands beside him. Elohim shouts, "Adam, see the woman we have formed for you. What will you call her?" Adam looks over his helpmate and answers, "Eve."

"Why will you call her Eve?" asks Elohim.

"Because she is the Mother of all living."

"True, Adam, she is the Mother of all living."

Elohim now addresses Jehovah: "We will plant a garden eastward in Eden, and there we will put the man whom we have formed." In Mormon theology this Garden of Eden was located in Independence, Missouri. This will also be the center of Zion in the millennium. Elohim tells the audience: "The brethren will now follow Adam and the sisters will follow Eve into the room representing the Garden of Eden." They pass through the curtain separating the rooms.

The walls of this room are decorated with painted trees, flowers, shrubbery. Birds and beasts are romping together in perfect harmony. The ceiling is painted to represent a blue sky with silver stars. At one end of this room is an altar upon which rests a Bible. At one side is "the tree of knowledge of good and evil."

Elohim addresses Adam: "Adam, see this garden which

we have planted for you. Of all the trees of the garden thou mayest freely eat, but of the fruit of the tree of knowledge of good and evil thou shalt not eat of it, for in the day that thou eatest of it thou shalt surely die. Now be fruitful and multiply; be happy and enjoy yourselves. We go away, but we will return and give you further instructions."

Elohim and Jehovah leave. In some temples they step onto a small elevator painted to resemble clouds. Adam speaks to the audience: "Now, brethren, let your minds be calm and be not surprised at anything you may see or hear. We shall be visited soon."

Sure enough, a man enters from the Creation Room and walks up the center aisle surveying the room. He usually wears a black suit, a silk hat, a cane and a Masonic apron, which is what a Worshipful Master wears in the Masonic Lodge. He is Lucifer.

LUCIFER: Adam, you have a nice new world here: it is patterned after the world where we used to live.

ADAM: I know nothing of any other world.

LUCIFER: Oh, I see, you haven't had your eyes opened yet.

He pretends to pluck some fruit from the tree of knowledge and invites Adam to take some of the same. "It will make you wise." Adam refuses and Lucifer turns to Eve to tempt her. She refuses at first and expresses surprise that he should ask her to disobey the Father. Lucifer assures her: "Ye shall not surely die but ye shall be as the gods; ye shall know good from evil, virtue from vice, happiness from misery."

"Is there no other way?" Eve asks. The devil says there is none and Eve takes a bite of the fruit. She tries to get Adam to taste it and he refuses. "Do you intend to obey all Father's commands?" asks Eve. "Yes, all of them," says Adam. "Well, you know our Father commanded us to be fruitful and multiply and replenish the earth. Now I have partaken of the forbidden fruit and shall be cast out, while you will remain a lone man in the Garden." He realizes this predicament and eats and now Eve recognizes Lucifer as the devil who was cast out of the presence of the Father for his rebellion.

"I see you are beginning to get your eyes open already," snarls Lucifer.

Adam asks Lucifer what apron he is wearing and he replies: "That is an emblem of my power and priesthood." Now Elohim and Jehovah return and Elohim begins to call for Adam.

Adam has hidden himself and he comes out of his hiding place, much ashamed: "I heard thy voice as I was walking in the garden and I was afraid because I knew that I was naked, and I hid myself."

ELOHIM: Who told thee that thou wast naked? Hast thou eaten of the fruit whereof I commanded thee thou shouldst not eat?

ADAM: The woman that thou gavest to be with me, she gave me of the fruit and I did eat.

ELOHIM: Eve, what hast thou done?

EVE: The serpent beguiled me and I did eat.

ELOHIM: Lucifer, what have *you* been doing here?

LUCIFER: Oh, the same as we have been doing in other worlds— I gave them some of the fruit to open their eyes.

ELOHIM: For this that thou hast done, thou art cursed above all cattle. Upon thy belly shalt thou go and dust shall be thy meat all the days of thy life on the earth.

LUCIFER: And I will take of the treasures of that earth, silver and gold, and buy up armies and navies, popes and princes, and I will reign with blood and terror.

ELOHIM: Begone!

Lucifer slinks out of the room but halts at the doorway, shakes his fist and stamps his heel. Adam now commands the audience, "In your bundles, brethren and sisters, you will each find an apron. You will now put it on." They are already wearing their robes.

To Eve, Elohim declares:

"Because thou hast hearkened unto the voice of the Tempter and hast eaten of the fruit whereof I commanded thee thou shouldst not eat, I will greatly multiply thy sorrow and thy conception; in sorrow shalt thou bring forth children. Nevertheless thou mayst be saved in child-bearing; thy seed shall bruise the serpent's head but he shall bruise thy heel."

Elohim turns to Adam:

"Because thou hast hearkened unto the voice of thy wife and hast eaten of the fruit of the tree, cursed is the ground for thy sake. In sorrow shalt thou eat of it all the days of thy life. In the sweat of thy face shalt thou eat bread till thou return unto the ground from whence thou wast taken: for dust thou art, and unto dust shalt thou return."

Elohim instructs Jehovah:

"Let Adam be cast out of the garden and cherubim with a flaming sword be placed to guard the way of the tree of life."

Jehovah repeats this message. Now Eve crosses the stage and stands next to Adam. Elohim promises:

"Adam, we will provide for you a Saviour and send you messengers to instruct you how you may return to our presence."

Elohim and Jehovah depart and Adam asks the audience:

"Brethren and Sisters, I would here ask if any of you have forgotten your new name that you hold up the right hand."

Ordinarily no one has been so forgetful. The men and women now unpack their bundles to prepare for the first degree. Adam speaks:

"You will now arise, push back the seats, place the robe on the right shoulder, put on your caps and moccasins, and receive the first token of the Aaronic priesthood. And you will not forget that the utmost secrecy is to be observed with respect to these proceedings. They are not to be even spoken of to each other."

Adam demonstrates the secret sign and the audience follows. The left arm is placed at the square, palm to the front. The right hand and arm is raised to the neck, holding the palm down and thumb under the right ear. Adam speaks:

"We, and each of us, covenant and promise that we will not reveal any of the secrets of this, the first token of the Aaronic priesthood, with its accompanying name, sign, or penalty. Should we do so, we agree that our throats be cut from ear to ear and our tongues torn out by their roots. All bow your heads and say 'Yes.' "

As the last words are spoken the right hand is drawn swiftly across the throat and the hands dropped from the square to the sides. The name is the name given with the garments; the grip is hands clasped, pressing the knuckle of the index finger with the thumb.

For comparison we may examine the oath for the first or Entered Apprentice degree of Freemasonry. The candidate concludes his oath with these words:

"All this I most solemnly, sincerely promise and swear, with a firm and steadfast resolution to perform the same, without any mental reservation or secret evasion of mind whatever, binding myself *under no less penalty than that of having my throat cut across, my tongue torn out by its roots,* and my body buried in the rough sands of the sea, at low-water mark, where the tide ebbs and flows twice in 24 hours, should I ever knowingly violate this my Entered Apprentice obligation. So help me God, and keep me steadfast in the due performance of the same."

Back in the Mormon temple Adam tells the assembled Mormons:

"The brethren will now follow Adam and the sisters will follow Eve into the room representing the Lone and Desolate World."

In the Salt Lake City temple, the brothers and sisters must go up a long flight of stairs to reach this room. The paintings on the walls depict a world in which chaos and disorder prevail. Wild vegetation, broken rocks, snarling wild animals locked in combat form the subject of the murals. Adam and Eve stand behind an altar at one end of the room. Adam speaks:

"When Adam was cast out of the Garden of Eden, he built an altar and called on the Lord, saying:

'O Lord, hear the words of my mouth!
'O Lord, hear the words of my mouth!
'O Lord, hear the words of my mouth!' "

As he speaks he raises his hands high above his head, then drops them to the square and then to his side. This resembles the Masonic sign of distress which Joseph Smith attempted to give as he was shot in the Carthage jail. The Masonic formula is "O Lord, my God, is there no help for the widow's son?" The words which the Mormon Adam utters are, "Pale, hale, hale" which are supposed to mean "O Lord, hear the words of my mouth" in pure Adamic language. Adam explains that he does not understand why he has given the sign of distress except that he has been told to do so when he needs help.

Lucifer enters and asks, "I hear you. What is it you want?"

Adam asks who he is and Lucifer replies, "The god of this world."

ADAM: Who made you the god of this world?

LUCIFER: I made myself. What is it you want?

ADAM: I was calling on Father.

LUCIFER: Oh, I see, you want religion. I'll have some preachers along presently.

In the earlier versions of the ceremony the Mormons introduced a number of "preachers" representing the Methodist, Presbyterian, Catholic, Quaker and other denominations. Their doctrines were broadly caricatured and the banter provided some comic relief in the lengthy ritual. Today one actor represents all the non-Mormon churches. The dialogue today goes something like the following:

PREACHER: You have a very fine congregation here.

LUCIFER: Oh, are you a preacher?

PREACHER: Yes.

LUCIFER: Have you ever been to college and studied the dead languages?

PREACHER: Why, certainly; no one can preach the gospel acceptably unless he has been to college and studied the dead languages.

LUCIFER: Well, if you will preach your gospel to this congregation and convert them, mind you, I'll give you —let me see, five thousand dollars a year.

PREACHER: That is very little, but I'll do the best I can.

The preacher greets Adam and says that he understands that he is looking for religion. The preacher sings several verses from a hymnbook as Lucifer keeps time with his feet. The preacher asks Adam:

"Do you believe in that great Spirit, without body, parts or passions, who sits on the top of a topless throne, 'beyond the

bounds of time and space,' whose center is everywhere and circum-
ference nowhere; who fills immensity with His presence and yet
is so small he can dwell in your heart. Do you believe this?"

Adam replies that he does not believe a word of it. The
preacher fumes:

"Then I am very sorry for you. But perhaps you believe in hell
—that great and bottomless pit which is full of fire and brimstone,
into which the wicked are cast and where they are ever burning
and yet never burn."

Adam answers, "No, I do not, and I am sorry for you."
Lucifer adds, "We are very, very sorry for you." He asks
Adam what he wants and Adam says, "I want nothing. I am
awaiting messengers from Father."

From another room voices of the gods can be heard by the
audience.

Elohim speaks to Jehovah: "Jehovah, the man Adam seems
to be true and faithful. Let us send down to him Peter, James
and John." The trio descends a flight of stairs at the rear of
the room. Lucifer advances to meet them.

Peter asks, "What is going on here?"

Lucifer explains, "We are making religion." Peter asks
what they are making religion out of and Lucifer says, "Newspapers, novels, notions of men and women sugared over with
scripture."

PETER: And how does it take with this congregation?

LUCIFER: Oh, pretty well with all except this man Adam; he
          doesn't believe anything.

PETER: (to Adam) Good morning, sir. How do you like the
          preaching of this gentleman?

ADAM: Not at all. He tells of a God without a body, and a
          hell without a bottom into which the wicked are cast
          and where they are forever burning and yet never
          consumed. I cannot believe it.

PETER: We do not blame you. We will visit you again shortly.

The three Apostles now go back up the stairs and Peter is heard talking to Elohim:

"We have been down to the man Adam. Lucifer is there with a preacher who is trying to teach him all manner of false doctrine; yet amid it all he remains true and faithful."

Elohim commands:

"Go down to the man Adam in your proper characters. Give him the second token of the Aaronic priesthood. Instruct him to place the robe on the left shoulder and come back and report."

The three return to the room by way of the stairs and introduce themselves to Adam. He asks, "Are you the Apostles of our Lord and Saviour Jesus Christ?" They declare they are.

Now the preacher points to Lucifer and says:

"Why, he said we should have no more Apostles and if any should come along professing to be such I was to ask them to cut off a leg or an arm and put it on again, just to show they had come with power."

Peter explains:

"He did that to deceive you. A wicked and adulterous generation seeketh after a sign. We do not satisfy people's idle curiosity. Do you know who that man is?"

PREACHER: Why, certainly! He's a great gentleman and is at the head of all the religious denominations of the day.

PETER: I can fully believe that. Why, that's Lucifer!

PREACHER: What! The Devil?

PETER: Yes, I believe that is one of his names. I would advise you to have a settlement with him and get out of his employ.

PREACHER: But if I get out of his employ, what is to become of
            me?

PETER: We will teach you the everlasting gospel in connec-
            tion with the rest of the sons of Adam.

The preacher taps Lucifer on the shoulder and asks to get
out of his service. The devil is disgusted anyway since the
preacher was not very effective in converting others but was
ending up converted himself.

Peter asks Adam if he has his tokens and Lucifer asks if
he has money, adding that you can get anything in this world
for money. Peter asks Adam: "Do you sell your tokens for
money? You have them, I believe." Adam answers: "I have
them, but I value them too highly to part with them for
money."

Peter orders Lucifer to leave and Lucifer asks by what
authority he gives this command. With his left arm to the
square, Peter declares: "In the name of Jesus Christ, my
Master." Lucifer follows the preacher out of the room.

Now Peter takes Adam by the right hand and asks, "What
is that?"

Adam says that it is the first token of the Aaronic priesthood. Peter now asks Adam for its name but Adam says he
cannot give it since "it is connected with my new name, but
this is the sign." He raises his left arm to the square.

Adam addresses the assembly:

"Brethren and Sisters, these are true messengers from Father.
Give heed to their instructions and they will lead you in the
ways of life and salvation."

The three Apostles leave to report to Elohim, who in turn
tells them:

"Peter, James and John, go down again in your own proper
characters and reveal to Adam the second token of the Aaronic
priesthood and place the robe upon his left shoulder."

Peter speaks:

"The brethren and sisters will now stand, push back the seat, place the robe on the left shoulder, and receive the Second Token of the Aaronic Priesthood.

"We and each of us do covenant and promise that we will not reveal the secrets of this, the Second Token of the Aaronic Priesthood, with its accompanying name, sign, grip or penalty. Should we do so, we agree to have our breasts cut open and our hearts and vitals torn from our bodies and given to the birds of the air and the beasts of the field.

"All bow your heads and say yes."

In the second or Fellow Craft degree of Freemasonry the candidate binds himself "under no less penalty than of having my breast torn open, my heart plucked out, and placed on the highest pinnacle of the temple there to be devoured by the vultures of the air."

The sign for the Mormon token is made by placing the left arm on the square at shoulder level, placing the right hand across the chest with the thumb extended and then drawing it from left to right and dropping it to the side. The name of the token is the given name of the candidate. The grip is given by clasping the hand and pressing the thumb in the hollow between the first and second knuckles of the hand.

Peter's voice is again heard as he reports to the gods: "We have been down to the man Adam, have given him the Second Token of the Aaronic Priesthood and instructed him to place the robe on the left shoulder." Elohim replies, " 'Tis well. Go down again, instruct him to place the robe on the right shoulder, give him the First Token of the Melchizedek Priesthood, and come back and report."

The three Apostles agree to do as they are instructed. Peter invites the men and women to follow Adam and Eve into the Terrestrial Room. It is also known as the "Blue Room" or "Upper Lecture Room." In the Utah temples the walls are hung with paintings of the life of Christ. Copies of the Bible and *Book of Mormon* rest on a prayer altar at the east end. A veil separates the Terrestrial Room from the final or Celestial Room.

Peter instructs the candidates to place the robes on their right shoulder and repeat the oath of the First Token of the Melchizedek Priesthood:

We and each of us do covenant and promise that we will not reveal any of the secrets of this, the First Token of the Melchizedek Priesthood, with its accompanying name, sign or penalty. Should we do so, we agree that our bodies be cut asunder in the midst and all our bowels gush out.

Candidates for the Master Mason degree make a similar pledge on the penalty "of having my body severed in two, my bowels taken from thence and burned to ashes. . . ."

The Mormon sign for this token or degree is made by bringing both hands to the square, palms to the front. As the last words of the oath are given the hands are dropped till the thumbs are in the center of the stomach and drawn swiftly across the stomach to the hips and then dropped to the sides. The name of this token is the Son, meaning the Son of God. Members of the Melchizedek or higher Priesthood belong to the Order of the Son of God. Initiates give the grip by placing the thumb on the back of the hand and the tip of the forefinger in the center of the palm. This represents the piercing of the hand by a nail as in the crucifixion and is called the "Sign of the Nail."

Next the Apostles administer the Second Token of the Melchizedek Priesthood after the usual conference with Elohim. No special penalty is attached to this token but the obligation of secrecy remains. The sign is made by elevating both arms above the head to represent the crucifixion. The words "Pale, hale, hale" are recited. The grip is given by grasping the hand with the forefinger on the center of the wrist and the little fingers locked. It is based on the tradition that the nail driven through Jesus' hand pulled out from the weight of his body and the executioner then drove the nails through the wrist. This grip is called the "Patriarchal Grip" or the "Sure Sign of the Nail."

Peter now administers a series of obligations to the candidates, who stand with the right arm at the square.

LAW OF SACRIFICE

You and each of you do covenant and promise that you will sacrifice your time, talents and all that you may now or hereafter become possessed of to the upbuilding of the Church of Jesus Christ of Latter-day Saints.

All bow your heads and say yes.

LAW OF CHASTITY FOR MEN

You and each of you do covenant and promise that you will not have sexual intercourse with any of the opposite sex except your lawful wife (or wives) who are given you by the holy priesthood. [Now that polygamy has been discontinued by the Church the phrase in parentheses is not recited.]

LAW OF CHASTITY FOR WOMEN

You and each of you do covenant and promise that you will not have sexual intercourse with any of the opposite sex save your lawful husband, given you by the holy priesthood.

When the Church openly practiced and promoted polygamy the following question would be put to the women:

Sisters, those of you who are willing to uphold and sustain the heaven-ordained principles of polygamy by allowing your husbands to have more wives than one, say "Aye," and those opposed, "Nay."

There seems little doubt that the oath of vengeance as given at Nauvoo after Smith's death and at the endowment house in Salt Lake City and the St. George temple included the phrase "on this nation." Today this oath is modified; a patriotic Mormon need not choose between his church and his nation as his grandfathers may have chosen.

LAW OF VENGEANCE

You and each of you do solemnly promise and vow that you will pray, and never cease to pray, and never cease to importune high heaven to avenge the blood of the prophets (on this nation), and that you will teach this to your children and your children's children unto the third and fourth generation.

The true order of prayer is now taught by what is known as the Prayer Circle. As many candidates as possible surround the altar and review the tokens of the Aaronic and Melchizedek priesthoods. The women are told to veil their faces and they lower the veil attached to the hood. In the Mormon burial service the temple veil is again pulled over the face of the corpse. It will be removed in the resurrection by her husband. The men, kneeling, take each other by the right hand in the Patriarchal Grip and place the elbow of the left arm on the shoulder of the person next to them, arm at the square, palm of the hand to the front. An elder kneels at the altar with his right arm at the square and his left arm extended with the hand cupped. He offers a prayer which is repeated by all those in the circle.

Elohim or some other official now mounts the platform in front of the veil and delivers the Endowment Lecture. He reviews the proceedings of the day and explains the signs and grips and symbols. The length of this lecture depends on the number who are going through the ceremony for the first time and the inclination of the speaker.

The veil is approached by three steps on either side of the altar. It covers a long archway which is supported by five pillars. The candidates give their grips, signs and token between the pillars in order to be admitted to the holy of holies.

Peter announces: "We will now uncover the veil."

At this time temple workers draw back the covering of the

veil, exposing the veil itself. It is known as the veil of the temple. The marks on the veil are the same as on the sacred undergarments: the compass on the left and the square on the right, the navel mark, and the knee mark which signifies that at the name of Jesus every knee should bow. Besides these cabalistic signs are four other "Marks of Convenience." Through one such hole the Lord puts his hand to test the knowledge of the candidate. Through two others the hands of the Lord and the candidate are thrust to be placed on each other's backs. Through the final hole the candidate whispers into the Lord's ear. As a man's name is called he takes his wife, his bride, or some other woman to the platform where they sit until their turn comes. Sometimes the man takes several women, unknown to him personally. A woman can go through the veil to the Celestial Room only with a man.

When his turn comes, the candidate is escorted to one of the openings between the pillars. A temple worker gives three raps with a mallet on the pillar. The Lord parts the veil slightly and asks what is desired. The temple worker declares: "The man Adam having been true and faithful in all things now desires to converse with the Lord through the veil." The Lord says, "See that his garments are properly marked, present him at the veil, and his request shall be granted."

The candidate advances to the veil itself. He is prompted in his answers by the attendants. The Lord sticks his hand through the veil and grasps that of the candidate, asking, "What is this?"

ENDOWEE: The first token of the Aaronic Priesthood.

LORD: Has it a name?

ENDOWEE: It has.

LORD: Will you give it to me?

ENDOWEE: I will, through the veil. (He whispers his Temple name.)

LORD: What is that?

ENDOWEE: The second token of the Aaronic Priesthood.

LORD: Has it a name?

ENDOWEE: It has.

LORD: Will you give it to me?

ENDOWEE: I will, through the veil. *(He whispers his given name.)*

LORD: What is that?

ENDOWEE: The first token of the Melchizedek Priesthood.

LORD: Has it a name?

ENDOWEE: It has.

LORD: Will you give it to me?

ENDOWEE: I will, through the veil. *(He whispers)* The Son.

LORD: What is that?

ENDOWEE: The second token of the Melchizedek Priesthood— the Patriarchal Grip or Sure Sign of the Nail.

LORD: Has it a name?

ENDOWEE: It has.

LORD: Will you give it to me?

ENDOWEE: I cannot for I have not yet received it. For this purpose I have come to converse with the Lord behind the veil.

LORD: You shall receive it upon the five points of fellowship through the veil. These are: foot to foot, knee to knee, breast to breast, hand to back, and mouth to ear.

The Five Points of Fellowship is among the oldest Masonic gestures. In the Master Mason's initiation the Worshipful Master raises the candidate by means of the Master Mason's grip and imparts the grand Masonic word—"Ma-hah-bone" on the Five Points of Fellowship. It is an identical posture in the Mormon temple.

The Lord whispers: "This is the sign of the token. Health to the navel, marrow in the bones, strength in the loins and sinews, and power in the priesthood be upon me and my posterity through all generations of time and throughout all eternity."

Without changing position, the Lord asks: "What is that?" The candidate answers: "The second token of the Melchizedek Priesthood" and repeats the formula which he has just heard.

The candidate is taken to the opening by the attendant who gives three more raps with his mallet. The Lord asks what is wanted and the attendant replies: "Adam, having conversed with the Lord through the veil, now desires to enter His presence." The Lord commands that he be admitted.

The Lord extends his hand and welcomes the candidate into the Celestial or Glory Room. Now the man takes the place of the Lord and examines the women for their knowledge of the tokens.

The Celestial Room in the Salt Lake City temple is the largest of all the rooms and the most richly furnished. Its walls are decorated with mirrors and portraits. It measures 60 by 45 feet. Rooms off the Celestial Room are devoted to sealings of both the living and the dead and the Holy of Holies which is reserved for rites of the higher priesthood.

Those who are going through the temple rites for their dead ancestors enter the Sealing Room for the Dead. They must present their credentials and wait their turn. They go through a proxy ceremony which seals man and wife or children to parents.

Bride and groom to be married for time and eternity enter the Sealing Room for the Living when their time comes. They may have been previously married for time in a ceremony in their hometown ward. If this is their one and only marriage ceremony they must present their wedding license to the temple officials. Parents of bride or groom who cannot qualify for a "recommend" from the bishop may be refused admission to the temple to witness the marriage ceremony. Living children who have been born to parents not married for eternity may be sealed to their parents in this room.

The bride and groom kneel at the altar and clasp their hands in the patriarchal grip. The president of the temple usually presides at these marriages. The formal ceremony goes as follows:

"Do you, Brother ———, take Sister ——— by the right hand to receive her unto yourself to be your lawful wedded wife and you to be her lawful wedded husband, for time and all eternity, with a covenant and promise on your part that you will fulfill all the rites, laws and ordinances pertaining to this holy matrimony in the new and everlasting covenant, doing this in the presence of God and angels and these witnesses, of your own free will and choice."

He addresses the bride in similar fashion and pronounces:

"In the name of the Lord Jesus Christ and by the authority of the holy priesthood, I pronounce you legally and lawfully husband and wife for time and for all eternity; and I seal upon you the blessings of the holy resurrection, with power to come forth in the morning of the first resurrection, clothed with glory, immortality and eternal lives; and I seal upon you the blessings of thrones and dominions and principalities and powers and exaltations, together with the blessings of Abraham, Isaac and Jacob. And I say unto you, be fruitful and multiply and replenish the earth, that you may have joy and rejoicing in your posterity in the day of the Lord Jesus. All these blessings, together with all the other blessings pertaining to the new and everlasting covenant, I seal upon your heads through your faithfulness unto the end, by the authority of the holy priesthood, in the name of the Father and of the Son and of the Holy Ghost. Amen."

In a polygamous union with the first wife present the officiating officer would ask: "Are you willing to give this woman to your husband to be his lawful and wedded wife, for time and all eternity? If you are, you will manifest it by placing her right hand in the hand of your husband."

In the Salt Lake City temple the first two floors are used for the endowment and marriage ceremonies. On other floors are special rooms for meetings of the elders, the seven presidents of the Seventies, and high council and stake presidencies, the Twelve Apostles and the First Presidency; a General Assembly room on the top floor of the temple seats 2,000 people.

These secret rites are performed in a dozen Mormon temples around the world of which the best known is certainly the great Salt Lake City temple. Construction of this temple began in 1853 but it was not dedicated until forty years later. As the federal army advanced on the Mormon capital in 1857 the Saints filled in the excavation and removed all evidence of masonry work. The site resembled a plowed field. When the threat abated, the workmen returned and continued their construction.

When Brigham Young died in 1877 the walls of the temple had risen twenty feet above ground level. Basement walls are eight feet thick and upper-story walls are six feet thick. Atop the tallest of the six spires is a statue of the Angel Moroni blowing a trumpet. Granite for the walls was hauled by teams of oxen from the Little Cottonwood Canyon twenty miles south of the city. The teams took four days to drag each load of blocks to the construction site. The Salt Lake City temple cost more than $4 million.

Nearby is the tabernacle which many of the million tourists who visit Temple Square each year confuse with the temple itself. This auditorium was begun in 1864 and com-

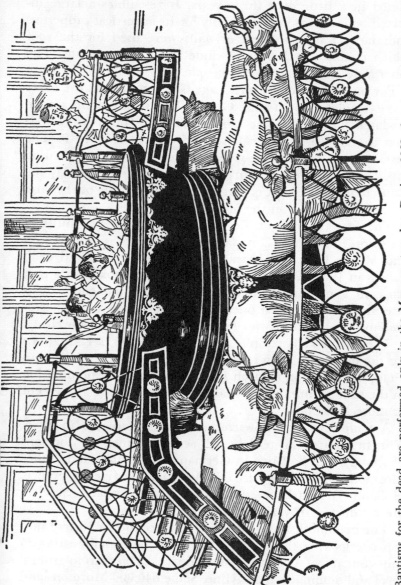

Baptisms for the dead are performed only in the Mormon temples. During 1962 there were 47,745 ordinances performed for the living in these temples and 2,566,476 ordinances for the dead.

pleted in a little over three years. It resembles a large inverted bowl and is known chiefly for its acoustical properties and the fact that no steel or nails were used for the roof which is held together by rawhide and locking beams. The tabernacle seats about 8,000 people.

For many decades the Salt Lake City temple and the other three temples in Utah at St. George, Logan and Manti accommodated the Saints. The next temple was built in Hawaii near the village of Laie, Oahu, and dedicated in 1919. The first Mormon elder went to Hawaii in 1850 and succeeding missionaries converted many of the natives so that today the Church of Jesus Christ of Latter-day Saints is one of the largest religious bodies in the 50th state.

The first temple outside of U. S. territory was built at Cardston in Alberta, Canada. Its architecture is along Incan and Mayan lines and it was first used for the sacred ordinances in 1923. The Mesa, Arizona, temple looks like a post office in a medium-sized city. It conducts the endowment rites in Spanish at least once a week and serves a number of Indians (Lamanites) who have joined the LDS Church.

The Idaho Falls temple, dedicated in 1945, set a pattern for the newer Mormon temples with a tall single spire. As in Utah, the Mormon Church is now the largest denomination in the state. A number of Idaho communities are 70 percent or more Mormon.

A temple in Bern, Switzerland, was completed in 1955. This first European temple will serve continental Mormons of whom about half live in Germany and Switzerland. Other Mormons who will go to the Bern temple live in France, Holland, Denmark, Sweden, Norway and Finland. Services are conducted in various languages.

The mammoth Los Angeles temple occupies a 13-acre hilltop overlooking the city; its spire can be seen by ships 25 miles out at sea. A statue of Moroni rises 257 feet from ground level and dominates the skyline. Some 640,000 Mormons and Gentiles toured the $6 million building before its dedication in 1956. They saw its stainless steel baptismal font supported by 12 brazen oxen, many of its 90 rooms, its third-floor Assembly Room which seats 2,600, and the Five Rooms on the second floor used for the Endowment. Each of these rooms accommodates 300 people.

Through intensive missionary work the LDS Church has become the dominant church among the Maori of New Zealand. Few of these converts could afford to travel to Hawaii for their endowments. The Church has built a temple near Hamilton, New Zealand, to serve 40,000 Saints in New Zealand and in the Tongan, Tahitian, Samoan and Australian missions. A number of Mormons from Utah went to New Zealand as labor missionaries to help with the construction. Like some of the newer temples, the New Zealand temple gets by with one lecture room and the Celestial Room instead of the Five Rooms.

A new temple for the British Isles has been built on a site 25 miles from London. It serves a rapidly growing Scottish and English membership. LDS missionaries have been laboring in England since 1837. The temple is expected to boost conversions in the Isles. The building of temples in Europe and New Zealand indicates that the Church no longer expects converts to gather in Zion in these latter-days. The temples demonstrate that a Latter-day Saint can live a full Mormon life without leaving his homeland.

Finally, a temple has been dedicated in Oakland to serve Mormons in northern California. It cost about $4 million and can easily be seen by ships entering the Golden Gate. No doubt many more temples will be built during the coming decades, including one to serve the Mormons in the eastern part of the United States.

Nothing in contemporary Mormonism would lead us to believe that these temples will ever be open to the general public. These rites are not meant to be witnessed by outsiders any more than are Masonic initiations. This secrecy has led some critics of Mormonism to suggest that the ceremonies are vulgar or obscene or treasonous. We believe that these charges are unfounded although Christians may well object to the theological basis of the rites. To the believing Mormon these rites are the key to salvation and exaltation for the living and the dead, the sacred ceremonies revealed by God to Adam and to Joseph Smith, Jr., the Prophet. To the Gentile student they seem to be adaptations of the Masonic ritual built around the story of Genesis rather than the story of Hiram Abiff and King Solomon's Temple which forms the basic Masonic myth.

Temple work reinforces the loyalty of the Mormon adult to his church. He becomes a sharer in esoteric rites unknown to the Gentile world. He believes that he is able to extend the good news of Mormonism to his dead relatives. The doctrines, the secret names, grips and tokens imparted in the temples become the passwords by which he hopes to enter the Celestial Kingdom.

12. *Mormonism and Freemasonry*

Smith's INTEREST and involvement in Freemasonry during the Nauvoo days turned Mormonism into a latter-day mystery religion. From those years on, Brighamite Mormonism carried on its central rites behind closed doors; only Saints in good standing could participate in these temple ceremonies. Any comparison of Masonic and Mormon ritual will reveal that the Prophet simply appropriated large chunks of the Masonic degree system into its endowment rites.

Mormonism developed in western New York, which was also the focus of the anti-Masonic movement sparked by the Morgan affair. In 1826 William Morgan disappeared from his Batavia, New York, home. He was said to have been preparing an exposé of Masonic secrets. His abduction to Fort Niagara was laid to Masonic culprits who wished to suppress the book. His body was never positively identified but many people believed that enraged Masons had murdered their captive.

His disappearance touched off the anti-Masonic crusade and prompted some politicians to establish an anti-Masonic party. This party actually carried Vermont in the national elections in 1832 and had polled 128,000 votes in an earlier election. The lodge was denounced from pulpit and platform. Thousands of Masons turned in their aprons. The lodge did not recover from this blow until after the Civil War.

No doubt young Joe Smith witnessed the presentation of burlesque Masonic ceremonies at anti-Masonic rallies near his home. If he did not enjoy such spectacles or hear exposés of Masonic initiations, he would have been one of the few people in that part of New York State to have escaped the pervasive influence of the anti-Masonic movement.

S. H. Goodwin, former Grand Master of the Utah lodge, in his study, *Mormonism and Masonry*, comments:

He [Smith], with others no doubt, attended the anti-Masonic mass meetings which were of frequent occurrence and of increasing and absorbing interest. He must often have listened to the highly colored and vicious attacks on the Fraternity which marked every public gathering of those days, and many times have witnessed the burlesqueing of Masonry and the alleged exemplification of various degrees by renouncing Masons.[1]

When Smith wrote (translated) the *Book of Mormon* he reflected the prevalent attitude toward the lodge. Several passages about "secret combinations" can only refer to Masonry. For example, in 2 Nephi 26:22 we read:

And there are also secret combinations, even as in times of old, according to the combinations of the devil, for he is the foundation of all these things; ... yea, and he leadeth them by the neck with a flaxen cord, until he bindeth them with his strong cords forever.

In the first degree initiation the candidate for Freemasonry is led into the lodge room with a cable tow around his neck. Here and elsewhere in the *Book of Mormon,* Satan is declared to be the father of the Masonic lodge, but fifteen years later Smith would petition to join the lodge in Nauvoo.

Anti-Masonic sentiments can be seen in the following *Book of Mormon* verses: 2 Nephi 10:15, 26:22; Alma, 37:29; Helaman 2:8, 3:23, 6:18, 19, 21-26, 30, 38, 39, 7:4, 25, 8:1, 28, 10:3, 11:2, 10, 26, 27; 3 Nephi 2:11, 3:9, 5:6, 7:9, 9:9; Mormon 1:18, 8:27; and Ether 8:15, 16, 18, 19, 22, 24–26, 9:5, 6–7, 10:33, 11:15, 22.

In the *Pearl of Great Price* we read another condemnation of the lodge in the story of Cain and Abel:

And Satan said unto Cain: Swear unto me by thy throat, and if thou tell it thou shalt die; and swear thy brethren by their heads, and by the living God, that they tell it not; for if they tell it, they shall surely die; and this that thy father may not know it; and this day I will deliver thy brother Abel into thine hands.

And Satan sware unto Cain that he would do according to his commands. And all these things were done in secret.

And Cain said: Truly I am Mahan, the master of this great secret, that I may murder and get gain. Wherefore Cain was called Master Mahan, and he gloried in his wickedness.

(Moses 5:29—31)

For Master Mahan read Master Mason and it is clear that Smith was developing his theme that Satan founded the Masonic lodge and that it was a nefarious and wicked alliance. This was written in December 1830, four years after the Morgan episode.

By the time the Mormons had established their settlement at Nauvoo, Smith had apparently changed his mind about the Masons. The anti-Masonic movement was petering out. Goodwin suggests that the Mormons might have thought to win Masonic friendship after their troubles in Kirtland and Missouri; lodge brothers in political office might have offered protection from their enemies. The Mormon writer, E. Cecil McGavin, makes the same judgment:

If he [Smith] and his brethren could attend Masonic conventions and freely mingle with the prominent jurists and lawmakers of the state, they would surely be spared the persecution they had witnessed elsewhere, they thought. They considered the Masonic fraternity a necessary means to this desired end.[2]

Many Mormon leaders were already members of the Masonic lodge before the Nauvoo lodge was organized. These included the Prophet's brother Hyrum, Brigham Young, Heber C. Kimball, and Dr. John C. Bennett. Granting of the dispensation to the Nauvoo lodge was opposed by members of Bodley Lodge No. 1 in nearby Quincy, but the Grand

Lodge of Illinois granted the dispensation on March 15, 1842. At this time Nauvoo had a population of between 8,000 and 10,000.

Smith's diary for March 15, 1842, states, "In the evening I received the first degree in Free Masonry in the Nauvoo Lodge, assembled in my general business office." The next day he wrote, "I was with the Masonic Lodge and rose to the sublime Degree." Both Smith and Rigdon were raised to Master Masons "at sight," that is, without going through the rituals themselves.

The Prophet indicated to some close friends that he planned to "celestialize" the lodge. George Arbaugh comments:

Furthermore, there is best evidence for believing that Joseph taught that Masonic principles and practices operated among the gods as well as on earth. His followers in Utah were taught that there is a sort of divine Masonry among the angels who hold the priesthood, by which they can detect those who do not belong to their order. Those who cannot give the signs correctly are supposed to be impostors . . .[3]

Smith later claimed that he only joined the lodge to discover how far the Masonic ritual had degenerated from the ritual of Solomon's Temple. His own ritual, insisted the Prophet, was revealed directly by an angel. Apparently he attended only three lodge meetings after his initiation; he took no higher degrees in Masonry than the first three.

Within less than six months the new lodge in Nauvoo and another Mormon-Masonic lodge in Montrose, Iowa, had initiated 286 Masons. Throughout the rest of Illinois the other eleven lodges enrolled only 227 brothers; the largest single lodge outside of Nauvoo was the 43-member Springfield lodge. The Gentile Masons naturally believed that the Mormons would soon dominate the Grand Lodge.

On complaint of neighboring lodges the Nauvoo lodge was ordered to cease work on August 11, 1842. A committee investigated the reported irregularities but allowed the Mormon Masons to resume lodge work on November 2, 1842.

There is some indication that Joseph Smith attempted to appeal to his Masonic brethren when he and the others were attacked by the mob in the Carthage jail. A number of men in the mob were known to be Masons. They knew Joseph and his brother were Masons in good standing on June 27, 1844, the date of the attack.

An editorial in the *Times and Seasons* for July 15, 1844, shamed the Masonic brothers for their participation in the murder:

They were both Masons in good standing. Ye brethren of "the mystic tie," what think ye! Where is our good Master Joseph and Hyrum? Is there a pagan, heathen, or savage nation on the globe that would not be moved on this great occasion, as the trees of the forest are moved by a mighty wind? Joseph's last exclamation was, "O Lord My God!"

Later in the editorial the writer explained:

With uplifted hands they gave such signs of distress as would have commanded the interposition and benevolence of savages or pagans.

In the Masonic third or Master Mason degree, the candidate swears:

"... I will not give the Grand Hailing Sign of Distress except in case of the most imminent danger, in a just and lawful Lodge, or for the benefit of instruction; and if ever I should see it given, or hear the words accompanying it, by a worthy brother in distress, I will fly to his relief, if there is a greater probability of saving his life than losing my own."

In giving this sign of distress the Mason raises both hands in the air and repeats: "O Lord, My God, is there no help for the widow's son?"

Heber C. Kimball, who had been a Mason since 1823, confirmed the fact that Joseph had tried to get help by means of the Masonic sign of distress:

"Joseph and Hyrum Smith were Master Masons, yet they were massacred through the instrumentality of some of the leading men of that fraternity, and not one soul of them has ever stepped forth to administer help to me or my brethren belonging to the Masonic Institution, or to render us assistance, although bound under the strongest obligation to be true and faithful to each other in every case and under every circumstance, the commission of crime excepted.

"Yes, Masons, it is said, were even among the mob that murdered Joseph and Hyrum in Carthage Jail. Joseph, leaping the fatal window, gave the Masonic signal of distress. The answer was the roar of his murderers' muskets and the deadly balls that pierced his heart." [4]

Zina D. Huntington Young was a divorcee who was sealed to Smith for eternity and to Brigham Young for time. In the *Latter-day Saints Encyclopedia* she related: "I am the daughter of a Master Mason; I am the widow of the Master Mason who, when leaping from the window of Carthage jail, pierced with bullets, made the Masonic sign of distress, but those signs were not heeded except by the God of Heaven."

Finally a Latter-day Saint author of more recent years has written:

When the enemy surrounded the jail, rushed up the stairway and killed Hyrum Smith, Joseph stood at the open window, his martyr-cry being these words, "O Lord My God!" This was not the beginning of a prayer, because Joseph Smith did not pray in that manner. This brave, young man who knew that death was near, started to repeat the distress signal of the Masons, expecting thereby to gain the protection its members are pledged to give a brother in distress.[5]

After Smith's murder and a little more than two years after the authorization of the Nauvoo lodge, the Grand Lodge lifted the dispensation and ordered the suspension of all Masonic work by the Mormons. From October 1844 on, any Masonic activity in the Mormon lodges was considered clandestine and unlawful by the Grand Lodge. As the beleaguered Mormons under the leadership of Young prepared to march to the West they abandoned all interest in the lodge. The Nauvoo Masonic temple was converted into a storehouse for grain. Once in Utah, the Church showed no inclination to reestablish the lodges which once flourished in Illinois and Iowa. Masonry did not protect Mormonism from the hostility of the Gentiles nor prevent the murder of the Prophet and his brother. The Church hierarchy saw no reason to inaugurate Masonic lodges in the western settlements.

The Prophet had administered the Temple ritual for the first time on May 4, 1842, six weeks after his initiation as a Mason. He was probably well acquainted with Masonic ritual for many years before this. The anti-Masonic crusade saw many enactments of supposedly secret Masonic rites, since removing the mystery of the lodge room seemed a good way to destroy the attractions of the lodge. Morgan's own exposé was widely circulated and we know that Kimball for one possessed a copy which he kept under lock and key. Finally, many of the Church leaders were Masons who would certainly disclose the details of the lodge ceremonies to a Prophet of the Lord if so requested.

An objective student of Mormonism such as Prof. Thomas O'Dea states simply:

To find appropriate materials for ritual development, his own non-liturgical religious background made it necessary to look outside strictly religious practices. Joseph went to Masonry to borrow many elements of ceremony. These he reformed, explaining to his followers that the Masonic ritual was a corrupted form of an ancient priesthood ceremonial that was now being restored.[6]

A Mason or student of Masonry will recognize many traditional Masonic symbols in a Mormon temple: the beehive, earth, moon, sun, stars, clasped hands, All-Seeing Eye. As in a lodge, the ceiling of the Garden Room of the temple is painted to represent the sky and clouds. Against the south wall is a platform reached by three steps; a Bible rests on the altar.

Embroidered on the right breast of the temple garment is a square and on the left a compass. The rents in the garment which are known as holy priesthood marks remind the wearer of the penalties for disclosing the secrets of the endowment ceremony.

As we have seen in our discussion of the temple rites in Chapter 11, the devil appears wearing a silk hat and a Masonic apron as would the worshipful master in a Masonic lodge. The penalties attached to the stages of the temple endowment correspond in numerous details to the penalties of the three Blue lodge degrees.

A publication of the Reorganized Church of Jesus Christ of Latter Day Saints asserts:

It is evident to any reader, from a description of the ceremonies used in the Mormon temples (and so many have told of them they are no longer a secret), that they are adopted largely, if not altogether, from the Masonic Lodge. The Masonic Lodge of Utah has issued pamphlets denouncing the Utah temple ceremonies as clandestine Masonry, and giving that as a principal reason for denying the right of any Mormon to join the Masonic Lodge in Utah.

It is a well-known fact that he [Young] made the Bee Hive a prominent emblem in his work, even making it the state emblem. The bee hive, the garments, the apron, the All-Seeing Eye, the constellation, and the square and compass on the garments and in the temples were all taken bodily from the Masonic Lodge. The grips, signs, and penalties are similar.[7]

Goodwin comments:

The observant Craftsman cannot be long among the Mormon people without noting the frequent use made of certain emblems and symbols which have come to be associated in the public mind with the Masonic fraternity. Now and again he will catch expressions and phrases in conversation and meet with terms in literature which are suggestive, to say the least. If he should continue his residence in Utah, he will sometimes be made aware of the fact, when shaking hands with a Mormon neighbor or friend, that there is a pressure of the hand as though some sort of "grip" is being given.[8]

Mormon apologists explain the remarkable similarities between the Masonic ritual and their own by claiming that both go back to that of the Temple of Solomon; Freemasonry's version has been corrupted and deformed while theirs was restored in its purity by Smith.

Once, while speaking at the St. George temple, Young declared:

"It is true that Solomon built a temple for the purpose of giving endowments, but from what we can learn of the history of that time they gave very few, if any endowments. And one of the High Priests was murdered by wicked and corrupt men who had already begun to apostatize because he would not reveal those things appertaining to the priesthood that were forbidden him to reveal until he came to the proper place."

The high priest to whom Young referred was, of course, Hiram Abiff, the central figure in the Masonic allegory.

McGavin accepts the most fanciful claims to antiquity put forth by such discredited Masonic historians as Mackey, Anderson and Oliver. These early Masonic writers were wont to claim Solomon, Adam, and most of the upright men of the Old Testament as early lodge brothers. Modern Masonic historians date the origin of the lodge in the early eighteenth century and recognize that these pioneer speculative Masons simply adopted the story of the building of Solomon's temple as a dramatic background for their initiations. Fred L. Pick and G. Norman Knight in their *Pocket History of Freemasonry* admit:

Up to the present time, no even plausible theory of the "origin" of the Freemasons has been put forward. The reason for this is probably that the Craft, as we know it, originated among the Operative Masons of Britain. No doubt it incorporated from the earliest times shreds of ritual, folk-lore and even occult elements of time-immemorial antiquity. But it is almost certainly a British product and of British origin.[9]

A few elements in modern Masonry here and there can be traced to the medieval guilds of working masons, but no one with a scholarly reputation would try to maintain that the degree system as it is worked now—and as it was worked in Nauvoo in 1842—could have possibly been derived from Solomonic rites.

McGavin insists simply that "Masonry did not have the slightest influence upon the endowment ceremony." He explains:

Joseph Smith definitely insisted that the Temple ritual was revealed to him, and that much of the pattern, symbolism, and design were taken from the Temple of Solomon. The font resting upon the backs of twelve oxen is but one of the many Solomonic features of Mormon Temples. In like manner we may say that all other "Masonic touches" were not borrowed from Masonry but from the parent of Masonry—Solomon's Temple.[10]

Antagonism between the Grand Lodge of Utah and the Church of Jesus Christ of Latter-day Saints persists to this day. The Grand Lodge refuses to initiate any known Mormon although Masonic lodges in other states do admit Mormons. When these Mormon Masons visit Utah they may not enter the lodge room.

As early as 1878 Grand Master J. M. Orr of Utah issued the following condemnation:

We say to the priests of the Latter-day Church, you cannot enter our lodge rooms—you surrender all to an unholy priesthood. You have heretofore sacrificed the sacred obligations of our beloved Order, and we believe you would do the same again. Stand aside; we want none of you. Such a wound as you gave Masonry in Nauvoo is not easily healed, and no Latter-day Saint is, or can become a member of our Order in this jurisdiction.

The Utah lodge issues the general instruction to its officers:

You will take notice that Mormons claiming to be Masons, be excluded from the right of visiting; and also that petitions for the degrees of Masonry shall not be received from any person who is known to be a Mormon.

An embarrassing situation took place some years ago when President Frederick M. Smith of the Reorganized Church, a prominent Mason, visited Salt Lake City and entered a local Masonic lodge. The doorkeeper did not question his religious affiliation but the matter came up during the lodge meeting to Smith's chagrin as well as his host's.

The stand of the Utah lodge is unique in American Freemasonry since it is the only Grand Lodge which applies a religious test to membership. Masonic lodges will initiate Catholics, Lutherans and others whose churches forbid Masonic affiliation even though such initiation involves automatic excommunication for the new Masons.

The lodge considers the Nauvoo episode a betrayal of Masonry and a bold attempt to take over the Illinois Grand Lodge by wholesale initiation of Mormons. The Masons resent the appropriation of so many Masonic symbols and rituals for use in the Mormon temples. The Mormons comprising a majority of the Utah population could dominate the Grand Lodge if no restriction or blackballs were employed to keep them out. As it stands now, the lodges in Utah serve as rallying places for the Protestant minority.

The LDS Church discourages all Mormons, Utahans or not, from entering the lodge. Any LDS Mason becomes ineligible to hold an office in the Church or advance in the priesthood. The Mormons too have their reasons for their stand. They recall the disregard of the Prophet's final signal of distress, the active part in the murder played by neighboring Masons, and the lack of compassion of Masons in the exodus from Nauvoo. They resent that the Illinois Grand Lodge outlawed the Mormon lodges and in effect suspended the Masonic affiliation of Brigham Young and the other Mormon Masons. The Latter-day Saints may also deem it unwise to allow men to go through both the temple endowments and the Masonic initiations lest they question the many similarities between the two and begin to doubt the official explanation that both originated in Solomon's Temple.

Recently the president of the Church urged Mormon men to seek fellowship in the priesthood quorums rather than the lodges:

President McKay also emphasized the place of the quorum in fostering fellowship and fraternity among the priesthood members. He declared the quorum should be to the priesthood of the Church what the lodges and fraternities are to the men of the world.[11]

Gentiles find it hard to accept the Mormon claim that their ritual came through revelation and owed nothing to Masonry. Few people have studied both the Masonic and Mormon rituals, but those who have cannot miss the striking parallels.

13. *Family Life and Welfare Program*

A MONG THE MORE ATTRACTIVE aspects of contemporary Mormonism is its emphasis on the family as the basic social unity. Certainly some of the recent converts to the Church must have been drawn to the image of the Mormon family as a happy, loyal, industrious, devout, and disciplined household.

Mormon theological concepts of marriage for time and eternity reinforce the ideal of marriage for all Mormon adults. Bachelors and spinsters have no status in Mormon society.

Unlike Roman Catholicism, Eastern Orthodoxy, and Anglicanism, the Church of Jesus Christ of Latter-day Saints places no premium on celibacy. The monk or nun, the unmarried schoolteacher or nurse, can lead satisfying lives in many Christian denominations but not in Mormonism. The Mormon who reaches maturity is subjected to intense community and religious pressure to get married and start raising a large family. Sometimes the elders of the Church feel compelled to have a talk with a Mormon bachelor who seems to prefer a life without family responsibilities. The celibate by choice or the homosexual is considered a shirker who is failing to bear his full responsibilities as a Mormon.

The *Doctrine and Covenants Commentary* declares:

Celibacy virtually denies the sacred character of the marriage relation. It is contrary to the Word of God. Men and women should be taught to marry young and to keep themselves pure.[1]

Marriage of a Mormon to a Gentile is strongly discouraged not only because such a mixed marriage may well lead to religious apostasy and indifference but also because such a marriage may not take place in the temple. The Mormon partner in such a union can be married only for time and not for eternity. He or she cannot attain full-fledged status unless the spouse is converted and the marriage later sealed in a temple ceremony. The Mormon husband in such a mixed marriage would find the road blocked if he desired to advance to the higher Church offices, while the Mormon wife in an interreligious marriage would have no claim to the blessings of the priesthood since she would not be married to a priest.

President Joseph F. Smith said:

... I would rather go myself to the grave than to be associated with a wife outside of the bonds of the new and everlasting covenant. Now, I hold it just so sacred; but some members of the Church do not so regard the matter. Some people feel that it does not make very much difference whether a girl marries a man in the Church, full of the faith of the gospel, or an unbeliever. Some of our young people have married outside of the Church; but very few of those who have done it have failed to come to grief. ... There is nothing that I can think of, in a religious way, that would grieve me more intensely than to see one of my boys marry an unbelieving girl, or one of my girls marry an unbelieving man.[2]

Despite the best efforts of the Mormon Church to encourage social relationships among Mormon young people the growth of mixed marriages will probably continue to concern Church officials. In cities like Salt Lake City, Gentiles now outnumber Mormons, and the former relative isolation of Mormon and Gentile is a thing of the past. Protestant and Mormon youngsters attend grade and high school together and a certain amount of dating is inevitable. Some Protestant ministers in Utah are frank to state that they would prefer a mixed Protestant-Catholic marriage to a Protestant-Mormon union. At least the Catholic and Protestant recognize each other's baptism and Christian status and share far more theological positions than the Mormon and, say, Presbyterian or Baptist or Methodist.

Strict chastity is expected of Mormon men and women during their dating and courting days. Masturbation, heavy necking, premarital sex relations, abortion, immodesty in dress or language are condemned outright as unworthy of a Saint. Adultery stands after murder as the most serious sin a human being can commit.

We have examined the Mormon marriage rites in Chapter 11. No stigma seems to attach to those couples who for reasons of economy or urgency prefer to get married for time only in the ward chapel and later arrange for a sealing in one of the temples. Sometimes several years elapse before the temple ceremony is scheduled.

Birth control is condemned by Church authorities but they have not undertaken the kind of active propaganda campaign against contraception which has characterized Roman Catholicism. Elder Richard L. Evans of the Council of Twelve answered an inquiry about birth control in the October 5, 1954 issue of *Look* magazine as follows: "The Church has always advocated the rearing of large families, and birth control, as commonly understood, is contrary to its teachings." Nevertheless the Mormon who admitted drinking beer or smoking cigarettes would incur a far greater censure than the one who confessed he and his wife used contraceptives. A standard Mormon theologian writes:

The doctrine that wedded man and woman should not beget children or should limit the number of children born to them, is contrary to the spirit of the Great Plan, and is a most erroneous one. Let the waiting spirits come! Let children be born into the earth! Let fatherhood and motherhood be the most honored of all the professions on earth.[3]

But Professor O'Dea notes:

Although the [Mormon] church generally frowns on divorce, it appears to compromise in practice; and while birth control may be found condemned in Mormon literature, it is today apparently ignored as a moral issue.[4]

The Mormon family with many children is presented as the model and the Church gives no attention to the so-called population explosion. The theological view is that there are billions of spirit children of the God of this planet awaiting mortality. Devout married Mormons will cooperate to give as many of these spirits bodies of flesh as they can support and educate. The extent of such cooperation is suggested by the 1962 Mormon birthrate of 33.16 per 1,000 compared to the national average of 24.9.

Dr. Wayne J. Anderson of the University of Minnesota wrote recently in the *Improvement Era:*

To them [Mormons] this means that as they as parents have children, they are fulfilling the purposes of God in providing opportunities for his spirit children so that they may go through this earthly schooling away from his presence. This is the reason that we, as a Church, believe in having large families, namely as many children as can be properly cared for.[5]

Distinctive family practices in Mormonism are fast day and Home Evening. Mormon families regularly skip two meals on the first Sunday of each month. The money which would have been spent for this food is donated to the Church to help feed the poor, ill and unemployed. Many Mormon families also designate one evening a week, usually Monday, as Home Evening. No one accepts engagements for this evening. It is devoted to family recreation such as music and community singing, games, reading aloud, hobbies, etc. The children get an opportunity to display their talents and engage in discussions of religious and secular topics.

Naturally the activities and social relationships in the local ward exert a strong influence on Mormon family life. The author attended the Sunday morning services recently at a ward composed mostly of university faculty members and students from a Big Ten school. Utah headquarters of the Church contributed 60 percent of the cost of the attractive chapel in a residential suburb.

The men of the ward assembled in the chapel at 9 o'clock for a hymn and prayer before breaking up into priesthood meetings. Each quorum met in a different room. At the meeting of the elders the presiding officer asked for volunteers to fertilize and cut the grass and announced the receipt of beans and rice for the two-year supply of rations suggested for each Mormon family.

The hour was spent in a discussion of the book *Jesus the Christ* by James E. Talmadge. The speaker covered two chapters and planned to cover the entire text during the year. He tried to answer the relatively few questions posed by the 17 other elders. After a brief recess some of the men along with several women got together to plan the Sunday school lessons for the day.

The entire congregation—men, women, and children—assembled in the chapel at 10:30. This happened to be Fast Sunday which meant that the Sunday school, sacrament meeting and testimonies would be scheduled consecutively until about 1 P.M. On other Sundays the people returned at 6:30 P.M. for the sacrament meeting.

Sunday school began with the singing of a hymn, an extemporaneous prayer, another hymn and a practice hymn: "There Is Beauty All Around When There's Love at Home."

Two recent women converts delivered their testimonies. The first had been baptized eight months before after a lifetime in the Lutheran Church. The other joined the Mormon Church six months before. Both declared their appreciation of the new understanding of doctrine they had received in the Mormon Church.

After these sermonettes the group divided itself into age

groups for the Sunday school. I sat in on the session for investigators although the class also included recently baptized Mormons and a few seeking a "refresher" course. The instructor was a graduate student in speech working for a Ph.D.; he intended to write his thesis on the public addresses of Joseph Smith, Jr. He led a discussion on baptism, the proper mode (immersion), the proper age (eight or older), and the need for proper authorization (by a Mormon priest).

Back in the chapel the congregation reassembled for the weekly sacrament or communion service. After a hymn and prayer, two elders who were undergraduate students at the university pronounced the words of blessing. During the prayer they had broken slices of bread into smaller pieces. Four deacons passed the trays of bread and trays containing paper cups of water to the people in the pews. Even children of two and three years of age partook of the bread and water although investigators were urged to wait until they had been baptized.

The personal testimonies followed. About 15 members stood and expressed their belief in the *Book of Mormon* and the claims of the Prophet, asked the congregation for forbearance of their faults, thanked God for their parents, spouses, children and friends, related incidents from missionary experiences, relayed messages from former members of the ward who had returned to Utah, etc. The pause between these testimonies sometimes stretched to two or three minutes. When all were heard, the meeting was adjourned at 1:10 P.M.

Nationwide about four Mormons out of ten attend the Sacrament meeting on any particular Sunday.[6] This would be a higher average attendance than most Protestant denominations but lower than the 60 percent attendance at Sunday Mass estimated by Catholic sociologists.

At three to six weeks of age a Mormon baby is given a blessing and his name is entered on the Church records. The children will be baptized into the faith at the age of eight.

This may take place in a river, a swimming pool, or a baptismal font in the ward chapel. The boys enter the ranks of deacon in the Aaronic priesthood at the age of twelve.

Mormons emphasize extended kinship relations to a greater degree than most American families. Grandparents, aunts and uncles, cousins, keep in touch with each other. Family reunions in Mormon communities during the summer months attract as many as 1,000 kinfolk. Descendants of pioneer Mormon families attach an importance to their families which some observers would be tempted to say borders on ancestor worship. Indeed some grandparents and great-grandparents may be thought to have achieved the godhead so that they are entitled to a high degree of honor and reverence. Mormon temple work for the dead and interest in genealogy adds to the interest in the larger family unit of the living and the dead.

Mormonism de-emphasizes contemplation and fosters an activist pragmatism. Children growing up in an orthodox Mormon home will be urged to apply themselves to their studies, to cultivate recreational interests such as music, art and hobbies, to take an interest in health and to apply the rule of moderation to all the facets of life. Regular church attendance is expected but speculation about theological problems or the religious answer to modern movements such as existentialism or Freudianism is discounted. This life is constantly seen as a preparation for eternity. Knowledge acquired now will be useful after death. Nothing could be further from the spirit of Mormonism than the Trappist monk—celibate, contemplative, withdrawn from the world. Although Calvinism was rejected by the Prophet and disparaged in the *Book of Mormon* the Calvinist ethic—work hard, save as much as possible, give away as much as possible—finds a welcome home in contemporary Mormonism.

The Mormon family is patriarchal today as it was in the days of polygamy although the secular pressures of American society constantly threaten to undermine this pattern of authority. In Mormonism the man, the father, holds the priesthood, and what benefits the wife derives from the priesthood come only through her marriage to the priest. For the woman, motherhood takes precedence over any secular career. The woman with only one or two children or with an outside job cannot expect to receive the recognition given to the mother who fulfills her feminine role by raising a large family of sons and daughters to be faithful Latter-day Saints.

Although many of the early Mormons came from Puritan backgrounds, the Church has traditionally encouraged such activities as dancing and the theatre. Taking their cue from 2 Nephi 2:25—"men are, that they might have joy"—the Mormons were said to have built dance halls right after they finished their ward chapels in Utah. The typical Mormon dance begins with a prayer and ends with a hymn; smoking, drinking and low-cut gowns are forbidden and the festivities usually end before midnight.

A network of religious educational and social organizations enrolls Mormons of all age groups. Primary Association offers religious and recreational instruction for young Mormons from four to twelve. The 60,000 adult teachers take care of about 350,000 participants including 18,000 non-LDS members, many of whom eventually ask for baptism.

All Mormons, not just young people, are expected to attend the classes of the graded Sunday school. The 5,000 schools of the Deseret Sunday School Union enroll 720,000 pupils. Mormons write and publish all their own Sunday school material rather than use material available to Protestant denominations. The school opens with a general exercise for all pupils, divides into classes arranged according to age, and reassembles for benediction. A distinctive feature of the school is the two- or three-minute talks given by two young members before the entire congregation each Sunday. This provides an opportunity for a boy or girl to get a taste of public speaking long before this would be allowed in the traditional churches.

Similar to the Protestant-oriented YMCA and YWCA, the Mormon Young Men's Mutual Improvement Association and Young Women's Mutual Improvement Association appeal mainly to teen-agers. Brigham Young founded these associations nearly 100 years ago and today they claim a worldwide membership of 400,000. They meet once a week for prayer, dancing, debates, musical programs, sports and drama. Most wards plan "fireside" meetings for teen-agers and young adults on Sunday evenings. The YMMIA sponsors the largest softball and basketball leagues in the world with 2,600 teams in each sport.

The Mormons were also the first religious denomination to sponsor the Boy Scout program and now enroll about 160,000 Scouts and adult leaders in their program.

Mormon girls participate in the parallel Beehive Girls with a membership of 38,000 in 8,000 units.

Except for schools in the Mexican mission and in the Mormon settlement of Colonia Juárez near Chihuahua, Mexico, the Mormon Church no longer maintains its own parochial school system. Instead, the Church has built a network of religious education centers adjacent to public high schools and colleges. On the high school level these part-time schools are known as seminaries. The 150 full-fledged seminaries and 850 other seminaries which lack their own buildings enroll 60,000 LDS high school students. This system dates back to 1912, predating the released time arrangements worked out by other denominations.

The seventh-grade Mormon boy or girl attending the seminary studies Biographies of Great Religious Leaders. In the eighth grade he studies the *Book of Mormon;* in the ninth, the Old Testament; in the tenth, the New Testament; in the eleventh, Church History and Doctrine; and in the final year of high school, Teacher Training, Priesthood Leadership, and Missionary Training.

Similar religious education centers near the public college campuses are known as Institutes of Religion. They provide programs much like the Newman Clubs or Hillel Centers. The 25 Institutes near college campuses in Utah, Idaho, Arizona, Wyoming and California serve 10,000 Mormon students. In some cases college credit is offered for these courses in Mormon theology.

The Mormon child who has participated in Primary, in Sunday school and church worship, in the YMMIA or YWMIA, in the high school seminary system, and in the Institute of Religion or in Brigham Young University or another Mormon college can step into his mission assignment at the age of nineteen or twenty with a knowledge of his religion rivaled by few young people in other churches.

Despite everything the Church has been doing to stabilize Mormon family life there are signs that divorce among the Mormons is increasing. The divorce rate in Utah is higher than in most states. In theory, only adultery is recognized as a legitimate reason for divorce but actually almost any reason acceptable to the civil courts is accepted as grounds for a temple divorce as well. Widtsoe comments:

The Church decries divorce, yet it holds that divorce is better than daily unhappiness in marriage. Those who for sufficient reasons secure divorces do not lose their standing or good repute in the Church. . . . The Church has no authority to grant civil divorces. This is a concern of the State. The Church, however, may dissolve that part of a marriage for time and eternity which pertains to the life after this. . . . Each request to have an eternal marriage annulled, must come before the President of the Church for action.[7]

One of the apostles, Spencer W. Kimball, warned the General Conference in 1962: "So long as the marriage covenant has not been legally severed, neither spouse morally may seek new romance or open the heart to other people. After the divorce becomes final, both freed individuals may engage in proper courting activities."

Mormons are constantly reminded that they are their

brothers' keepers. The Mormon family knows it will be called upon to assist other Mormons who, because of advanced age, physical handicap, unemployment or sickness, may need help. Likewise the Mormon family knows that should misfortune strike its own house it could expect such help from fellow Mormons.

Early Mormon attempts to form a communistic or cooperative society such as envisioned by the Prophet in the United Order floundered. The ideal of charity remained and was put to many tests in the mutual hardships faced in Missouri, Nauvoo, the march to the West, and pioneer Utah. During the Great Depression the Mormon authorities announced the consolidation of charitable agencies in an overall Welfare Department. Since 1936 this department has helped hundreds of thousands of Latter-day Saints tide themselves over bad times and misfortunes.

The myth that no Mormon ever took relief during the Depression or worked on the WPA is belied by an examination of the Utah welfare rolls. As a matter of fact, the large numbers of Mormons accepting government handouts in the early 1930's prompted President Heber J. Grant and his aides to work out the Welfare Program now fully established. The Church believed then and still believes that relief payments strip a man of his self-respect and do nothing to rehabilitate him and his family.

Throughout the western states and in some foreign countries are 140 bishops' storehouses which stock food, clothing and shoes. No one can buy any of this merchandise. It is given to needy Mormons who present an order from their bishop. Much of the food for these storehouses is grown on 650 farms operated by various wards and stakes with volunteer labor. Canneries process fruits and vegetables under the DESERET label. A coal mine furnishes fuel for the needy.

Largest of these storehouses is Welfare Square in Salt Lake City. It resembles a huge supermarket or department store with the exception that no money changes hands. To avoid

the embarrassment of recipients and the debilitating idea of
the dole, the unemployed in good health are expected to contribute their labor in the storehouses, canneries, or farms.

Those items which cannot be grown on Church farms are
purchased with money derived from the "fast money" contributed by Mormon families. In a recent year the Church
disbursed more than $4 million in cash. A total of 100,000
Saints were helped with cash, jobs, provisions. Some Mormons out of work are given jobs on Church building projects.

In a well-run ward the poor and needy Mormons should
not have to apply to the bishop for help. He should be close
enough to the members of the congregation to spot such cases.
The teachers and deacons who make regular calls on all Mormon families report situations which call for assistance. Some
needs may be met by the Relief Society, the ladies' auxiliary
of the Church.

The Mormon Church seeks to do more than bail out members who need help. It engages in a continuous educational
program to help Mormon families save part of their incomes,
avoid getting into debt or piling up installment payments,
frittering money away on luxuries. Organizations for girls
and women stress budgeting, sewing, economical cooking,
etc.

The Church even makes outright loans to members for
useful purposes. In these cases the individual would have to
report that he could not obtain a regular bank loan. All
Church loans are on character only. They might be made
to a Mormon who wanted to buy seed, make a down payment
on a small business, etc.

Mormons and others donate discarded clothing, furniture,
appliances and the like to the Deseret Industries, which operates much like the Salvation Army or Goodwill Industries.
The aged and handicapped repair the contributed items
which are then given away or sold at a nominal price in 13

retail stores. Deseret Industries also operates a factory which manufactures rugs, overalls, coats, and blankets.

Church authorities encourage all Mormon families to stock a full year's supply of food, clothing and fuel in their homes. This would tide them over during almost any emergency. The program has been lauded by the Civil Defense authorities. Some families try to stock two years' supply of food in their basements and attics. Occasionally a bishop announces a drill for his ward which means that all families stop buying any groceries and try to live on what they have squirreled away. These drills reveal deficiencies in the family storage plans which can be corrected.

We should not underestimate the attraction of this integrated Church-sponsored social security program for prospective converts to Mormonism. In a world which many people see as a dog-eat-dog affair, the picture of a 2,400,000-member fellowship interested in both the spiritual and material welfare of its members facilitates the work of the thousands of young Mormon missionaries. Thus the Mormon slightly dissatisfied with the Church would think twice or more before cutting himself off from the security represented by the welfare program as well as the informal help he could expect from his bishop and coreligionists in the ward.

The emphatic Mormon position on self-sufficiency and the suspicion of government welfare work help explain why almost all top Church officials are Republicans of the right wing. Many rank-and-file Latter-day Saints vote Democratic, but the president or apostle or member of the Mormon hierarchy who frankly espoused the concept of the welfare state or could be classified as a New Dealer, Fair Dealer, or New Frontiersman would be a lonely man.

The announced goal of the Church today is that no Mormon need ever apply to the State or Federal Government for assistance because of old age, sickness or unemployment. The Church tries to take care of its own. It seems clear that such an objective can be maintained during a recession but whether the Church, wealthy as it may be, could support any sizable number of its members during a prolonged depression is another matter. Meanwhile, the Church's philosophy on welfare cannot but influence the political atmosphere in several western states and the votes of Mormon senators and congressmen. The acceptance of this philosophy in an extreme form probably explains the political phenomenon of a J. Bracken Lee, Gentile ex-governor of Utah and right-wing spokesman.

The Welfare plan of the Church frees the Mormon from some of the economic worries which plague his Gentile neighbors and helps cement his loyalty to his church. Despite an observable trend toward mixed marriages, divorce and acceptance of contraception, the Mormon family remains a strong pillar of the Church. The many ties which bind the family members to the Church—spiritual, educational, recreational, economic—do not allow a Mormon family to apostatize or join a Protestant or Catholic denomination without considerable inconvenience. If the Mormon family must face new problems in a mixed society it is nevertheless more stable and united than the family units typical of many other churches, not to mention those without any spiritual grounding.

14. *The Word of Wisdom*

MANY BAPTISTS AND METHODISTS abstain from liquor and tobacco for religious reasons, but the Latter-day Saints insist also on abstinence from coffee, tea and cola drinks. This prohibition and other dietary regulations stem from a revelation given to Joseph Smith at Kirtland on February 27, 1833. It appears in *Doctrine and Covenants* as Section 89 but is more familiarly known as the Word of Wisdom.

With the discontinuance of polygamy the distinguishing marks which set the Mormon secularly apart from the Gentile community are his dietary habits and tithing. Mormons who succumb to the temptation of a bottle of beer or a cup of coffee have disobeyed God Himself and persistent lapses will relegate such offenders to the status of "Jack Mormons."

Actually the Word of Wisdom makes no mention of coffee or tea. The prohibiton is written against "hot drinks"—"hot drinks are not for the body or belly." The extension of this to mean coffee and tea and cola drinks is a matter of interpretation. In his *The Life of Joseph F. Smith,* Hyrum Smith declares: "In the 'hot drinks' of the Word of Wisdom tea and coffee are included." [1] Again the same author repeats: "Again hot drinks are not for the body or belly. There are many who wonder what this can mean, whether it refers to tea or coffee or not. I say it does refer to tea and coffee." [2]

The further extension of the divine prohibition to cola derives from the caffeine which such drinks contain. The *LDS Reference Encyclopedia* states that such cola drinks "are as damaging to the human system as coffee." [3] The same book even warns against the use of cocoa since it contains theobromine, "a near relative of caffeine," and irritates the kidneys.[4]

The fact that a drink is hot or cold does not seem to matter much. Iced tea and iced coffee are prohibited but hot chocolate, warm lemonade, and broths are allowed. Beverages with the caffeine removed, such an Sanka, could presumably be drunk hot or cold.

The Word of Wisdom forbids the use of wine or strong drink except for the Sacrament and "for the washing of your bodies." The pertinent articles of Section 89 read:

That inasmuch as any man drinketh wine or strong drink among you, behold it is not good, neither meet in the sight of your Father, only in assembling yourselves together to offer up your sacraments before him.

And, behold, this should be wine, yea, pure wine of the grape of the wine, of your own make.

And, again, strong drinks are not for the belly, but for the washing of your bodies.

Total abstinence has become a test of Christian fellowship for the Latter-day Saints, although the use of liquor by others is tolerated. The Church itself owned a brewery in Nauvoo, and in Church-owned hotels in Salt Lake City today customers can bring their own liquor bottles and order setups of cracked ice and mixes to concoct drinks in the dining rooms. The Church-owned radio and TV stations carry advertisements for cigarettes, beer and wine, and coffee. Utah was the 36th state to ratify the 21st Amendment, which technically abolished national prohibition. At that time over 87 percent of the people of the state were Mormons.

Originally the Word of Wisdom was given as counsel, but President Heber J. Grant elevated it to the position of a commandment. He explained:

The Word of Wisdom is today a commandment of the Lord to us, first given to us "not by constraint or commandment," but of later years given to us by the Prophet Brigham Young and by the Prophet Joseph F. Smith as a commandment to this people.[5]

That Joseph Smith, Jr. himself did not regard the Word of Wisdom as a commandment at the time is evident from his drinking wine in the Carthage jail the night before he died. The *History of the Church of Jesus Christ of Latter-day Saints* by B. H. Roberts reports the events of that day as related by John Taylor. Taylor recalled:

"Sometime after dinner we sent for some wine. It has been reported by some that this was taken as a sacrament. It was no such thing; our spirits were generally dull and heavy, and it was sent for to revive us. . . . I believe we all drank of the wine and gave some to one or two of the prison guards." [6]

The growing Mormon abhorrence of alcohol has led the denomination to substitute water for wine in the Sunday sacrament service, although the original Word of Wisdom prescribes wine for this communion. Protestant denominations, such as the Methodist Church, which object to wine have used grapejuice instead. Neither the New Testament, the *Book of Mormon* or *Doctrine and Covenants* makes any reference to the use of water instead of wine in the communion service. Of course, it was quite impossible for the Jews gathered in the spring for the Last Supper to serve unfermented grapejuice. Outsiders have wondered how the Mormon Church can be so insistent on immersion as the only proper and scriptural mode of baptism while arbitrarily changing the communion element from the fruit of the vine to simple water. As a matter of fact, *Doctrine and Covenants* specifically commands the use of wine.

Brigham Young declared, "No matter how many generations come and go, believers in him are required to eat bread and drink wine in remembrance of his death and sufferings until he comes again." [7]

Tobacco also comes under the list of prohibited items. Article 8 declares that "tobacco is not for the body, neither for the belly, and is not good for man, but is an herb for bruises and all sick cattle, to be used with judgment and skill." Exactly what value tobacco might be to bruises and sick cattle is uncertain; neither physicians nor veterinarians have discovered any particular curative powers in the weed.

The pages of the *Improvement Era* often contain temperance admonitions. In 1948 President McKay warned:

I think tobacco is a vice which should be shunned as the bite of a rattlesnake. When I say that, I am not unaware of the fact that though seemingly there are some young men who can use tobacco without serious injury, there are many others who are poisoned, their characters weakened, and their health undermined by the ingredients of that cigarette. The Lord has said that tobacco is not good for man. That should be sufficient for Latter-day Saints.

Recent evidence linking cigarette smoking with lung cancer and other disorders confirms the wisdom of the Word of Wisdom for Mormon believers. Available evidence seems to indict only the cigarette; those who have been smoking pipes and cigars do not seem to be in much danger from lung cancer. At the time of the revelation—1833—the usual form in which tobacco was used was in pipes or as snuff or chew. President Heber J. Grant thundered that "smoking is absolutely no good morally, intellectually, physically, or in any other way."

Strictly speaking, Mormons who follow the Word of Wisdom will be vegetarians in the spring, summer and fall. Section 89 limits the use of meat to "times of winter, or of cold, or famine." All meat should be eaten sparingly.

And again, verily I say unto you, all wholesome herbs God hath ordained for the constitution, nature, and use of man—

Every herb in the season thereof, and every fruit of the season thereof; all these to be used with prudence and thanksgiving.

Yea, flesh also of beasts and of the fowls of the air, I, Lord, have ordained for the use of man with thanksgiving; nevertheless they are to be used sparingly;

And it is pleasing unto me that they should not be used, only in times of winter, or of cold, or famine.

All grain is ordained for the use of man and of beasts, to be the staff of life, not only for man but for the beasts of the field, and the fowls of heaven, and all wild animals that run or creep on the earth;

And these hath God made for the use of man only in times of famine and excess of hunger.

All grain is good for the food of man; as also the fruit of the vine; that which yieldeth fruit, whether in the ground or above the ground—

Nevertheless, wheat for man, and corn for the ox, and oats for the horse, and rye for the fowls and for swine, and for all beasts of the field, and barley for all useful animals, and for mild drinks, as also other grain.

The devout Mormon should not join his fellow Americans around the backyard barbecue pit during the summer months, since this is a time when meat should not be eaten. For the average Mormon the warning against the use of meat does not have the force of the prohibitions against alcohol, tobacco, coffee and tea.

In an earlier revelation (*D. & C.* 49:18–19) the Lord seemed to command the use of meat:

And whoso forbiddeth to abstain from meats, that man should not eat the same, is not ordained of God;

For, behold, the beasts of the field and the fowls of the air, and that which cometh of the earth, is ordained for the use of man for food and for raiment, and that he might have in abundance.

A group of ultraorthodox Mormons in Salt Lake City call themselves the "Eighty-niners" and try to observe every article of Section 89 to the letter. Some Mormons stay away from pepper and spices although this is not commanded.

Mormon apologetical literature makes frequent reference to health surveys which indicate that Mormons live longer and suffer from fewer diseases such as cancer, tuberculosis and parasitic disease than the general American population. Unfortunately no significant comparisons are available because the Mormon statisticians do not use a genuine control group. Even excluding the Negro population, the disease and death rates of people in city slums, of recent immigrants from Puerto Rico, and of southern sharecroppers are obviously going to be considerably higher than those of a generally rural population in the Rocky Mountain states. To be statistically significant the comparison should be drawn between a group of Mormons and a control group of white Presbyterians or Lutherans or Baptists living in the same area.

This is not to say that the general health level of a people who abstain from liquor, tobacco and all stimulants may not be higher than that of men and women who do indulge. But the medical evidence that an adult who takes a glass of wine with his steak followed by a cup of coffee and a cigar will suffer poor health compared to a vegetarian and total abstainer is not conclusive.

Physicians would be inclined to smile at Brigham Young's violent denunciations of Word of Wisdom violators:

"Says the mother—'Do eat, my little daughter, you are sick; take a piece of pie, toast, or meat, or drink a little tea or coffee; you must take something or other.' Mothers in Israel, such a course engenders disease, and you are laying a foundation that will cut off one-half to two-thirds of the lives of your children." [8]

Quite apart from the religious and health motivations for observing the Word of Wisdom prohibitions are the economic motivations. Prof. Leonard J. Arrington of the economics department at Utah State University explains the strict enforcement of the prohibitions after 1867 as a necessary measure to develop and maintain a self-sufficient economy in the Mormon settlements. The Saints could ill afford to spend what little cash they had to import tobacco, tea, coffee, etc. In an article entitled "An Economic Interpretation of the 'Word of Wisdom'" Professor Arrington observed:

President Young came to be unalterably opposed to the expenditure of money by the Saints on imported tea, coffee, and tobacco. It was consistent with the economics of the time that he should have had no great objection to tobacco chewing if the tobacco was grown locally. It was also consistent that he should have successfully developed a locally produced "Mormon" tea to take the place of the imported article.[9]

To those who follow its counsel and commandments the Word of Wisdom promises "health in their navel and marrow to their bones." They "shall find wisdom and great treasures of knowledge, even hidden treasures. And shall run and not be weary, and shall walk and not faint." Finally, the faithful Mormon is told: "And I, the Lord, give unto them a promise, that the destroying angel shall pass by them, as the children of Israel, and not slay them. Amen."

The dietary aspects of the Word of Wisdom contribute to an *esprit de corps* among Mormons just as similar regulations help solidify Jewish, Catholic and Islamic communities. The Mormon emphasis on the value of health and long life finds a parallel in the concern of the New Thought and Christian Science movements for well-being. On the other hand, the Word of Wisdom denies full Church membership to thousands of born Mormons who conform to the general eating and social habits of the American middle class. The Church has discovered no formula by which these "Jack Mormons" can enjoy a cigarette or highball without rejecting their religious heritage.

The Word of Wisdom also enables many Mormon families to pay their tithes without undue hardship, since Gentile families may spend a considerable percentage of their income on liquor, tobacco, tea and coffee. As a nation we spend far more on alcohol alone than we do on education.

O'Dea comments:

Abstention from the practices forbidden in the Word of Wisdom appears to have replaced plural marriage as the badge of Zion, the sign of the gathered, in these days of accommodation to and integration into the larger Gentile community.[10]

Some liberal Mormons object to the emphasis given to the literal adherence to the Word of Wisdom prohibitions. Nevertheless, it appears that such strict adherence will continue to be a basic test of faithfulness and, along with tithing, a requirement for all who would enter a Mormon temple.

15. *Mission System*

SEVERAL YEARS AGO my wife was entertaining some of the ladies of the neighborhood at a midmorning coffee break when two dark-suited young men rang the doorbell. They introduced themselves as ministers and asked if they might chat for awhile. She invited them in and introduced them to the other women.

"Care for a cup of coffee?" my wife asked.

"No, thank you," replied one of the visitors with a smile.

"Cigarette?"

"Oh, no," said the other with a firm shake of his head.

Then the pair identified themselves as elders of the Church of Jesus Christ of Latter-day Saints and explained their stand against coffee, tea, tobacco and other vices being flaunted at this neighborhood orgy.

These two gentlemen, both about twenty, interrupted their college educations to accept calls by the Mormon Church to serve as missionaries. During their period of service they were being supported by their families in Utah. They happened to be assigned to the medium-sized Indiana community where we live.

The missionaries put in a full schedule. They are expected to work sixteen hours a day, seven days a week. The missionary who has already spent a year in the field instructs the new arrival. Both call on householders, leave pamphlets and tracts, try to sell the *Book of Mormon,* instruct investigators, and baptize converts. While on this assignment they may not date or dance.

They were only two out of more than 12,000 such missionaries stationed around the world besides 7,000 part-time
local or home missionaries. The Church itself need not draw
on its income from tithes and investments to support these
young men and women. It costs about $2,000 to support a
missionary in the field for two years: the Church pays trans-
portation from but not to the assigned missions. If their own
families cannot afford to support them in the mission field
they may be "adopted" by wealthy Mormon businessmen.

Recently the Church has been sending teams of labor
missionaries overseas to help in the construction of Mormon
meetinghouses. They have assisted with the building of the
New Zealand temple and with chapels in northern England
and Nice, France.

Most of the volunteer Mormon missionaries are in their
late teens or early twenties. When called they agree to serve
anywhere in the world for from 18 to 30 months. Their only
theological education is what they have learned in Sunday
school, the after-hours high school seminaries and perhaps
in religion courses at Brigham Young University. Just before
leaving for their posts they attend a one-week short course in
missiology at Salt Lake City. For their terms as missionaries
they are considered ordained ministers with authority to
baptize, marry, and conduct funerals.

Obviously the theological equipment of most such missionaries is limited. Their knowledge of Roman Catholicism
and Protestantism as rival commitments is sketchy. Coming
from small towns and farms in Utah and its neighboring
states, they bring an unsophisticated and rather provincial
attitude into the cities of the Eastern Seaboard and Europe.

Their theological naïveté can also embarrass the Church
at times. A few years ago about 30 missionaries in France
decided to reform the Church itself. They began to preach
the almost forgotten doctrines of blood atonement and polygamy. The Church ordered them all back to Utah, but some

persisted in their rebellion and have tried to woo converts among the orthodox Saints.

Mormon missionaries generally labor among people who already profess some belief in Christianity. Clergymen of other denominations often accuse the eager Mormon missionaries of sheep stealing but the Mormons believe that they are simply building on a previous belief in God, in Jesus Christ, and in the Bible to bring the potential convert to a knowledge of the restoration of the true Church in these latter-days.

The living example of these thousands of young men and women, the cream of Mormonism, postponing their educational, vocational and even marital plans to serve their church without pay probably exerts a greater influence on the Gentile public than their apologetical skills. Even if they made no converts at all they would be helping to reshape the image of Mormonism which in nineteenth-century America meant only polygamy and suspected treason.

Because Mormonism drew most of its early converts from the British Isles and Scandinavia, and because few of its missionaries have mastered a foreign language, the Church favors sending them to English-speaking areas. It has been reaping an impressive harvest of converts in England where in 1962 the Mormons baptized 16,830 members. The Church is building 25 to 30 ward chapels each year throughout the British Isles and recently dedicated a Mormon temple near London.

Mormonism has been seeking converts in England for more than a century. Smith sent seven missionaries to England in 1837; they and their successors baptized 77,000 English converts during the next two decades and encouraged most of them to emigrate to Zion in Nauvoo and Utah. Of course, this emigration also stripped the Church of most of its natural leaders in England, so that by the end of the century the number of converts barely reached 300 a year.

The man who sparked the modern resurgence of the LDS

Church in England is T. Bowring Woodbury V, who began his job as mission president in 1958. He immediately appealed for more missionaries to supplement the 160 assigned to England. Before long he was directing the activities of 1,100 proselytizers. He trimmed the indoctrination period before baptism from weeks to days. He urged the young missionaries to organize baseball teams for the children as a way to reach the parents. By 1963 the Mormon Church counted between 50,000 and 55,000 members in the United Kingdom.

Many of the Mormon converts were active or inactive members of the Church of England. In 1961 the Church of England assembly called the Mormon missionaries "undesirables." The Anglican chaplain at the University of Durham has criticized the "well-meant but over-zealous attempts of overeager Mormon missionaries."

The Anglican bishop of Durham, Dr. Maurice Harland, warned his diocesan conference against "the attraction, especially to young people, of well-equipped Mormon buildings and social activities which alienate them from the Christian faith." He said that the Mormon religion "seems so absurd that we have not taken it seriously" but that "American money and accent and young attractive American men have an undoubted appeal." Mormons have never paid much attention to their clerical critics from the historic Christian churches and they have ignored these Anglican attacks as well.

Only during the past decade has the Mormon Church firmly established itself in Scotland. President McKay flew to Glasgow at the age of eighty-nine to organize the Glasgow stake which now numbers 3,500 people. The Latter-day Saints have built their first ward chapel in Glasgow and are planning chapels in Edinburgh, Aberdeen and other Scottish cities. Presbyteries of the Church of Scotland have watched the invasion of 250 Mormon missionaries into Scotland and Ireland and have expressed the same concern as their Anglican colleagues in England.

The Presbyterian Church of Scotland issued a report in 1963 warning its members against the Mormon missionaries:

> Their most insidious approach is to young people, attracted as always to what is romantically American, taking them free to football games, organizing American baseball teams and offering them other similar inducements. Thus they play on youthful interest in what is free, what is bizarre, what is novel.

About a dozen years after starting the English mission the Mormon Church sent its first missionaries to Scandinavia and to the Society Islands. It achieved considerable success in these areas and then dispatched additional missionaries to Switzerland and Italy. The Swiss listened to the Mormon claims and a number requested baptism, but the Italians ignored the claims of the restored gospel. In 1851 the Church launched missions in France, Germany, Australia and Latin America, and in 1852, in India, New Zealand, and Malta. The South African mission dates from 1853.

Mormon missionaries have had considerable success in New Zealand where 80 percent of their converts are Maoris. The New Zealand National Council of Churches refused to consider the LDS Church for membership, declaring: "Their conception of God is anthropomorphic. To them He is really a glorified man."

Mormons divide their mission organization into three categories: foreign nations; areas in the United States, Canada and Mexico where Mormonism is weak; and home areas in the Rocky Mountain states. The Mormons are notably weak in converting Gentiles who live in predominantly Mormon communities. The stake mission was started in 1936 and seeks to reclaim lapsed Mormons and convert Gentiles; stake missionaries need not leave home and family to engage in this work in their spare time.

Foreign missions today are organized in Argentina, Australia, Brazil, Great Britain, Denmark, France, Japan, Netherlands, Norway, New Zealand, Israel, South Africa, Sweden, Switzerland, Tahiti, Tonga, and West Germany. A president and two counselors preside over each mission. The mission itself is divided into districts and the districts into branches.

During 1962, Mormon missionaries harvested a bumper crop of 115,000 converts, an all-time record. Of this number, 105,000 were baptized in the mission fields and 10,000 in the stakes. The previous record was set in 1961 with 88,807 convert-baptisms.

The Mormon Church began missionary work in South America only 38 years ago. Half of the more than 29,000 LDS in South America joined the Church during the past two years. Most live in Brazil, Argentina and Uruguay. As late as 1959 the annual harvest of converts on this continent averaged fewer than 1,000. The Church enrolled 3,000 members in Brazil in 1958; only five years later their number had risen to 15,000. More than 300 Mormon missionaries labor in this area.

The seven South American missions reported 8,906 converts. The Indian and Mexican missions brought in 10,336 new members and the Polynesian missions baptized 4,365.

Naturally the Mormons make no special effort to convert the Negroes of Africa, since these converts would be ineligible to enter the priesthood because of the "curse" of their race.

A new Mormon mission has been opened in Nigeria, but the missionaries will confine their ministrations to the white settlers. The only other African area being worked by LDS missionaries is in South Africa.

While Hitler banned Jehovah's Witnesses and clamped many Witnesses into concentration camps, he did not disturb the Latter-day Saints missionaries in Germany and Europe.

Of course, Mormon missionary activity almost ceased during World War II. Most of the young men who would have gone on missions went instead into the American armed forces. During the war the number of missionaries leaving Salt Lake City dropped to twenty-five a month and most of these were girls.

The early Mormon missionaries were often directed to undertake a mission assignment by a revelation; *Doctrine and Covenants* includes numerous specific revelations addressed to individuals. Brigham Young himself was sent to England in 1839 and served for two years. During the first year there he and the other missionaries baptized between 7,000 and 8,000 converts and published many thousands of copies of the *Book of Mormon,* hymnbooks, and tracts.

When Young became president of the Church he appointed most new missionaries personally by calling out their names during the general conferences at the Tabernacle. This was the first knowledge they had that they would have to leave Utah and go to the ends of the earth to preach the restored gospel.

Today the bishop investigates the qualifications of the young men and women in his ward, discovers if the individual can support himself on the mission and if the family can get along without him. He forwards a recommendation to the stake president. If he approves the "recommend" he sends it to the First Presidency. One of the General Authorities or an assistant interviews the applicant at one of the quarterly stake conferences. The call itself is signed by the president of the Church, and the arrival of this document is a high point in the life of the young Mormon. The call also indicates the date on which he is to report at the Mission Home in Salt Lake City.

The course actually lasts less than two weeks. Missionaries get free room and can buy their meals at a cafeteria operated by the Church. Their days are filled with lectures, a physical examination, tests, and orientation programs. Finally they receive their assignments and the travel arrangements which have been made for them.

Specific instructions regulate most aspects of the life of a missionary. As a missionary elder he "should keep himself pure, sweet, and unspotted from the sins of the world." The thought is reiterated that the missionary represents his church, his family, the Mormon priesthood. He is told: "If you have the privilege of 'sight-seeing' within the larger cities, you should refrain from visiting the 'districts' of bad reputation. If you cannot assist in correcting evil, avoid it entirely."

He is counseled to continue his studies and to read the "Jewish, Nephite and Latter-day revelations." The missionary is warned against spending his time debating obscure points of doctrine with fellow missionaries or with the people he calls upon. "Guard against familiarity with persons of the opposite sex. Any departure from this rule may lead to immorality; and a fallen brother not only condemns himself but brings misery and woe to the kindred of both parties concerned. Sexual sin is a heinous offense, there are few sins more enticing and none more dangerous and deadly." He is warned against baptizing a married woman without the consent of her husband, or children without the consent of their parents.

The instructions warn: "Never say in public or in private that you do not know the gospel is true." The missionary elders must keep careful records of all the baptisms, confirmations, blessings and naming of children—ordinances which they may confer. Manifestations of healing and speaking in tongues should be reported by witnesses and sent to the office of the mission presidents.

Missionaries live in pairs and travel from house to house in pairs. They seek lodging in private homes rather than in hotels so that they may save money and witness to their landlords. Basic rules govern the conduct of the elders with women. They must never be alone with a woman, never call a woman by her first name, and never touch a woman except to shake hands.

By careful economies a missionary can get along on as

little as $60 a month. On their rounds they usually walk and seldom if ever drive an automobile. They are advised to dress in dark suits and hats. The copies of the *Book of Mormon* they distribute are sold at cost, about 50 cents, as are other bound books.

The basic prebaptismal instruction is given in six lessons which can be taken a week or a few days apart. The format of these lessons is memorized by the missionaries and followed closely in all house-to-house calls. To enable the missionary to master this format the Church has published a manual entitled *A Uniform System for Teaching Investigators* (1961). A perusal of this manual gives some insight into the religious and psychological approach which the LDS Church believes will convince inquirers. Many of the principles could be applied to any sales presentations. For example, the missionary is encouraged to "Have the 'Attitude of Success,'" to "Relax. Be at ease with your contacts. Show genuine interest in your contacts. Praise them for their achievements," and "Motivate your contacts by expressing confidence in their ability. Do not rely on forceful speech or logic alone." [1]

Considering the limited theological training which many elders have undertaken, the manual advises them to "stick to the logic and scriptures in the dialogues [given in the Manual]." They are instructed to "answer objections with questions." [2]

Elder Franklin D. Richards, assistant to the Council of the Twelve, told the assembled Saints at the General Conference in October 1962:

"The discussion plan is not designed to convince intellectually, but rather the discussions are instruments through which the Holy Ghost can work to awaken a spiritual awareness and bring a personal testimony into the hearts of the listeners that Joseph Smith is a Prophet and the Church is true."

Part of each lesson consists of a testimony, a personal affirmation of the truth of the Mormon gospel. The elders are told to set their testimony apart from their instruction. They are advised to pause slightly, look the contact in the eye, and bear the testimony in a natural tone of voice. The appropriate moment for the spontaneous testimony is indicated in each of the six lessons.

The booklet tells the elders how to address the potential convert:

In all discussion except the first, the contact probably should be called "Brother Brown" rather than "Mr. Brown." This is never offensive, and it makes the contact feel much closer to being a member of the Church, since he knows that the members refer to each other in this way. People enjoy being called "brother" and "sister." [3]

As in all effective teaching the Mormon system emphasizes repetition. For example, in every lesson the inquirer is questioned about the invalidity of any previous baptism in a Protestant or Catholic church. He is given to believe that the opportunity now presented for genuine baptism by holders of the Mormon priesthood is an incomparable gift from God.

Missionary elders today use the flannel board as an audiovisual aid in their teaching. The materials themselves are furnished by the Church. The Church can also supply a flip-board and it plans to prepare a film strip for similar use.

Not only must the young missionaries memorize the dialogues in the booklet but also a specified number of passages from the Old and New Testaments and the Standard Works of the Church.

In the first discussion with an inquirer the missionaries attempt to prove that God the Father and Jesus Christ have bodies of flesh and bones, that Joseph Smith was the Prophet, that the Christian Church must be identical to the Church of apostolic times and that apostles and prophets must be found in any authentic church. The missionary tries to show the need for a priesthood and the lack of a valid priesthood in any other church. The prospect is asked to admit that after the death of the original Apostles the Christian Church went into apostasy. Smith, however, was the instrument in the restoration of the priesthood and the true Church.

At one point the missionary asks his prospect: "In your own mind, what is the priesthood, Mr. Brown?"

"The authority of God to teach and baptize," replies Brown.

"Why is the priesthood so important?"

"Because a man must have it to do those things." Brown gets a bit of coaching to arrive at the proper answers, if necessary.

The missionary agrees with Brown's observation but asks, "Suppose a priest or minister baptizes without the priesthood, what does that mean in the sight of the Lord?"

Brown replies, "It doesn't mean a thing," and the missionary asks why.

"Because he would lack the necessary authority."

The missionary says, "Right. So even though a minister might be sincere, unless he has the priesthood, will the Lord recognize a baptism performed by him?" The inquirer answers that the Lord will not.[4]

Throughout the rest of the lessons the elder comes back to the point that the non-Mormon not only does not belong to the true, restored Church but has not even been baptized in the sight of God. Not only those Christians who have been baptized in infancy by pouring lack valid baptism, but those who were baptized by immersion as adults have not really been baptized unless they were so baptized by Mormon priests.

Later after declaring that the death of the original Apostles resulted in the apostasy of the early Church, the elder declares:

"I know that the Church of Jesus Christ was taken completely from the earth. Once this true Church had been lost, other churches began; they continued to use his name and some of his teachings. These are the modern Catholic and Protestant churches." [5]

None of the present Christian churches except the LDS Church is said to have apostles, authority to teach or baptize, or the valid priesthood. This frontal attack on all other Christian churches is what arouses the Church of England clergymen and others. Except in a few Pacific islands and Japan, the Mormons concentrate their mission activities among people who are at least nominally Christian.

At the end of the first discussion the elders mention the date of the next baptismal service and ask the inquirer if he will attend church at the Mormon ward chapel the next Sunday morning and evening. They leave two pamphlets: one is a recital of Smith's experiences in discovering the golden plates, and the other is a tract entitled "Which Church Is Right?"

The inquirer is invited to ask some of his friends or relatives to attend the next home lesson. The elders then ask him to kneel and lead them in prayer. If he does not know how to pray they include a brief instruction on prayer techniques. The instructions note: *It is vital that he offers the prayer. Ask more than once until he finally does, expressing confidence in him, then bowing heads in prayerful expectation that he will do it.* If he yields, the elders are told to "make the contact feel happy that he prayed, and express gratitude to him, even if he did poorly." [6]

On the second visit the elders review the points covered in the first discussion and carry the inquirer further into Mormon teachings. He is led to affirm that God the Father and Jesus have bodies of flesh and bones, while the Holy Ghost is a personage of spirit. The apostasy of the Catholic and Protestant churches is reemphasized as well as their lack of authority and priesthood. Now the convert is introduced to the *Book of Mormon,* about which he has read in the pamphlet about Joseph Smith. The elders give a brief outline of its contents and offer to sell or lend the book to the prospect. They ask him to promise to read 50 to 100 pages before their next session. This second discussion is concluded by extracting a further promise that the contact will inaugurate a period of family prayer in his household.

The third session begins with the usual review of previous points. The authenticity of the *Book of Mormon,* the role of Smith the Prophet, the total apostasy of the churches of Christendom, the need for a baptism recognized by God, are covered catechism style. Now the convert learns about the Word of Wisdom which forbids liquor, tobacco, coffee and tea. In the case of a cigarette addict, the elders offer to take his supply of cigarettes with them to get rid of temptation. They leave a pamphlet on the prescriptions of the Word of Wisdom, ask further questions on the contact's reading in the *Book of Mormon,* and kneel for the final prayer.

By the time of the fourth meeting the contact is expected to have read 225 or 250 pages of the *Book of Mormon.* The usual disparagement of the Catholic and Protestant churches is included in the discussion and the date of the contact's baptism as a Latter-day Saint is worked into the conversation. Now the elders delve a little deeper into Mormon theology. They explain that the result of Adam's fall was physical death, but that the more important spiritual death by which man is estranged from God is the result of his own, not Adam's, sin. Jesus, a spirit son of God, overcame both physical and spiritual death. The Lord removes man's sins when man obeys the commandments, repents and receives Mormon baptism. By the end of this discussion the contact is expected to have committed himself firmly to accepting baptism. If he has not, the elders are instructed to use an additional dialogue which includes a flat challenge to accept baptism.

Particular Mormon doctrines such as baptism for the dead

are expounded in the fifth discussion. Early in the discussion the elders ask: "As our physical bodies grow, we become like our earthly fathers. But what happens as our spirits mature by gaining the attitudes of godliness?" The contact answers: "We become like God."

ELDER: "As we become more like God, we are obeying a law called the law of eternal progression. Why is it important for us to continue to grow and progress even after we leave this life?"

CONTACT: "If we did not grow, our existence would not have any purpose."

ELDER: "And what is the final object of our eternal progression?"

CONTACT: "To become like God." [7]

By now the contact is expected to accept the Mormon belief in pre-existence. All men lived as spirit creatures of God and agreed to receive physical bodies on earth. God drew a veil over their memory of their previous existence with Him.

The elders explain that every man without exception must accept the first principles—faith in Jesus Christ, repentance, Mormon baptism, and the laying on of hands for the gift of the Holy Ghost. But those who die without hearing the Mormon gospel can accept it in the spirit world. Baptism can only be conferred in this physical world, however, so that someone must undergo a proxy baptism for the dead if they are to be saved. The elders quote the only biblical reference to baptism for the dead—I Cor. 15:29. The elders briefly mention the three degrees of glory in the hereafter: celestial, terrestrial, and telestial. They leave a tract entitled "The Plan of Salvation."

By the time the inquirer reaches the sixth and final discussion he will have read the *Book of Mormon* through, attended church twice on Sunday for a month, observed the Word of Wisdom, arranged daily family prayer. He has learned some of the elementary Mormon doctrines. Now the elders review the Ten Commandments. They point out that "picnics and movies and various forms of recreation destroy the spirit of the Sabbath."

The final instruction concerns the law of tithing. After observing that many people are greedy about money the elder explains: "Tithing means one-tenth. Members of the Church are expected to give one-tenth of their income to the Church to help build new meetinghouses and schools and for other church purposes. Why is that such a wonderful way to use our money?"

Contact answers: "Because we know it is being used for good and unselfish purposes." [8] He receives a pamphlet on tithing. The elders complete arrangements for the convert's baptism.

Such is the six-lesson course of instruction completed by more than 100,000 men and women last year. Little is left to chance. The young missionaries are not encouraged to depart from the prescribed dialogue. The basis is simple memorization of dialogue and appropriate passages from the Bible and the *Book of Mormon*. The subjects about which the typical Gentile may be most curious, such as polygamy and the Mormon temple rites, are not even mentioned.

The structure of the discussions reveals the efficiency of American business methods. The elders work in pairs; any fund raiser or salesman knows the psychological advantage of a two-to-one ratio. They follow a tried and tested series of lectures. They use audio-visual aids which enable the contact to see as well as hear the points being made. They leave printed material for study during the week between lessons. They involve the prospect step by step into the Mormon Church until the only step which remains is baptism. They plant the idea in his mind in the first and all succeeding lessons that his previous baptism is invalid and that he will surely wish to receive a baptism recognized by God.

The missionary experiences of these thousands of men

and women help solidify their loyalty and that of their families to the Mormon Church. The constant repetition of testimonies to the truth of Smith's claims and the authenticity of the Mormon scriptures reinforces the Saint's personal commitment. The returned missionaries bring a cosmopolitan outlook to the Church, to Salt Lake City, and to BYU, which helps overcome to some degree the natural provincialism of a state such as Utah which is far removed from the crossroads of the world.

If the converts made by this six-lesson system soon lapsed into their former indifference or if the measure of commitment were slight we could question its effectiveness. But we have no evidence that many of these converts leave the Mormon Church after baptism. The tight Mormon organization keeps them involved in Church activities, and the day-by-day commitment involved in regular prayer, church attendance, observance of the Word of Wisdom and tithing provides a satisfying way of life for many thousands who once called themselves Anglicans and Methodists and Catholics and Baptists.

16. *Mormonism and the Negro*

ONLY TWO AMERICAN cults elevate race to the theological plane: the Black Muslims who believe the Negro race is superior to the white, and the Mormons who believe the Negro is cursed by God. The traditional Catholic and Protestant positions assume the equality of all men before their Creator.

Mormonism, which ordains three out of four adult members to its priesthood, refuses to admit any Negro or anyone with Negroid blood to the priesthood. Negroes who might still join the Church of Jesus Christ of Latter-day Saints cannot marry for time and eternity in a Mormon temple. In the Mormon scheme of salvation this deprives Negroes of the opportunity to reach the highest kingdom.

This Mormon attitude toward the Negro is based on revelation to Joseph Smith, Jr. The Old Testament describes the slaying of Abel by his brother Cain and states that Cain was cursed, but it gives no explanation of the character of the mark of Cain. Nothing would prevent a scripture scholar from speculating that Adam and Eve were black and that the mark of Cain was a white skin or vice versa, but he could find no substantiating passage in the Bible.

In Smith's *Book of Moses,* which forms part of the *Pearl of Great Price,* he revealed the nature of the mark of Cain. In Smith's account we read: ". . . and there was a blackness came upon all the children of Canaan, that they were despised among all peoples" (Moses 7:8). And again: "And Enoch also beheld the residue of the people which were the sons of

Adam; and they were a mixture of all the seed of Adam save it were the seed of Cain, for the seed of Cain were black, and had not place among them" (Moses 7:22). Later in his *Book of Abraham,* Smith explains that one of Noah's sons, Ham, perpetuated the seed of Cain and that his wife, Egyptus, was apparently a Negro. Ham and his descendants were forbidden to hold the priesthood.

Prof. John J. Stewart, in his book *Mormonism and the Negro,* quotes these passages from Smith's translations and comments:

In the above scripture from Abraham, then, we have a reliable account of the early genealogy of the Negro race, and in Abraham's comments we have further evidence of the divine direction in the LDS Church policy of not allowing the Negro, the seed of Cain and Ham, to bear the Priesthood.[1]

But why are certain individuals born into this world with the curse of Cain, i.e., a black skin, and so ineligible to enter the Mormon priesthood which is the key to salvation? For the answer to this the Mormons refer to their belief in pre-existence.

Mormons are quite able to affirm that all men are created equal but they maintain that this creation happened many thousands of years ago, long before any living man was born as a human being. Before birth all men lived as spirit entities with the God of this world. In fact even before being "organized" as a spirit child by God each man existed as an intelligence co-eternal with God.

During this premortal life all men had the power to do good or evil. Mormons believe that approximately one-third of these billions of spirit creatures rebelled against God and allied themselves with Lucifer. They are the Sons of Perdition.

Other spirit children defended God in this rebellion and were allowed to assume human form as a necessary step on the road to godhead for themselves. The choicest blessings

were foreordained for those fortunate ones who would eventually become humans, accept the restored gospel of the
Church of Jesus Christ of Latter-day Saints, enter the Mormon
priesthood or marry a Mormon priest.

If some souls were so favored, others were less favored.
They would become mortals but live in ignorance of the Mormon gospel or even reject it. Still others, because of their
attitudes and actions in the spirit life, would be unfit as
humans to enter the Mormon priesthood or a marriage arrangement for time and eternity. They were neutrals in
the great battle of heaven, they could not decide which side
to join. They were allowed to enter mortality but with the
curse of a dark skin.

A more sophisticated Mormon view is that no one knows
exactly why Negroes were so cursed but that it was not necessarily that they stood on the sidelines. In fact some spirits
were so lacking in virtue that they do not even qualify for
the stage of mortal existence but must continue throughout
eternity as angels.

Stewart attempts to console the Negroes and liberals in the
LDS Church who find this doctrine hard to swallow:

While the Negro and others of Negroid blood cannot hold the
Priesthood, in this stage of life, apparently because of a lack
of valor in the pre-mortal existence, neither are any of them likely
to become Sons of Perdition—as many of the Priesthood bearers
might become.[2]

To support this view he quotes the New Testament: "For
of him unto whom much is given much is required; and he
who sins against the greater light shall receive the greater
condemnation." (Also *D & C,* 82:3.)

Mormons defend their denial of the priesthood to Negroes
on the same basis as Roman Catholics, Anglicans, and Eastern
Orthodox deny ordination to women. This prohibition is
divinely revealed and not subject to debate. The difference
is that it is relatively easy to distinguish a man from a woman

whereas it may be difficult or impossible to determine whether a man or woman has "Negroid blood." In fact, scientists know nothing about white, black or yellow blood; all blood falls into one of four types—A, B, AB, and O—and an individual of any race may receive a transfusion from an individual of another race who possesses the same blood type.

Anthropologists differ on definitions of race. Depending on which characteristics are chosen—of which skin color is one of the least significant—anthropologists classify the human species into three, five, or as many as thirty "races." Their definition of a Negro is not what the Mississippi legislature may decide is a good definition. To any scientist a man seven-eighths white and one-eighth Negro is properly a white man, but to some southern legislatures a man one sixty-fourth Negro is a Negro by law. What transgression or lack of valor in the spirit world would qualify a man as one sixty-fourth a Negro? Why should this one sixty-fourth bring down on his head the curse of Cain and Ham?

Mormons forbid intermarriage of a white person with a Negro or anyone with "Negroid blood." Stewart explains:

> There is nothing in Church policy that forbids nor discourages it from extending brotherly Christian love to the Negro. This, however, does not and should not include intermarriage, for we would bring upon our children the curse of Cain, or rather, we would bring unto ourselves children from those spirits destined to be of the seed of Cain.[3]

This stand could make life difficult for a Mormon in Brazil, the Caribbean, some of the South Sea islands or other areas where most of the population possesses some Negro ancestors. Despite careful genealogical research, mistakes could happen and young men with "Negro blood" could advance through the Mormon priesthood. To detect such traces of Negroid blood the Mormons rely on the miraculous. They believe the patriarch who is called to give his blessing on a baptized Mormon will be able to tell whether the individual has Negro blood which would make him ineligible for ordination or marriage to a white person.

Mormonism's attitude toward the Negro naturally influenced its history in Missouri and Illinois. Negroes were owned as slaves during the years in which Smith devised his theological system; the LDS Church originated in an area strongly abolitionist. Most early Mormons were probably opposed to the institution of slavery.

The *Book of Mormon* gave no hint of the later LDS policy on Negroes. In 2 Nephi, 26:33, we read, ". . . and he inviteth them all to come unto him and partake of his goodness; and he denieth none that come unto him, black and white, bond and free, male and female; and he remembered the heathen; and all are alike unto God, both Jew and Gentile."

But the Church soon found itself trying to establish an outpost in a slave state, Missouri. An editorial in the July 1833 issue of the *Evening and Morning Star* was interpreted by the Missouri slaveholders as an invitation to free Negroes to settle in Jackson County with Mormon assistance. Attacks on Mormons followed, Bishop Edward Partridge was tarred and feathered, and the newspaper hastened to get out an extra dated July 16. The Mormon editor explained:

> Our intention was not only to stop free people of color from emigrating to this state, but to prevent them from being admitted as members of the church. Great care should be taken on this point. The saints must shun every appearance of evil. As to slaves we have nothing to say. In connection with the wonderful events of this age, much is doing towards abolishing slavery, and colonizing the blacks in Africa.
>
> We often lament the situation of our sister states in the South, and we fear, lest, as has been the case, the blacks should rise and spill innocent blood: for they are ignorant and a little may lead them to disturb the peace of society. To be short, we are opposed to have free people of color admitted into the state; and we say, that none will be admitted into the church, for we are determined to obey the laws and constitutions of our country, that we may

have that protection which the sons of liberty inherit from the legacy of Washington, through the favorable auspices of a Jefferson, and Jackson.

This retreat did not fully pacify the Missourians, who continued their harassment of the Saints. The troubles with the Missourians stemmed in part from the belief of the old settlers that the Mormons inclined toward an abolitionist position.

Smith cautioned the Saints against adopting the abolitionist position, but once they had left Missouri for Illinois he advocated his plan that the Government purchase Negroes from their masters at a fair price and set them free.

When Smith launched his campaign for the Presidency of the United States, he advocated the freeing of the slaves. In his manifesto, *Views on the Powers and Policy of Government,* he wrote:

Petition also, ye goodly inhabitants of the slave states, your legislators to abolish slavery by the year 1850, or now, and save the abolitionist from reproach, and ruin, infamy and shame. Pray Congress to pay every man a reasonable price for his slaves out of the surplus revenue arising from the sale of public lands, and from the deduction of pay from the members of Congress. Break off the shackles from the poor black man, and hire them to labor like other human beings; for "an hour of virtuous liberty on earth is worth a whole eternity of bondage."

A few Negroes joined the Mormon Church but no efforts were made to proselytize among them. Three Negroes are said to have gone with the Saints on the march to the West from Nauvoo.

When Horace Greeley interviewed Young in Salt Lake City he quoted the Mormon patriarch as saying: "We consider slavery of divine institution and not to be abolished until the curse pronounced on Ham shall have been removed from his descendants." [4]

One Negro was ordained an elder by William Smith while

on a mission in New York State. An octoroon, Elijah Abel, joined the infant Mormon Church in 1832, was ordained an elder in 1836 and a Seventy in 1841. He practiced his profession of mortician at Nauvoo and went to Salt Lake City where with his wife he managed a hotel. He served as a missionary in Canada and died in Ohio on Church business in 1884.

At a meeting in the home of President A. O. Smoot on May 31, 1879, it was decided that Negroes could be baptized into the Church but could not hold the priesthood. One Mormon attending this meeting testified that Smith had told him: "... the spirit of the Lord saith the Negro has no right nor cannot hold the Priesthood." Another reported that when Smith discovered Abel's Negro ancestry he demanded that he be dropped from the Quorum and another be appointed.

Brigham Young carried out the wishes of Smith regarding the prohibition of ordination of Negroes. He said:

"... The first man that committed the odious crime of killing one of his brethren will be cursed the longest of any one of the children of Adam. Cain slew his brother. Cain might have been killed and that would have put an end to that line of human beings. This was not to be, and the Lord put a mark upon him, which is the flat nose and black skin ... after the flood, ... another curse is pronounced upon the same race—that they should be the 'servant of servants' and they will be, until that curse is removed; ... How long is that race to endure the dreadful curse that is upon them? That curse will remain upon them, and they never can hold the Priesthood or share in it until all other descendants of Adam have received the promises and enjoyed the blessings of the Priesthood and the keys thereto ... They were the first that were cursed, and they will be the last from whom the curse will be removed." [5]

Again Young elaborated the official LDS view of the "curse" on the Negro people: "Why are so many inhabitants of the earth cursed with a skin of blackness? It comes in consequence of their fathers rejecting the power of the Holy Priesthood, and the law of God. They will go down to death. And when all the rest of the children have received their blessings in the Holy Priesthood, then that curse will be removed from the seed of Cain, and they will then come up and possess the Priesthood, and receive the blessings which we now are entitled to." [6]

Young had harsh words on the subject of racial inter-marriage:

"Shall I tell you the law of God in regard to the African race? If the white man who belongs to the chosen seed mixes his blood with the seed of Cain, the penalty, under the law of God, is death on the spot. This will always be so." [7]

The *Deseret News* (April 3, 1852) commented:

...his White friends may wash the race of Cain with Fuller's soap every day, they cannot wash away God's mark; yet the Canaanites may believe the Gospel, repent, and be baptized, and receive the Spirit of the Lord, and if he continues faithful until Abel's race is satisfied with his blessings, then may the race of Cain receive a fullness of the priesthood, and become satisfied with blessings; and the two of them become as one again, when Cain has paid the uttermost farthing.

President Wilford Woodruff dissuaded a colored sister from seeking to go through the temple endowments in 1894. He praised her for her devotion to the gospel but outlined her disadvantages as one of the descendants of Cain. When President Joseph F. Smith preached at her funeral some years later, he declared that at the resurrection "Aunt Jane" would attain the longings of her soul and become a white and beautiful person.

Considering the condescending attitude of Mormons to-ward the Negro and his skin color, it is not surprising that few Negroes have sought baptism in the Mormon Church. A white skin is considered synonymous with God's favor, physical beauty, and the pristine state of mankind.

That such a policy is not a relic of the early days of Mormonism is made clear by a statement of the First Presidency on the Negro Question, dated August 17, 1951. The statement reaffirmed the denial of the priesthood to Negroes but added: "Why the Negro was denied the Priesthood from the days of Adam to our day is not known." The statement asked the readers to remember several "known facts about our pre-earth life and our entrance into mortality." Among these were that not all intelligences reached the same degree of attainment in the pre-earth life; man will be punished for his own sins and not for Adam's transgression, which also means that the Negro is not punished for Cain's transgression but "came to earth through the loins of Cain because of his failure to achieve other stature in the spirit world"; "all spirits are born innocent into this world"; and "the Negro was a follower of Jehovah in the pre-earth life." This last point clarified the question of whether there were neutrals in the battle between God and Lucifer.

President McKay had likewise answered the letter of a prominent sociologist, Dr. Lowry Nelson, who wrote in 1947 to ask why those of Negroid blood could not receive ordination. McKay admitted that only one verse in the Book of Abraham (1:26) could be interpreted to deny the priesthood to Negroes, but he went on to elaborate the reasons from the Mormon belief in preexistence. In other words, he appealed more to tradition and the authority of the Church than to the Mormon scriptures.

President McKay wrote in part:

From the days of the Prophet Joseph even until now, it has been the doctrine of the Church, never questioned by any of the Church leaders, that Negroes are not entitled to the full blessings of the Gospel.

Furthermore, your ideas, as we understand them, appear to

contemplate the intermarriage of the Negro and White races, a concept which has heretofore been most repugnant to most normal-minded people from the ancient patriarchs till now. God's rule for Israel, his Chosen People, has been endogamous. Modern Israel has been similarly directed.

We are not unmindful of the fact that there is a growing tendency, particularly among some educators, as it manifests itself in this area, toward the breaking down of race barriers in the matter of intermarriage between whites and blacks, but it does not have the sanction of the Church and is contrary to Church doctrine.

The Mormon position on race continues to embarrass Mormon sociologists, anthropologists, missionaries, and politicians. The sociologists and anthropologists understand how vague and imprecise are the terms "race" and "Negro." They may question whether God would have chosen such a means as race to punish the descendants of Cain and Ham. Of course, they cannot disown the doctrine without denying the continuous revelation claimed by the Church.

One Mormon apologist explains the Church's stand as an example of God's mercy. According to him, Satan tries to tempt Mormon priests especially and he could use the added weapons of social stigma and prejudice against Negro priests.

No one likes to believe that he has been singled out along with his parents and relatives to be cursed by his Creator. A Negro who would join the Mormon Church might be thought to have a strain of masochism in his personality. He would be a spiritual pariah to the others in the congregation because he is only suffering the just deserts of his actions in his premortal life.

Mormons chide Gentile critics of the Church's race policies. Why worry about the denial of the priesthood to Negroes if you do not attach any particular value to that priesthood? The critics might reply that a total abstainer could still object if a bartender refused to serve a Negro, and a vegetarian could still protest if a waiter refused to take a Negro's order for a steak.

A report of the Utah State Advisory Committee to the U. S. Commission on Civil Rights in 1959 made this observation:

The Mormon interpretation of the curse of Canaan ... together with unauthorized, but widely accepted statements by [Mormon] leaders in years past, has led to the view among many Mormon adherents that birth into any race other than white is the result of inferior performance in pre-earth life, and that by righteous living dark-skinned races may again become "white and delightsome."...[8]

The Mormon politician running for office in a northern state or in a national election finds that his political opponents can make a popular issue out of his religious view on race. Even a master politician would have trouble explaining to a large minority of voters that although he belongs to a church which considers the Negro cursed, he himself has no animosity toward cursed people. Despite the racist position of his Church, Governor Romney claimed to have received 30% to 40% of the Negro vote in Michigan in the 1966 gubernatorial election.

Removal of the bar against ordination of Negroes was being considered by the top leadership of the Mormon Church in 1963. Such a doctrinal revision would rank in magnitude with the abandonment of polygamy in 1890.

Hugh B. Brown, one of President McKay's four counselors, reported: "The whole problem of the Negro is being considered by the leaders of the Church in the light of racial relationships everywhere. We don't want to go too fast in this matter. We want to be fair."

Brown further explained: "We are in the midst of a survey looking toward the possibility of admitting Negroes." The decision to reverse the historic ban would have to be announced by McKay. Said Brown: "Believing as we do in divine revelation through the President of the Church, we all await his decision."

Lifting the bar against ordination of Negroes to the Mormon priesthood would no doubt also allow Negro members to enter temple marriages, but it would not necessarily change the Church's ban against marriages between Negroes and those of other races.[9]

Some Nigerians received copies of the Book of Mormon in 1953 and have formed a schismatic LDS Church. These 7,000 Nigerian Mormons have ordained themselves priests and some have adopted polygamy. The Nigerian government refuses resident visas to any LDS missionaries from the United States because of the Church's racial policies. The head of the schismatic church has declared: "Nigerian priests will run their own branch. This is their creation, and they are in their own country."[10]

Meanwhile many of the Negroes in Utah are bitter. According to the 1960 census they number only 4,148 out of the state's 900,000 population. An Associated Press report quoted one such Negro: "It's bad enough being a Negro anyplace, but in Utah you're told you're bearing some damned curse to boot." [11]

A NAACP leader in Salt Lake City, Charles Nabors, maintains that Utah "has potentially the worst race problem in the United States." The state of Utah is the only state outside of the Deep South without any civil rights legislation on its books. A survey of public facilities in Salt Lake City in 1961 revealed that the Negro is barred from 72 percent of the hotels, 12 percent of the restaurants, 49 percent of the motels, and 80 percent of the beauty shops.

Negro leaders threatened to picket the semiannual conference of the Church in the fall of 1963 unless Church leaders finally denounced segregation. A conference between Negroes and Church representatives headed off the demonstration. President Hugh Brown told the conference: "We would like it to be known that there is in this church no doctrine, belief or practice that is intended to deny the enjoyment of full civil rights by any person regardless of race, color, or creed."

At about the same time that Negroes in Utah were asking for a Church statement, *Time* magazine commented that Mormons "are unsympathetic toward the Negro, largely as a consequence of the strange church doctrines formulated by the first Mormon Prophet, Joseph Smith, and amplified by his successors." [12]

Although the Church believes in the basic principle of continuous revelation, President McKay has never said that he has received any such revelations. His probable successor, Joseph Fielding Smith, has never shown any particular sympathy or understanding toward the Negro. He recently told a *Look* magazine writer: "I would not want you to believe that we bear any animosity toward the Negro. 'Darkies' are wonderful people, and they have their place in our church." [13]

Nevertheless there is the possibility that a new revelation may solve this race problem as it did the problem of polygamy in 1890. J. D. Williams, thirty-seven, a professor of political science and former bishop in Provo, believes, "The change will come and within my lifetime. The Mormon liberal has for years felt a deep uneasiness over his church's doctrine that Negroes are not worthy to hold the priesthood."

Liberal LDS members no doubt wish the Church could jettison this stand and open the doors to all races. They see that the Church's attitude toward Negroes was formed in pre-Civil War America when the few Negroes with whom Smith and Young came into contact were by their lack of education and culture understandably thought to be the victims of a curse. This view becomes harder to hold with the passing years and its only possible value might be to help convert diehard southern segregationists who find their own Baptist and Methodist churches preaching the equality under God of all races.

17. *Brigham Young University*

In PROVO, UTAH, the Mormons operate what has become
the largest church-related university in the nation, larger
than Notre Dame, Southern Methodist, Fordham, or any
Catholic or Protestant institution in full-time enrollment.

Brigham Young reported a total of 21,354 students on
campus in 1966 in daytime and evening sessions. The University now offers the Ph.D. and Ed.D. in 16 fields and enrolls more than 1,600 men and women in its Graduate School.

The BYU campus overlooks the city of Provo, third largest
in the state with a population of about 40,000. Mount Tim-
panogos forms a majestic 12,000-foot backdrop for the
campus, which now occupies 614 acres besides the various
farm properties. Provo is only 45 miles south of Salt Lake
City; its mountains, Utah Lake and canyons provide outdoor
recreational facilities for BYU students.

Approximately 94 percent of the University's students
belong to the Church of Jesus Christ of Latter-day Saints,
but all students regardless of religious affiliation must agree
to abstain from alcohol and tobacco and submit 16 credits
in LDS theology courses for graduation. Non-LDS students
need not refrain from coffee and tea but they will find none
served in BYU residence halls or student union. All students
also sign an honesty pledge which covers all tests and home-
work assignments.

The BYU catalogue states: "The maintenance of standards
of honor and integrity, of graciousness in personal behavior,

of Christian ideals in everyday living, of a high standard of morality, and of abstinence from alcohol and tobacco is required of every student. A student's having improper associates or visiting places of questionable repute will not be tolerated."

BYU is not the only institution of higher education operated by the Church but it is the capstone of the Mormon system. Once the Church ran a chain of junior colleges throughout the state but gave these to the state in 1933 and set up adjacent Institutes of Religion which offer courses in LDS theology. For far less expenditure the Mormons got just about the same indoctrination for their young people. Mormons established the University of Deseret in Salt Lake City in 1850; the school received a new charter and a new name—the University of Utah—in 1892. It is now a state university.

The Church staffs a small junior college in Rexburg, Idaho, known as Ricks College. This school was established as Bannock State Academy in 1888 and once offered a four-year program. It now registers between 800 and 1,000 students. The LDS Church also maintains the LDS Business College in a renovated mansion in Salt Lake City, and the LDS Church College in Hawaii. It is making plans to open a university in the British Isles.

Probably no private college or university in the country offers a greater educational bargain than BYU. Tuition and fees for all regular college and graduate students in 1967-68 were only $400 for LDS members and $650 for non-LDS. During the same year MIT had to charge $1,900, New York University charged $1,500, and Brandeis University $1,450. In most private colleges student tuition forms the largest part of the cost of education, with the balance coming from gifts and income on endowment. At BYU the Church uses the regular tithes of its members to provide 71 cents out of every dollar spent by the University to educate a BYU student. Tuition pays for only 23 cents, and other sources of income provide the remaining 6 cents.

In addition students who belong to the Church may apply for financial aid from the Church Student Loan Fund. Loans up to a maximum of $2,100 will be made to qualified applicants, who can delay repayment until they leave school.

Estimated annual cost of attending BYU is put in the catalogue at only $1,050, which is well under the average of $1,600 spent by students at other private colleges and universities. As a matter of fact, many students attending prestige institutions can hardly get through the academic year for less than $2,500 or $3,000. BYU discourages students from owning or operating automobiles which add considerably to the cost of student living.

BYU allows no fraternities or sororities. All students live in University residences or in approved off-campus rooms or apartments. Twenty-four Heritage Halls provide accommodations for 1,548 women. These halls are unique in college housing since they are actually apartment-type buildings in which six girls occupy each unit and prepare their own meals. Specialists help the coeds with their budgeting, food-buying, and meal-planning problems. The rental for each girl is $250 a year in addition to groceries which are purchased cooperatively by the residents.

A church which encourages early marriage and large families must expect a large number of married college students. The University has just finished construction of 462 units in a married-student housing project.

Religious activities on campus are highly organized. The Church enrolls LDS students in three campus stakes which embrace 37 wards of between 200 and 300 students. All single students from LDS homes belong to one of these wards while married students may join a BYU ward or retain membership in their regular wards. Every Wednesday the school schedules a devotional assembly; during the academic year every member of the First Presidency and of the Quorum of the

Twelve Apostles is expected to appear on the program. These 15 men also comprise the board of trustees of BYU.

In the 1963 spring semester, 2,875 returned missionaries were enrolled at BYU. They had served from 18 to 36 months in 70 mission areas. Their travel and experiences in foreign countries helped break down the provincial atmosphere of the campus.

A religious survey of one of the three stakes at BYU in 1960–61 revealed that 95.8 percent of those married were married in the temple. The average attendance at Sacrament meeting was 77 percent, while 86 percent of the total stake membership of 2,744 held ward and stake positions. Even students are not exempt from tithing and the report showed that 63 percent paid a full tithing and 6 percent paid a part tithe; most of the others presumably did not earn any income and so were not required to tithe.

BYU graduates more certified teachers than any other college or university in the United States according to a report of the Department of Health, Education and Welfare. Next is Wayne State University, followed by Michigan State University and Brooklyn College. President Wilkinson announced in 1963 that 5,447 BYU students had expressed their desire to be trained as teachers. They could major in any subject and take enough education courses to qualify for teacher certification in any state.

In addition to a large College of Education, BYU has Colleges of Biological and Agricultural Sciences, Business, Family Living, Fine Arts, Humanities and Social Sciences, Nursing, Physical and Engineering Sciences, Physical Education, and Religious Instruction. BYU also enrolls students in a General College and Graduate School. Traditionally the LDS Church has emphasized sociology, family life, recreation and the agricultural sciences.

The University itself awards master's degrees in most departments and the Ph.D or Ed.D in the following fields: chemistry, Bible and Modern Scriptures, educational administration, educational psychology, geology, history, history and philosophy of religion, human development and family relationships, musicology, physics, psychology, sociology, bacteriology, botany, and zoology and entomology. It also gives two-year certificates in agriculture, business, engineering, genealogy, and industrial technology.

An Institute of Mormon Studies, established in 1961, will conduct research in areas of Mormon theology, history, organization, but will not engage in teaching. A new Asian Studies program will carry on research about that part of the world. BYU enrolls more foreign students from Asian countries than from Europe.

For a university of its size BYU has a rather small library of 400,000 volumes. It recently completed a new library building designed to hold a million books. The new library boasts five floors of stacks and reading areas, each the size of a football field. BYU has a long way to go to match Stanford's 1,300,000 volumes or Northwestern's 1,200,000, much less Harvard's 6,000,000-volume collection.

Students may also use the LDS Genealogical Society Library in Salt Lake City which shelves 55,000 books and 150,000 rolls of microfilm. These are mainly family histories, biographies and autobiographies, military records, cemetery inscriptions, and official records. They are used by Saints to trace their ancestors so that they may undergo baptism by proxy in a Mormon temple. BYU is one of the few universities in the nation to offer a major program in genealogy.

An analysis of the 576 faculty members during the 1961–62 year reveals that only 56 completed their undergraduate work outside of the state of Utah. The high degree of faculty inbreeding is indicated by the fact that 318 of the instructors and professors at BYU are BYU graduates themselves. Almost all faculty members are Latter-day Saints; the government even manages to send mostly LDS officers to staff the Air Force ROTC program at BYU. The University of Utah and Utah State University claim 202 alumni at the Provo school.

About half the BYU faculty have their Ph.D. degrees, compared to a national college and university average of 37.8 percent. Some of the best graduate schools in the nation are represented among the BYU faculty, including Stanford, Harvard, Cornell, California, Wisconsin, Purdue, Columbia, Ohio State, Princeton, California Institute of Technology, Pennsylvania, Michigan, and UCLA.

Perhaps the most distinguished member of the BYU faculty is Dr. Harvey Fletcher, former director of research for Bell Telephone. One of the fathers of radio, television and stereophonic sound, he is also the first Mormon to be named to the National Academy of Science.

Mormon dedication to education goes back to its earliest days. The School of the Prophets at Kirtland was one of the pioneer adult education ventures in the nation. The Church founded the University of Nauvoo soon after draining the swamps along the river.

Doctrine and Covenants urged the Saints to further their education:

... seek ye out of the best books words of wisdom; seek learning, even by study and also by faith (88:118).

Brigham Young founded the forerunner of BYU in 1875 and picked a German convert, Dr. Karl G. Maeser, to take over as principal in its first full year. The deed or trust specified that "pupils shall be instructed in ... such branches as are usually taught in an academy of learning" and also in the Old and New Testaments, the *Book of Mormon* and *Doctrine and Covenants*. When Dr. Maeser asked for his instructions from Young he was told simply, "Only this. I want you to remember that you ought not to teach even the alphabet or the multiplication tables without the spirit of God. That is all. God bless you. Good-bye." Years later the school adopted as its motto the oft-quoted passage from *Doctrine and Covenants* (93:36): "The glory of God is intelligence."

President Maeser served as principal of the Brigham Young

Academy for sixteen years. He was succeeded by Benjamin Cluff in whose reign the name of the school was changed from "Academy" to "University." George H. Brimhall served as president for seventeen years and Franklin S. Harris held that office from 1921 to 1945, the longest tenure of any BYU chief official. The superintendent of Salt Lake City schools, Howard S. McDonald, served from 1945 to 1949 and was succeeded by an acting president until 1951.

Most of BYU's remarkable physical expansion has taken place under the direction of President Ernest L. Wilkinson. A BYU alumnus, he received a law degree from George Washington University and a Doctor of Juridical Science from Harvard. He taught law, joined a law firm of which Charles Evans Hughes was senior member, and then organized his own law firm in Washington, D. C. He obtained judgments of $32 million for the Ute Indians, which was the largest judgment ever entered in the U. S. Court of Claims against the United States. He receives $1 a year for his services as BYU president. A political conservative like most LDS officials, President Wilkinson belongs to the board of directors of the National Right to Work Committee. This employers' organization seeks to enact right to work laws in all states; Utah has had such a law since 1955.

During Wilkinson's first decade as president, BYU experienced an increase of more than 100 percent in enrollment. By 1943 the enrollment had dropped from 2,000 to only 800 students. It became the largest church-related university in 1953 and continues to widen its lead over its competitors. In 1957 the University authorized the granting of doctoral degrees. The campus now has over 100 major academic and housing buildings; 73 of these have been completed since 1950. In 1954, Mormon officials came to the campus to dedicate 22 new buildings and they returned in 1957 to dedicate a dozen more.

Alumni of BYU now number more than 80,000, which includes all who have attended one quarter or more. They are found in all 50 states and U. S. territories as well as in 52 foreign countries. The University boasts that 97 percent of its predental students and 70 percent of its premed students have been accepted by dental and medical schools compared to a national average of only 50 percent. One of the University's most distinguished alumni is President O. Meredith Wilson of the University of Minnesota.

In 1960–61, fewer than half the BYU student body was from Utah: 5,293 out of 12,953 students. The next largest concentration of students was the 1,250 from neighboring Idaho. Foreign students were enrolled from Canada (292), Mexico (54), Hong Kong (44), Iran (26), India (18), Japan (13), New Zealand (14), and a number of other countries including even Ethiopia and Kenya.

Each full-time student, LDS or Gentile, must take two hours of religion each semester. For example, all freshmen must complete a course in "Introduction to the *Book of Mormon*." Transfer students from Ricks College, and LDS Institutes of Religion at state universities or other LDS schools can receive credit for religion courses taken elsewhere. Students with religion or Bible credits from Protestant or Catholic colleges may use these credits as electives but must still take the required BYU religion courses each semester.

Religion courses in the College of Religious Instruction are grouped in five separate departments: Bible and Modern Scriptures, Biblical Languages, History and Philosophy of Religion, Religious Education, and Theology and Church Administration. At one time the Church sent some of its scholars to obtain advanced degrees from theological departments at other universities such as the University of Chicago. This introduced a degree of liberalism and resulted in several apostasies. Today LDS specialists in religion are likely to receive all their training through the Ph.D. at BYU. The currents of ecumenism, Biblical study, and liturgical revival which wash over Catholic and Protestant theological departments and seminaries bypass Provo.

Professor O'Dea of the University of Utah comments:

While the [LDS] institutes and seminaries have been manned by people who often tend toward a liberal position or at least have a conservative-liberal attitude in theology, the Division of Religion at Brigham Young University has of late years been conservative. Recently it has produced an erudite, scholarly, and even esoteric scholasticism, to support conservative literal theology of a most fundamentalist nature.[1]

By "Bible" the BYU catalogue means the Old and New Testaments, and by "Modern Scripture" it means the *Book of Mormon, Doctrine and Covenants,* and the *Pearl of Great Price.* There are eleven courses in Bible on the undergraduate level and five in Modern Scripture. The same ratio of two to one is maintained on the graduate level. The Biblical Languages Department offers courses in Hebrew, Aramaic, Syriac, Akkadian, and Ugaritic but not in Reformed Egyptian.

BYU is one reason why Utah and the Church of Jesus Christ of Latter-day Saints are able to report such a high percentage of college graduates in their constituencies. An education at BYU is actually cheaper than that offered by most state universities to residents of the state. Many Roman Catholic parents are paying more for tuition at a Catholic high school than a BYU student pays for his university education. Of course, the difference in cost is probably more than made up over the years by the payment of tithes by the BYU student and his family.

The Church of Jesus Christ of Latter-day Saints is making an enormous effort to bring BYU to the forefront of American universities. It has the enrollment, the financial wherewithal, the progressive leadership, and the physical plant necessary to success. Its limitations too are obvious. It is generally parochial in its faculty and student body, inbred, isolated in its theology department, weak in library facilities, far removed from the New England, Middle West or West Coast universities which lead the nation in scholarship, research and scientific achievement. Nevertheless, by any standards the effort of President Wilkinson and his colleagues to upgrade BYU standards and academic prestige is impressive.

18. *Other Latter-day Saints*

ALL MORMONS are Latter-day Saints but not all Latter-day Saints are Mormons. The name "Mormon," originally a nickname like Quaker and Shaker, has been generally accepted by the Church of Jesus Christ of Latter-day Saints with headquarters in Salt Lake City. But other followers of Joseph Smith, Jr., who also accept the authenticity of the *Book of Mormon,* reject the leadership of the Utah church as well as the name "Mormon."

Largest of these other Latter-day Saints bodies is the Reorganized Church of Jesus Christ of Latter Day Saints with headquarters in Independence, Missouri. They are often known as Josephites while the Utah Mormons are called Brighamites since they accepted Brigham Young's leadership. Not a single direct descendant of the Prophet belongs to the Utah church but some 145 of Smith's grandchildren and great-grandchildren belong to the Reorganized Church.

Far outnumbered by the Utah church, the Reorganized Church nevertheless reports more than 180,000 members in 1,144 branches. As such, the Reorganized Church claims more adherents than the Mennonites or Unitarians or Quakers in the United States but is little known as a church distinct from the larger Mormon Church. President of the Reorganized branch is W. Wallace Smith, a grandson of the Prophet who was born when his father, Joseph Smith III, was sixty-eight.

When Smith was killed in the Carthage jail, the city of Nauvoo was thrown into a panic. The logical successor,

Hyrum Smith, was also killed by the mob. Smith's son Joseph was only twelve years old at the time and obviously could not rally the disorganized Saints. Sidney Rigdon sought to assume the leadership he coveted for many years, but failed to convince the Saints of his claims. Other would-be prophets arose —James Strang, Lyman Wight, Alpheus Cutler, among others —and attracted small groups of Saints.

As we have seen, most of the Saints in Nauvoo acclaimed Brigham Young as the Prophet's successor and began the trek to the Great Salt Valley in the spring of 1846. But should we accept the Prophet's own estimate of his followers given shortly before his death—180,000 to 200,000—we must agree with the Reorganized Church that only a minority of Saints followed Young. Thousands of others, especially in Illinois, Iowa, Wisconsin and other midwestern states, stayed where they were and looked for some sign that the Lord had preserved His church. Emma Smith herself remained in the ghost town that was Nauvoo, remarried, and raised her family.

Basic to Reorganized claims is that the mantle of the Prophet passed in lineal descent from Joseph Smith, Junior. In two instances, they maintain, Smith laid his lands on the head of his son which indicated his desire to bestow his spiritual authority. They declare that the president of the Church should be called by revelation and approved by democratic action of the entire Church.

In the only two court cases involving claims of rival Latter Day Saints bodies, the courts have decided in favor of the Reorganized Church. In a suit for possession of the Kirtland temple in 1880, Judge L. S. Sherman in the Court of Common Pleas, Lake County, Ohio, declared:

That the said Plaintiff, the Reorganized Church of Jesus Christ of Latter Day Saints, is a Religious Society, founded and organized upon the same doctrines and tenets, and having the same church organization, as the original Church of Jesus Christ of Latter-day Saints organized in 1830, by Joseph Smith, and was organized pursuant to the constitution, laws and usages of said original Church, and has branches located in Illinois, Ohio and other states.

That the Church in Utah, the Defendant of which John Taylor is president, has materially and largely departed from the faith, doctrines, laws, ordinances and usages of said original Church of Jesus Christ of Latter-day Saints, and has incorporated into its system of faith the doctrines of celestial marriage and a plurality of wives, and the doctrine of Adam-God worship, contrary to the laws and constitution of said original Church.

And the Court do further find that the Plaintiff, the Reorganized Church of Jesus Christ of Latter Day Saints, is the True and Lawful continuation of, and successor to the said original Church of Jesus Christ of Latter-day Saints organized in 1830, and is entitled in law to all its rights and property.

In another decision regarding the Temple Lot case in 1894, Judge John F. Philips in the Circuit Court of the United States, for the Western District of Missouri, Western Division, stated:

The Book of Mormon itself inveighed against the sin of polygamy.... Conformably to the Book of Mormon, the Book of Doctrine and Covenants expressly declared "that we believe that one man should have but one wife, and one woman but one husband." And this declaration of the church on this subject reappeared in the Book of Doctrine and Covenants, editions of 1846 and 1856. Its first appearance as a dogma of the church was in the Utah Church in 1852.

Claim is made by the Utah Church that this doctrine is predicated on a revelation made to Joseph Smith in July, 1843. No such revelation was ever made public during the life of Joseph Smith, and under the law of the church it could not become an article of faith and belief until submitted to and adopted by the church. This was never done ...

The Utah Church further departed from the principles and doctrines of the Original Church by changing in their teaching the first statement in the Article of Faith, which was, "We believe in God, the Eternal Father, and in his Son, Jesus Christ, and in the Holy Ghost," and in lieu thereof taught the doctrine of "Adam-God worship.". . .

In 1852 the scattered fragments of the church, the remnants of those who hold to the fortunes of the present Joseph Smith, son of the so-called "Martyr," gathered together sufficiently for a nucleus of organization. They took the name of "The Reorganized Church of Jesus Christ of Latter Day Saints," and avowed their allegiance to the teachings of the ancient church; and their epitome of faith adopted, while containing differences of phraseology, in its essentials is but a reproduction of that of the church as it existed from 1830 to 1844.

A number of Saints who had remained in the Middle West gathered at Beloit, Wisconsin, in 1852 to "reorganize" the Church. The two chief founders, Jason W. Briggs and Zenas H. Gurley, had both been associated with the movement led by James J. Strang, later known as King James of Beaver Island.

Briggs joined the Latter-day Saints a few years before Smith's death but remained in Wisconsin. After the martyrdom Briggs joined Strang and in 1849 organized the Waukesha branch of the Strangite Church. In 1850 he affiliated with the church started by William Smith, the Prophet's brother, but when this disintegrated he got together with Gurley to found the New Organization. Eventually he and Gurley would withdraw from the Reorganized Church in 1886 in a doctrinal dispute.

More prominent among the Saints than his partner Briggs, Zenas H. Gurley was ordained a Seventy in Nauvoo in 1844 and was chosen senior president of the Seventies the next year. He also spent some time in the Strangite movement.

The Saints who met at Beloit in 1852 not only rejected the

leadership of Brigham Young but also the doctrines of polygamy, plurality of gods, secret endowment ceremonies, blood atonement, baptism of the dead, and celestial marriage. They insisted that all these doctrines had been introduced by Young and would have been disowned by the Prophet.

The New Organization established a United Order of Enoch in Decatur County in southern Iowa, founded Lamoni, and bought about 3,000 acres of land. They formed a number of congregations in the Middle West among Saints who refused to follow Young to the Rocky Mountains and among some converts. After 1866 they added the word "Reorganized" to their church name to disassociate themselves from polygamy, which was bringing the Utah church into disrepute.

Joseph Smith III, the Prophet's eldest son, had not been involved in the founding of the New Organization, but he and his mother, now remarried to a Nauvoo tavern keeper, visited conferences of the Church. In 1860 at Amboy, Illinois, Smith's son accepted the presidency of the Reorganized Church, declaring: "I come by a power not my own." He was accepted as Prophet, Seer, and Revelator; his mother and two brothers also joined the Reorganized group. He continued in that office until 1914.

Three of his sons have held the same office. Dr. Frederick M. Smith attended the Universities of Missouri and Kansas and received a Ph.D. in sociology from Clark University in 1916. He served from 1914 to his death in 1946 when he was succeeded by his brother, Israel A. Smith, an attorney and former member of the Iowa legislature. Israel was killed in an automobile accident in 1958 and his brother W. Wallace Smith, a 6-foot 6-inch former basketball star at the University of Missouri, assumed the presidency of the Reorganized Church.

The Reorganized Church owns the Kirtland temple, the original manuscript of the *Book of Mormon* handwritten by

Cowdery and Emma, and the graves of Joseph, Emma and Hyrum in Nauvoo. Also in Nauvoo the Reorganized Church maintains the Joseph Smith Homestead, Mansion House and Nauvoo House.

In 1860 the Church claimed 500 members but in a bare eight years it grew to 10,000. The prestige of the Prophet's son attracted Midwestern Saints and disgruntled Utah Mormons. For eighteen years the Reorganized Church continued its headquarters in Plano, Illinois. Then the Church moved to Lamoni, Iowa, where it still operates Graceland College, an accredited four-year institution. In 1920 the Reorganized moved back to Independence which Smith (as well as the Utah Mormons) declared would be the center of Zion in the latter-days.

Mother church of the denomination is the Stone Church in Independence with 2,000 members but there are 21 other congregations in the Independence-Kansas City area. The Church also supports a 202-bed hospital, a publishing house, a home for the aged, a social service center, and the School of Restoration which is a training center for Reorganized ministers.

General Church conferences are held in the 5,800-seat auditorium. This building was started in 1926 but work was halted by the Depression, World War II, and a lack of available funds. More than 20,000 people attended the dedication service in 1962 and received communion at successive services. It features a 6,300-pipe organ; its Messiah Choir rivals the more famous Tabernacle Choir in Salt Lake City. The choir's Christmas program has been carried by 900 radio stations.

The Reorganized Church believes that a temple can be built only at the specific command of God. With the Nauvoo temple destroyed it believes that it has possession of the only temple which meets this test: the Kirtland temple, which the Reorganized have held since 1880.

The Kirtland Temple remains the one house of the Lord standing thus, built in obedience to direct divine commandment as a temple to his service; and consistent with our position it has descended by legal decision to the possession of the Reorganized Church as the successor in full accord with the teaching and practices of the church under Joseph the Martyr. [1]

Even this temple is open to the public, unlike the Mormon temples which are closed to all but Mormons in good standing. A Reorganized pamphlet states:

In the Kirtland Temple of the Reorganized Church, there are no secret meetings of any kind, no secret rites, ceremonies, oaths, or practices. All meetings are open to the public, and no parts of the building are closed to the public; everything may be visited under guide service.... Not one of the sacraments and ordinances: baptism, confirmation, blessing, administration to the sick, marriage, and the sacrament of the Lord's Supper, is secret. Their nature may be freely revealed to the world. They are not guarded by secret oaths or obligation or secret covenants. [2]

In other words, the Reorganized Church has no endowment service in the temple, no wearing of temple undergarments, and none of the borrowed Masonry practiced in the 12 Mormon temples.

Although the Reorganized Church has not launched a volunteer missionary program like the Utah system, it sends salaried missionaries to Canada, England, Holland, Germany, Scandinavia, French Polynesia, New Zealand, Latin America and Australia. It is starting to seek converts in Japan and Korea.

Unlike the Utah church it bars no one from its priesthood because of race. A revelation given to President Joseph Smith III in 1865 declared:

"Be not hasty in ordaining men of the Negro race to offices in my church, for verily I say unto you, All are not acceptable unto me as servants, nevertheless I will that all may be saved, but every man in his own order, and there are some who are chosen instruments to be ministers to their own race. Be ye content, I the Lord have spoken it."

A Utah Mormon critic, Joseph Fielding Smith, comments:

The Lord did not tell Abraham [in Smith's Book of Abraham] that the children of Ham were cursed as pertaining to the Priesthood, and then command Joseph Smith of the "Reorganization" to be slow in ordaining them. In the "Reorganized" Church they have a few, at least, of the Negro race, that they have "ordained to the priesthood" but it is contrary to the word of God. This Reorganite revelation is spurious. [3]

In the United States, the Reorganized Church is strongest around Kansas City, Los Angeles, and Detroit. For many years it sent missionaries to convert Mormons in Utah, and the Brighamites in turn tried to win the Reorganized to the true faith. Today the Reorganized distribute certain Utah Mormon books through their Herald House publishing company. Relations between the two major Latter-day Saints branches are cordial, but doctrinal differences run so deep that they preclude any possibility of merger. To win the Reorganized to their cause the Utah Mormons would have to open their temples, abandon their endowments, discard their belief in plurality of gods, deny the authenticity of the revelation on polygamy, etc.

Two other sons of the Prophet, Alexander and David, visited Utah in the 1850's as emissaries of the Reorganized Church. They wanted to know if the Brighamites might now accept the presidency of Joseph Smith III. Brigham Young received the two men, dismissed their request for recognition of the Smith line, and added that their mother, Emma, was "the damnedest liar that lives."

Like the Utah church, the Reorganized Church expects its members to tithe but interprets the tithe more liberally. The Reorganized member contributes a tithe of 10 percent on his "increase," i.e., on what he has left after paying for his food, shelter, clothing, etc. This provides the Reorganized Church with far less money, but what funds it does receive go strictly into religious activities rather than into business ventures.

Reorganized Latter Day Saints accept the Bible, the *Book of Mormon,* and their own *Doctrine and Covenants* as authoritative. They reject the *Pearl of Great Price,* which teaches plurality of gods and polygamy. Unlike the Utah church, the Reorganized Church also uses the so-called Inspired Version of the Bible which was Smith's attempt at scriptural revision. They claim that Smith's version anticipated many changes in later translations such as the Revised Standard Version. The 464-page original manuscript of the *Book of Mormon* is kept under temperature and humidity control in a bank vault in Kansas City, Missouri.

Like the Utah church the Reorganized president is assisted by two other high priests and a Quorum of Twelve Apostles. The apostles direct the Church's missionary activity with the help of the Quorums of the Seventy. Delegates meet biennially at Independence to vote on matters of doctrine, policy, and legislation.

Local congregations rely on volunteer service by priests and elders of whom there are about 13,000. During the past 13 years, 300 new congregations have been established in the United States alone. In 1906 the Reorganized Church reported 40,851 members in the United States; in 1962 it claimed four times this number.

One of the Reorganized Church's major contentions is that Smith never taught or practiced polygamy. They flatly deny Young's assertion that the revelation he announced in 1852 was written by the Prophet while he was alive. Their denial that Smith ever had more than one wife is based on the facts that the only civil marriage ever recorded was that to Emma Hale, that the only children born to Smith and bearing his name were Emma's, that Emma always denied that her husband had any other wives, and that the *Book of Mormon* and other revelations condemn polygamy.

Although the Reorganized Church accepts the additional testimony of the *Book of Mormon* and the Prophethood of Smith, it stands much closer to historic Protestantism than the Utah church. The Reorganized idea of the nature of man and of God is nearer orthodox Christianity than the eternal progression ideas developed in Utah. Elbert A. Smith of the Reorganized Church states the basic difference concisely:

Between the idea of a progressive God on the one hand and on the other that of an unchangeable God, there seems to be no compromise. Until one church or the other is converted from its present position there will remain an insuperable theological barrier between them. It need not be debated with any degree of heat or enmity—but it is inescapably there.[4]

The adherence of Smith's descendants to the Reorganized Church, the two court decisions, and the historic property owned by the Reorganized branch embarrass the larger and wealthier Utah church, but the average Brighamite pays little attention to the other Latter-day Saints. He will be more concerned about the Fundamentalists in Utah, Arizona, and California who persist in practicing plural marriage than about the Reorganites.

Of course, the Utah church denies the Reorganized claims. It upholds the selection of Young as the leader of the church, maintains that Smith was a polygamist and the author of the revelation on polygamy, and upholds polytheism as a Smithian doctrine. Joseph Fielding Smith, answering Reorganite claims, wrote:

Joseph Smith the Prophet taught a plurality of Gods, and moreover that man, by obeying the commandments of God and keeping the whole law, will eventually reach the power and exaltation by which he also will become a God. And if Reorganites do not accept this truth, they have departed from the teachings of the Prophet Joseph Smith. The doctrine of plurality of

Gods did not originate with Brigham Young, but was taught him by Joseph Smith.[5]

The Utahans dismiss the priesthood of the Reorganite branch:

An ordination in the "Reorganized" church is of no more effect than is an ordination in the Methodist, Presbyterian, or Catholic church, for those officiating do not hold the Priesthood and are not recognized of God.[6]

The Reorganized Church believes in an open canon of its *Doctrine and Covenants*. Its presidents continue to receive and publish revelations whereas the Utah church has not published a revelation since the single revelation to Brigham Young in 1847 (*D. & C.*, 136). The Manifesto suspending the practice of polygamy in 1890 is not considered a revelation in the same sense as Smith's revelations. Nevertheless the Utah church insists that the blessing of continuous revelation by God to the Church presidents is one of the distinguishing characteristics of the restored church from the apostate churches of Christendom. Joseph Fielding Smith held a low opinion of the Reorganite revelations:

The "revelations" given by the Reorganite president to the "Reorganized" Church need only to be read to convince one of their spurious character. They are weak, puerile, and it takes very little of the spirit of discernment to know what source they are of.[7]

At the same time, the Utahans accept the revelation setting up Independence as the center of Zion. Smith declares: "We accept the fact that the center place where the City New Jerusalem is to be built, is in Jackson County, Missouri. It was never the intention to substitute Utah or any other place for Jackson County." [8]

Not only did Joseph Smith declare that Independence and Jackson County would be the center of the New Jerusalem but on August 3, 1831, he and eight elders dedicated the spot on which the great temple will be erected. However, neither the Utah church nor the Reorganized Church owns that real estate known as the Temple Lot. It is owned by still another splinter group of Saints, the Church of Christ (Temple Lot).

Three or four congregations around Bloomington, Illinois, refused to follow Young, Rigdon, Strang or any other claimant to Smith's office. They began to doubt whether the office of president was even a legitimate one, since the New Testament mentions only apostles and not "presidents." These Bloomington Saints sold their land in Illinois in 1867 and moved in a body to Independence where they began to raise money to buy the Temple Lot of some 2½ acres. When Smith dedicated the plot, the Church did not own the land. It belonged to the State of Missouri and later was purchased by one Jonas H. Flourmoy.

Elder Granville Hedrick edited their early newspaper and they have also been known as Hedrickites. They accept Smith's revelations up to February 1834 but consider some of the later revelations of doubtful character. They oppose baptism for the dead, polygamy, the exaltation of men to be gods, the idea that God was once a man like other men, and the doctrine of the lineal right to office.

Later the Reorganized Church contested the title to the Temple Lot. One court awarded them title in 1891, but the Church of Christ appealed and got it back in 1894. A Reorganized appeal to the Supreme Court was denied and the Church of Christ (Temple Lot) still owns the coveted property. They claim that the Utah church has offered them as much as $5,000,000 for the Temple Lot.

For a time this church engaged in merger talks with the Reorganized Church but talks were broken off in 1926. A number of Reorganized people entered the Church between 1915 and 1926 so that it grew from several hundred to several thousand. It has 12 churches with 3,000 members today and still cherishes dreams of building a temple on the lot in Independence which is now almost completely surrounded by property of the Reorganized Church.

Another tiny group of Latter-day Saints belong to the Church of Jesus Christ headquartered in Monongahela, Pennsylvania. Their doctrinal position approximates that of the Reorganized Church but they are more inclined to consider Smith a fallen prophet. Their founder was William Bickerton, who was baptized by Rigdon the year after Smith's death. Bickerton joined the Utah Mormons for a while but by 1852 he was denouncing Young for adultery and other crimes. Bickerton organized some small congregations in Pennsylvania and West Virginia and was eventually acknowledged to be a prophet himself. Meetings of Bickertonites often featured speaking in tongues.

Today the Bickertonites claim 2,447 members in 45 churches in the United States and conduct missionary work in Italy and Nigeria as well as among the American Indians. They have converted a number of Italian-Americans and publish the *Book of Mormon* in Italian as well as English. A recent report indicates they have won about 3,500 converts in Nigeria. W. H. Cadman was president of the Church of Jesus Christ and edited its monthly magazine, the *Gospel News,* until his death in 1963.

Only a handful of Latter-day Saints continue to revere James J. Strang, the one-time king of Beaver Island, as the legitimate successor to Joseph Smith. They form the Church of Jesus Christ of Latter Day Saints (Strangites) and have six churches and about 250 members. The high priest lives in Artesia, New Mexico.

Strang was baptized in Nauvoo but sought converts for the new faith in Wisconsin. Five months after his baptism Smith was killed but Strang hurried back to Nauvoo to claim the right of succession. He produced a letter, supposedly written by Smith, which appointed him the new Prophet and commissioned him to establish a new city in Wisconsin to be known as Vorhee or "Garden of Peace." Young and his party declared the letter a forgery and Strang a fake. But the bold Strang won over John C. Bennett, the Prophet's brother William, and two of the apostles.

He gathered a following and began to build his new city on the banks of the White River. More Mormons left Nauvoo to cast their lot with Strang. To reinforce his claims he commanded his followers to accompany him to a hill over-looking the river. "Dig here," he ordered. At three feet the diggers came upon a flat rock which covered a clay container. Inside the container were brass plates covered with mysterious markings. For five days the plates were exhibited in Vorhee and then Strang went into seclusion to translate them. Like Smith he claimed to have received a Urim and Thummin. The "find" was declared to be the sacred book kept in the Ark of the Covenant. It clearly named Strang as the successor to Joseph Smith.

Strang set up a kingdom among his followers and called himself the "Imperial Primate" of his secret society, The Halcyon Order of the Illuminati. At a banquet on New Year's Day in 1847, he invited 130 of his followers to swear allegiance to him as "Actual Sovereign Lord and King on Earth." He in turn made them knights.

In the spring of 1849, Strang and his subjects migrated to Beaver Island, a government-owned island with timber, a good harbor, and rich soil. They built a sawmill and a road. Originally Strang forbade polygamy, but converts from Nauvoo began to arrive with extra wives. Strang announced the receipt of 18 more plates, the plates of Laban, which authorized plural wives. Strang himself toured the East with a concubine disguised as a male secretary and known as "Charlie Douglas." When "Charlie" became pregnant he could no longer conceal his second marriage. Later he took three additional wives. King James decreed that all the women in the community would wear a standardized gar-ment of modesty and when two women refused, he had their husbands flogged. On June 19, 1856, while strolling along the shore of his harbor, Strang was shot by the two flogging victims from a rowboat.

Panic ensued. Many Strangites fled and boats evacuated the other 2,500 before a drunken mob arrived to fire the buildings. Strang lingered on, his followers gone and his empire in ashes, until he died on July 8.

The remnant of the Strangite Church provided the following statement for publication in the *Census of Religious Bodies 1936,* published in 1940. It outlined the objective of the Strangite movement:

Its aim is not to try to make a large number of baptisms appear on the records but to make those baptized into sound converts, able to reason with and to meet all comers and give a reason for the hope that is in them. Further, to build a body of elders, high priests, priests, teachers, and deacons, trained, experienced, sound in the law of the Gospel against the day when God again sees fit to send the Gospel to the world; which most elders teach will occur between 1944 and 1956, a generation after the fullness of the Gospel was restored under Joseph Smith and James J. Strang.[9]

The tiny Strangite sect could not resist a dig at the prosperous Utah church:

Time has been a tattletale on those prophets who do not prophesy; seers who see nothing; translators who translate nothing; and revelators who reveal nothing, and who can only tell you what Joseph Smith said.[10]

A small body of Strangites, descendants of the original settlers, live in Burlington (Vorhee) Wisconsin. They worship on Saturday, try to observe the Law of Moses, circumcise, and offer animal sacrifices to God. They number about 100.

Finally, thousands of so-called Fundamentalists claim to be Latter-day Saints and true followers of Joseph Smith even though they have been excommunicated by the Utah church for espousing and practicing polygamy. Most of these schismatics insist that the Mormon Church erred in capitulating to the Federal Government in 1890 and outlawing plural marriage. Another group of Fundamentalists maintains that President John Taylor called five men together and charged them with preserving plural marriage no matter what the Church might say or do to placate the civil authorities. They consider this a revelation and say they are carrying out the command of Taylor.

The Fundamentalists maintain that Taylor received this revelation to preserve polygamy while in hiding in Centerville on September 26, 1886. The five men charged with the responsibility were said to be John W. Woolley, Lorin C. Woolley, J. Leslie Broadbent, John Y. Barlow, and Joseph Musser. Today Roy Johnson is Prophet of this sect and Guy Musser is President. Besides the settlement in Short Creek, Arizona, this group has established a colony in Mexico below El Paso.

Mormon authorities and middle-class Mormons are embarrassed by the existence of the polygamous Mormons and often ally themselves with the state to discover and convict these polygamists. When the LDS Church uncovers a polygamist he is summarily excommunicated. Their subsequent marriages must be performed in secret by a member of the Fundamentalist priesthood.

Individual Mormons may prefer to let the polygamists go their own ways. Perhaps their own fathers or grandfathers lived in plural marriage and they cannot bring themselves to inform on modern day polygamists. The Fundamentalists then arouse both sympathy and indignation in the Mormon Church. Certainly the existence of plural households in Utah, California and Arizona cities is known to long-time residents. The outsider investigating polygamy gets about the same degree of cooperation accorded a visitor to the Kentucky hills who asks about the local stills.

The Fundamentalist movement as such does not date from the 1890 Manifesto. It was started in the early 1920's by John Y. Barlow and Joseph Musser, now both deceased. The movement is splintered into half a dozen sects. Fundamentalists run a co-op store in Bountiful, a motel and two beauty shops in Salt Lake City, and a coal mine at Dragerton, Utah. Most polygamists work in factories or till small plots.

One group of Fundamentalists is known as the Church of the First Born of the Fullness of Time. They do not preach the doctrine of polygamy in the United States but reportedly practice polygamy in their colony in Mexico which has a population of about 1,000. Joel LeBaron, head of this sect, claims that Joseph Smith adopted his great-great-grandfather, Benjamin F. Johnson, and told him that he would be his successor as head of the Church.

Members of the Order of Aaron are all former Mormons who do not practice polygamy but are pacifists. They live on 8,000 acres near the Nevada state line.

A Fundamentalist may maintain several households under one roof, set up apartments in different parts of town or even in different cities, or live in a polygamous settlement such as Short Creek, Arizona. He and other Fundamentalists gather in private homes for corporate worship. The Fundamentalists even publish their own journal, *Star of Truth*.

Of course, the Fundamentalists find plenty of ammunition for their position in official Mormon documents. Until 1890 the LDS Church defended plural marriage in the strongest terms. Smith, Young, John Taylor, Wilford Woodruff, Lorenzo Snow, Joseph F. Smith and Heber J. Grant were all presidents of the Church and all polygamists. The Fundamentalists differ from the regular LDS in insisting that polygamy was an essential element of Mormonism rather than an incidental one which could be suspended.

Some Fundamentalists claim that there is as much polygamy now in the LDS Church as there was in pre-1890 days in terms of percentages. Fundamentalists claim that for every Fundamentalist discovered and excommunicated for polygamy there are ten Mormons in good standing who have more than one wife. Throughout the West, they say, thousands of women known outwardly as widows, divorcees, spinsters, or wives of traveling salesmen or servicemen are actually plural wives. Attorney General Walter Budge of Utah has estimated there are at least 20,000 men, women and children living in plural marriages in his state alone.

Newsweek magazine agreed with this estimate in an article on the polygamous Mormons in 1955. The magazine used the figure of 2,000 Fundamentalist husbands who with their wives and children would number about 20,000. It quoted State Attorney General E. R. Callister who said, "Utah's jails aren't big enough to hold them all." *Newsweek* also observed that "many a Utah Mormon takes quiet pride in his polygamous forebears and is inclined to be lenient toward the Fundamentalists." [11]

A student of the Fundamentalist movement, Samuel W. Taylor, observes:

The Fundamentalists gain converts from deeply religious people—as does any other sect; the man who hasn't felt any spiritual needs nor given a second thought to his soul is barren soil for the missionary. And here is the elemental basis for the violence of Mormon reaction to the Fundamentalist creed. It is born of fear. Modern Mormons believe in plural marriage, but not its practice. The more deeply immersed a Mormon becomes in his religion, the thinner the line may become between belief and practice. The threat of Fundamentalist doctrine is to the most devout.[12]

Fundamentalists risk arrest and imprisonment if discovered, since unlawful cohabitation has been declared a felony in Utah since 1935. The existence of children is enough to prove unlawful cohabitation. To protect themselves, the Fundamentalists have planted spies in the LDS Church and police departments to tip them off about raids. The LDS

Church too is said to keep a surveillance on Fundamentalist activities by means of informers.

The spy network did not warn the Fundamentalists of the raid on March 7, 1944. Police swooped down on polygamists in three states. In Salt Lake City, 15 men were sentenced to terms up to 5 years for unlawful cohabitation. Other polygamists were sentenced for violating the Mann Act and the Lindbergh Kidnapping law. Some of these sentences were later reversed by higher courts but the 15 men went to prison. Among them they had 55 known wives and 287 children. They actually made some converts to their cult in prison, since prison was one place where people could speak freely about their "crimes."

Short Creek, Arizona, has been the most famous polygamous settlement in modern America. Located in the barren desert known as America's Tibet, the town is only 90 miles from Kingman, the county seat, but because of the barrier of the Grand Canyon the trip to Short Creek is 400 miles by road. Unlike most other Fundamentalists, the Short Creekers were frankly and openly polygamous. Fundamentalist sympathizers around the nation poured money into the little community much as American Zionists have subsidized Israel. The Short Creek group has tried to revive the United Order under the name "United Effort," but so far results have been disappointing.

One hundred law officers, social workers, politicians, newspaper reporters and photographers swooped down on Short Creek one hot day in July 1953. The raid was planned under top secret conditions but the raiders found the entire population assembled in the school yard singing "America." The state presented warrants for the arrest of 36 men and 83 women. Eventually the men received suspended sentences. Arizona has no laws against polygamy. In fact, the Navajo Indians of the state continue to practice polygamy as their forefathers did.

Although polygamy is much more deeply entrenched than

those outside the intermountain area suspect, its growth is hampered by several factors. For one thing the cost of supporting multiple households limits the practice to the wealthy or those willing to accept a subnormal standard of living. No one is likely to enter the Principle today for reasons of lust. Fundamentalists are Puritanical in many respects and insist that sex be used only for procreation. This means that a Fundamentalist husband will ordinarily have intercourse with any particular wife only once a month. If she becomes pregnant he may not resume marital relations until after the baby is weaned. Sex activity ceases when the wife reaches the menopause. Finally, Mormons involved religiously and socially in the Church hesitate to take a step which sets them against the LDS hierarchy and invites immediate excommunication. They believe that God has favored polygamy but they also accept the principle of continuous revelation. This revelation now tells the General Authorities to try to stamp out the practice in order to conform to the laws of the nation.

What growth the Fundamentalists have can be attributed to the enormous families they raise. Many of the children follow their parents into the Principle although some choose monogamy.

Recently a group of citizens, Mormons and Gentiles, formed the Anti-Polygamy Citizens League in Bountiful, Utah, a suburb of Salt Lake City. Social workers say there are 600 people living in plural marriage in Davis County alone.

President W. S. Draves heads the Church of Christ (Fettingites) and regularly receives visits from John the Baptist. His followers refer to the Book of Mormon as the "Nephite Record." This group broke away from the Church of Christ (Temple Lot).

The Lukeites of Independence, Mo., accept only the Bible and the Book of Mormon as authoritative. They ordain women to their priesthood.

Zion's Order of the Sons of Levi has established a United

Order in the Ozark Mountains near Mansfield, Mo. They are led by President Marl V. Kilgore.

Remnants of still other Latter-day Saints churches can be found here and there around the country. The Church of Jesus Christ (Cutlerites) is reduced to a single congregation in Clitherall, Minnesota. By far the most important branches outside of the Utah church are the Reorganized Church and the Fundamentalists and they could hardly disagree more violently on the central doctrine of plural marriage. One denies that Smith ever taught or practiced these doctrines and the other insists that Smith established a new order of Christian marriage which neither the state nor the Church hierarchy can forbid.

Although the Reorganized Church would reject the suggestion, it might be said that the Reorganized Church is in a sense a reform of Mormonism and a return to more orthodox Protestantism. Without its special attachment to the *Book of Mormon* and the prophetic office of Joseph Smith, it could easily pass for another Protestant church.

19. *Mormonism Faces the Future*

During its first 130 years Mormonism has successfully weathered harassment, defections, the murder of its Prophet, the threat of armed force, adverse public opinion, the storm over polygamy, and the Gentile penetration of Utah. Today the Church of Jesus Christ of Latter-day Saints counts more than 2 million adherents; it sees its wards and stakes, investments, missionary force and converts growing every month.

To the casual observer, the Mormon Church is riding the crest of popularity and prosperity and in view of the vitality displayed by the Church in past decades, it would be rash to predict that the fortunes of this church would take a turn for the worse in the near future. Nervertheless, a number of signs of tension within Mormonism can be seen on the horizon.

The Mormon policy of encouraging higher education has produced an intelligentsia which finds it increasingly difficult to accept the myths and biblical fundamentalism of the Church. A cult such as Jehovah's Witnesses can propagate a crude biblical literalism without disturbing its followers; the Witnesses attract only a handful of college graduates and direct their own children away from the distractions of the campus. But the Mormon Church instills a love of scholarship in its young people, imposes a social pressure on high school graduates to continue their educations, pours millions of dollars into Brigham Young University and the Institutes of Religion on secular campuses in the West.

The religious genius of Mormonism which provided nine-teenth-century converts with a direct revelation of God to man and the answers to specific questions, such as the origin of the American Indian, fails to satisfy a growing number of Mormon intellectuals.

These Latter-day Saints, some with master's degrees and doctorates from Eastern and Middle Western universities, honor their pioneer ancestors and the achievements of the Saints in making the desert bloom. They find a warm fellow-ship in the ward and try to incorporate many of the values of Mormonism in their daily lives and that of their families. Nevertheless, they know that they cannot question or re-interpret any of the Standard works of the Church or doubt the accepted version of Smith's translation without under-mining the cornerstone of their faith.

For example, the Mormon intellectual must accept the LDS Church's racial doctrine which holds the Negro to be cursed by God as punishment for his lack of fervor in his pre-existence. Perhaps many white Christians in the nineteenth, or for that matter, the twentieth century held a similar view of the Negro's inferiority, but his church as such did not incorporate any such view as part of its theological beliefs. The practical application of the doctrine of racial equality and brotherhood may lag behind acceptance of the theory, but no Protestant or Catholic can appeal to official Church statements to support the doctrine of spiritual inferiority. The Mormon may treat Negroes with perfect justice but he dare not contradict the LDS position on race.

The college-educated Mormon who does not confine his reading to Church books realizes that new discoveries in archaeology and advances in philology and biblical studies cast further doubt on the authenticity of the *Book of Mormon*. No one outside of the LDS Church accepts the Hebrew origin of the American Indians. Few Christian theologians or scripture scholars have ever even skimmed through the *Book of Mormon*. The continued growth and expansion of proselytizing activities of the LDS Church may force Catholic and Protestant scholars to subject the *Book of Mormon* to closer examination, using modern techniques of textual analysis. Even computers may be called upon to establish the date of authorship of the *Book of Mormon* and to compare the style of *Doctrine and Covenants* which Smith claimed to write with the *Book of Mormon*, which he only translated.

The system of Church organization in Mormonism favors the choice of older, successful businessmen for the top posts. Many of these men are intelligent, shrewd, personable, well-to-do and energetic but they lack the philosophical and theological equipment possessed by leaders of other denominations. What theology they know has been picked up in off hours and through leisure-time reading. Their only systematic religious education has come through the Sunday school. When we read their statements we become aware of their lack of familiarity with the ancient languages in which the scriptures were written, with religious history before the nineteenth century, with the doctrines and practices of Catholicism and Protestantism. To expect these presidents and apostles to present the Mormon answer to the profound problems which concern Christian and secular scholars—existentialism, the threat of nuclear annihilation, biblical criticism, automation, the role of the city, psychoanalysis—is to expect too much.

Within the Christian world the stirrings of the ecumenical movement have touched almost every denomination. The ideal of unity has expressed itself in the organization of the World Council of Churches, the merger of a number of churches and the calling of the Second Vatican Council by Pope John XXIII which was continued by Pope Paul VI. The fragmentation of Protestantism seems to have been halted. Within Roman Catholicism the 400-year Counter-Reformation period is seen to be drawing to a close as that Church enters a new era. Theologians such as Barth, Tillich, Niebuhr, and Bultmann have won a new respect for their discipline after a period in which Protestant theologians were busy defending the Bible against Darwin. All these developments within the historic Christian churches seem to have little or no effect on contemporary Mormonism. One result is that the picture of Protestantism and Catholicism drawn in Mormon books and depicted in Mormon sermons bears less and less resemblance to reality.

President McKay's appreciation of the ecumenical spirit is revealed by his statement in 1962: "I'm all for unity provided everyone joins the Mormon Church." [1]

The *Church News* asked in 1963:

Will amalgamation of the churches restore truth? If all come together in unity and consolidate their diversity of errors into one united but misconceived and uninspired faith, will it bring salvation? They will but compound their error!

Mormonism needs trained theologians, yet the Church hesitates to send its potential theologians to study at Protestant seminaries. Instead it tries to provide its own specialists in a Ph.D. program at BYU. Such a closed system in a period such as this which is witnessing rapid expansion of knowledge in such fields as biblical criticism cannot keep up.

The Mormon Church seems to fear contamination from Gentile theologians and scholars:

At times texts produced by scholars of the world become popular among our teachers and speakers. Often these texts deal with doctrinal discussions which are not in keeping with Latter-day Saint views. They become misleading, and when used, are the cause of trouble in our classes.

There must be no infiltration of sectarianism among us. If and when there is, even in a small degree, it is our own fault. The other churches do not force their views upon us. If their doctrines come among us it is because we bring them in ourselves.

Some of our teachers feel that in order to stay abreast of the world, they must accept the world's teachings, but that is where

they make a great mistake. Our teachings are not of the world—
they are of modern revelation.

No matter how bright and intelligent other teachers of religion
may be, we cannot accept their doctrines and dogmas which go
contrary to our revealed knowledge. Uninspired men do not
have the light of revelation to guide them. Therefore, we cannot
regard them as authorities on doctrine. They may do research on
history or geography pertaining to the Holy Land, and may know
more about these topics than Latter-day Saints, who have not
made such research, and we are glad for the information they
produce.

But doctrine is another matter. Because they may be authorities on geography or history does not make them authorities on
doctrine or interpretation of scripture.[2]

If constructive self-criticism can serve as a barometer of
organizational health the Mormon Church may be heading
for serious difficulties. The student of contemporary Mormonism cannot help but observe the almost complete absence
of such self-criticism. A Roman Catholic belongs to a church
which, like the Mormon Church, claims to be the one true
Church of Christ; the Pope claims infallibility when speaking
ex cathedra in areas of faith and morals. Yet the American
Catholic in the 1960's hears and reads widespread criticism
of Church practices and personalities in many diocesan newspapers, in books published with imprimaturs, in periodicals
such as *Commonweal, America, Jubilee, Ave Maria,
National Catholic Reporter,* and *Catholic Worker* which
simply has no counterpart in Mormonism. Likewise, the
Protestant can see analyses of the Church's stand on peace,
education, race, labor relations, ecumenism, in publications
such as the *Christian Century.* It appears that honest criticism
of the Mormon Church or its hierarchy has only one outlet.
This is *Dialogue,* a quarterly magazine, founded by 24 Mormon intellectuals, mostly graduates of Stanford and Harvard.

For decades, especially under Brigham Young and his immediate successors, the LDS Church attempted to preserve the agricultural base of Utah. Mormons were discouraged from exploiting the mineral wealth of the state, with the result that Gentile investors reaped most of the benefits from the eventual development of these underground resources. The agricultural orientation of the Church hierarchy is still obvious although now most Mormons probably live in urban areas.

In 1960, Utah ranked 10th among the 50 states in the percentage of population classified as urban (in cities of 2,500 or more). The values of the farm village are offered as solutions to the serious problems of an industrial society and it is no wonder that many of these solutions seem irrelevant. Nothing approaching the *Mater et Magistra* and *Pacem in Terris* encyclicals of John XXIII could be expected from the present leadership of the Mormon Church.

The general authorities of the Mormon Church are not only theologically but politically conservative. A few Mormons such as Brigham H. Roberts were drawn to the New Deal, but it is an open secret in Utah that the Church officials are conservative Republicans almost to a man. President Hugh B. Brown may be an exception.

Even Mormon apologists admit that President McKay blundered when he wrote a personal letter to 11 Mormons in Congress in 1965 asking them to vote against repeal of right to work laws. Seven out of the 11 congressmen voted against the prophet's wishes.

Today a number of Mormon leaders such as Ezra Taft Benson actively promote the John Birch Society and other extreme anti-Communist organizations. Apostle Benson has called the Birch Society "the most effective non-church organization in our fight against creeping socialism and godless communism." This prompted Dr. Harold E. Fey, editor of the *Christian Century,* to write:

In Utah, we are told, the Mormon Church is riding the rightist line so hard that its excess is consolidating moderate opinion behind mainline Protestant groups. One Utah minister defines Mormonism as "an economic empire with a vaporized religion, held together by autocratic controls." [3]

This political attitude intensifies the inner conflict of the Mormon professor or intellectual who, like his colleagues in other colleges and universities, probably favors the liberal position.

Not all Mormons welcome this identification of their church with ultraconservative political movements and philosophies. Ezra Taft Benson addressed a Los Angeles dinner in September, 1963, honoring Robert Welch, founder of the Birch Society. He called Welch one of America's great patriots. Secretary of the Interior Stewart Udall, saying he spoke "as much in sorrow as in anger," publicly criticized Benson's action and said that Apostle Benson did "some harm to his—and my—church."

Next month, speaking at a United Nations birthday banquet at Brigham Young University, President Hugh Brown observed:

"Listening to some of our fellow citizens, one would suspect that the Communists are scoring all the points in the cold war, that Africa and Asia are lost, that the U.N. is a failure, that foreign aid is wasted, and that Castro is about the greatest threat our country has faced since Pearl Harbor.

"A lot of this nonsense gets disseminated by the professional, self-styled anti-Communists who make a comfortable living scaring people all over the country and who have a financial stake in making the Communists look stronger than we."

The impressive financial empire of the Church fills many Mormons with justifiable pride but it dampens the enthusiasm of others. The conscientious Mormon will contribute more than a tithe to the Church. Besides this 10 percent he will contribute 2 to 3 percent to his local ward, forward his fast offerings for Church relief, and respond to other financial appeals such as building funds. With the increasing burden of federal, state and local taxes some Mormon families grumble that Church demands are too heavy. To donate these dollars for missionary work or welfare is one thing, but to sacrifice to this extent so that the Church can purchase office buildings, cattle ranches, factories and the like is something else. Recent issues of Mormon periodicals have devoted space to chastising such grumblers as materialists and malcontents who do not demonstrate a real faith.

Mormonism may be entering its diaspora stage. The Mormons already find themselves a minority in their own Salt Lake City. Within twenty years it is quite possible that the Church may enroll fewer than half the residents of Utah. One Mormon writer predicts that by the year 2000 there will be more Latter-day Saints in Los Angeles than in Salt Lake City and that the world membership of the Church will reach 6,000,000.[4] Young Mormons from farm families realize that they cannot earn a satisfactory living from the land; they leave for work in the city, sometimes outside of the Rocky Mountains area. BYU graduates accept employment opportunities around the country. The construction of Mormon temples on other continents gives sanction to the idea that a Mormon can lead a full Mormon life without ever contemplating a migration to Zion.

That not all is well in Zion is obvious to Mormon and Gentile citizens of Salt Lake City. Nationwide the crime rate increased 6 percent between 1961 and 1962 but in Salt Lake City the rate went up 21.4 percent. In the City, murders increased 350 percent over 1961, rape increased 73 percent, and aggravated assault increased 77 percent. Grand Rapids is slightly larger than Salt Lake City but reports about half as many crimes. Spokane has about the same population as Salt Lake but it reported half as many murders, one-eighth as many rapes, one-fourth as many robberies and larcenies.[5]

Justly or unjustly such social disorganization will reflect un-
favorably on the church which founded and for long dominated the city.

While an immersion in Gentile culture impels some Mormons toward a practical apostasy, it no doubt strengthens
the faith of others. For the first time these Mormons begin
to appreciate the values of their religious traditions and enter
into the life of the ward in Chicago or Detroit or Atlanta.

The Church's desperate striving for respectability is nowhere more evident than in its attitude toward polygamy.
What was once a divine revelation and the hallmark of
Mormon peculiarity is now skipped over as a more or less
curious episode in frontier Mormonism. The number of
Mormons who lived in polygamous households is minimized.
And today when tiny groups of Fundamentalists try to live
according to the Principle, the descendants of polygamists
denounce them as lawbreakers.

Did Brigham Young foresee the current "popularity" of
Mormonism when he warned:

...I am satisfied that it will not do for the Lord to make this
people popular. Why? Because all hell would want to be in the
Church. The people must be kept where the finger of scorn can
be pointed to them. Although it is admitted that we are honest,
industrious, truthful, virtuous, self-denying, and, as a community,
possess every moral excellence, yet we must be looked upon as
ignorant and unworthy, and as the offscouring of society, and be
hated by the world. What is the reason of this? Christ and Baal
can not become friends. When I see this people grow and spread
and prosper, I feel that there is more danger than when they are
in poverty. Being driven from city to city or into the mountains
is nothing compared to the danger of our becoming rich and
being hailed by outsiders as a first-class community.[6]

The emphasis on the practical and pragmatic has also de-
prived the Mormon Church of creative artists who might
enrich its culture. Over the years Mormonism has produced

few composers, poets, artists, dramatists or novelists. It seems content with the doggerel of Eliza Snow. Except for the familiar "Come, Come Ye Saints," the Mormon Tabernacle Choir draws its repertoire from the musical compositions of the apostate churches of Christendom and the spirituals of the Negro. The Church seems to honor the businessman, farmer, recreation and youth leader, and politician, but offers little recognition for the artist.

One question which only time will answer is whether the amazing increase in converts to the Church is a permanent or temporary phenomenon. In 1952 the Church baptized 16,813 converts, but ten years later it reported more than 115,000 in a single year. Will this growth rate continue and will these converts persevere?

Mormonism has some attractive selling points. Unlike many Protestant denominations it does not tell the prospective convert that he is sinful and depraved, the heir of original sin. He can progress in this life and the next until he actually reaches the status of a god himself. What is more, the LDS Church offers the male convert the opportunity to enter the Mormon priesthood. The Protestant doctrine of the priesthood of all believers becomes a reality for Mormon males over the age of twelve. Finally, the Mormon Church entices the convert by the same element of secrecy which draws men to join lodges and fraternal orders. Anyone can enter St. Peter's Basilica in Rome but only a Mormon in good standing can enter a Mormon temple and participate in the secret rites performed within its walls. Those who receive their endowments form a select body of men and women among the billions who inhabit the planet but cannot become privy to the mysteries of the Lord.

Another question which remains to be answered is whether the Mormon birthrate will continue to surpass the national average by any significant margin. As Mormons leave the farms and move to the cities we may expect some lowering of

the average family size. The ballooning costs of higher education may prompt younger Mormon couples to reevaluate
their family plans, since they would expect to send all or
most of their children to college. The Church itself wages
no very aggressive campaign against contraception although
it proposes the ideal of a large family.

We should also mention that the Mormon Church is
slow to purge its rolls of inactive members. In some wards
fewer than half the membership can qualify for a "recommend" to enter the temple, but the entire Church publishes
formal notices of excommunication against only 100 or so
former members a year. Cases have been reported in which
former Mormons have been active in Protestant churches for
many years before the Mormon Church got around to excom-
municating them.

If Mormonism can hold the allegiance of the intelligentsia
it has developed, if it can adjust its thought patterns from an
agrarian to an urban situation, if it can retain the broad base
of the priesthood while making room for a professionally
equipped corps of theologians, it should be able to resolve
some of these tensions.

Many prophets have appeared over the years in America,
gathered a few followers, and then passed from the scene:
John Humphrey Noyes, Ann Lee, Guy Ballard, John Alexander Dowie, Benjamin Purnell. Only remnants of believers
continue to study their messages or try to interest others in
their claims. But Joseph Smith, Jr. succeeded where others
had failed. Ralph Waldo Emerson once declared that Mormonism was "the only religion of power and vitality that has
made its appearance for the past 1,200 years." And yet Ernest
Sutherland Bates could write: "If there is one fact in American history that can be definitely established it is that the
engaging Joe Smith was a deliberate charlatan." [7]

His church reflects not only his own eclectic personality but also many of the dominating characteristics of American life. The student of Mormonism who would predict an early reversal of its expansion and growth would have to anchor his judgment on evidence other than that provided by its first 130 years.

NOTES

CHAPTER 1

1. *Christian Century* (Jan. 23, 1963), pp. 102-3. Copyright 1963 by Christian Century Foundation. Reprinted by permission.

CHAPTER 2

1. David Whitmer, *An Address to All Believers in Christ* (Richmond, Mo., David Whitmer, 1887), p. 12.
2. *Millennial Star* (Feb. 6, 1882), pp. 86-7.
3. John A. Clark, *Gleanings by the Way* (Philadelphia, 1842), pp. 256-7.
4. Fawn Brodie, *No Man Knows My History* (New York, Alfred A. Knopf, 1946), p. 81.

CHAPTER 3

1. Richard Burton, *The City of the Saints,* Fawn Brodie, ed. (New York, Alfred A. Knopf, 1963), p. 284.
2. Orson Pratt, *Divine Authenticity of the Book of Mormon* (Liverpool, 1850), p. 1.
3. *Improvement Era,* June, 1911.
4. Lucy Mack Smith, *Biographical Sketches of Joseph Smith the Prophet and His Progenitors for Many Generations* (Liverpool, 1853), p. 87.
5. Thomas F. O'Dea, *The Mormons* (Chicago, University of Chicago Press, 1957), p. 24. Copyright 1957 by the University of Chicago.
6. *Millennial Harbinger,* February, 1831, p. 85.
7. Melvin R. Brooks, *LDS Reference Encyclopedia* (Salt Lake City, Bookcraft, 1960), p. 95.
8. Brodie, op. cit., p. 69.
9. Ibid., p. 62.
10. Walter R. Prince, "Psychological Tests for the Authorship of the Book of Mormon," *American Journal of Psychology* (July, 1917), pp. 373-395.
11. Leslie Rumble, *A Reply to the Mormon Counter Attack* (St. Paul, Minn., Radio Replies Press, undated), p. 21.

12. Ross T. Christensen, *Newsletter of the University Archeological Society* (Jan. 30, 1960), p. 3.

CHAPTER 4

1. Brodie, op. cit., p. 174.
2. Ibid., p. 282.
3. *Times and Seasons* (May 15, 1843).

CHAPTER 5

1. Juanita Brooks, *John Doyle Lee* (Glendale, Calif., Arthur H. Clark Co., 1962), p. 376.
2. Burton, op. cit., p. 276.
3. Ibid., p. 265.

CHAPTER 6

1. *Journal of Discourses* (Liverpool, 1854-1886, 26 vols), Vol. 7, p. 333.
2. Sterling M. McMurrin, *The Philosophical Foundations of Mormon Theology* (University of Utah Press, Salt Lake City, 1959), p. 8.
3. Orson Pratt, *The Seer,* Vol. 1, p. 37.
4. Brigham H. Roberts, *Documentary History of the Church* (Salt Lake City, 1901-1906), Vol. 6, p. 305.
5. James E. Talmage, *Articles of Faith* (Salt Lake City, 1901), p. 48.
6. John A. Widtsoe, *Rational Theology* (Salt Lake City, 1915), pp. 23-4.
7. *Journal of Discourses,* Vol. 3, p. 93.
8. Ibid., Vol. 11, p. 286.
9. Glenn L. Pearson, *Know Your Religion* (Salt Lake City, Bookcraft, 1961), p. 24.
10. McMurrin, op. cit., p. 12.
11. Ibid., p. 29.
12. *Journal of Discourses,* Vol. 1, p. 50.
13. Talmage , *Articles of Faith,* p. 41.
14. James E. Talmage, *Jesus the Christ,* p. 104.
15. *Millennial Star,* Vol. 15, p. 770.
16. Widtsoe, *Rational Theology,* p. 148.
17. *Journal of Discourses,* Vol. 6, pp. 274-5.
18. Parley P. Pratt, *The Key to the Science of Theology* (Liverpool, 1855), p. 140.
19. *Improvement Era* (December, 1962), p. 905.
20. Orson F. Whitney, *Saturday Night Thoughts,* pp. 310-1.

21. Austin and Alta Fife, *Saints of Sage & Saddle* (Bloomington, Ind., Indiana University Press, 1956), pp. 234-5.
22. *Journal of Discourses*, Vol. 1, p. 50.
23. Ibid., Vol. 3, p. 247.
24. Ibid., Vol. 4, p. 219.
25. Ibid., Vol. 4, p. 51.

CHAPTER 7

1. Horton Davies, *The Challenge of the Sects* (Philadelphia, Westminster Press, 1961), p. 118.
2. Talmage , *Articles of Faith*, p. 479.
3. John A. Hardon, S.J., *The Protestant Churches of America* (Westminster, Md., Newman Press, 1958), p. 179.
4. Gustave Weigel, S.J., *Churches in North America* (Baltimore, Helicon Press, 1961), p. 92.
5. Gustave Weigel, S.J. and Robert McAfee Brown, *An American Dialogue* (Garden City, N.Y., Doubleday, 1960), p. 154.
6. George H. Tavard, A.A., *The Catholic Approach to Protestantism* (New York, Harper & Row, Publishers, Inc., 1955), pp. 43-4.
7. Konrad Algermissen, *Christian Denominations* (St. Louis, B. Herder, 1953), p. 871.
8. *Journal of Discourses*, Vol. 12, p. 313.
9. Ibid., Vol. 16, p. 43.
10. Ibid., Vol. 17, p. 262.
11. Gordon B. Hinckley, *What of the Mormons?* (Salt Lake City, Church of Jesus Christ of Latter-day Saints, 1947), p. 5.
12. LeGrand Richards, *A Marvelous Work and a Wonder* (Salt Lake City, Deseret Book Co., 1950), p. 2.
13. Pearson, op. cit., p. 132.
14. Ibid, p. 133.
15. *Time* (Nov. 16, 1959), p. 60.

CHAPTER 8

1. Kimball Young, *Isn't One Wife Enough?* (New York, Holt, Rinehart and Winston, 1954), pp. 101-2.
2. *Times and Seasons*, Vol. 5, p. 474.
3. Joseph H. Weston, *These Amazing Mormons* (Salt Lake City, Weston Publishing Co., 1948), p. 84.
4. Mark Twain, *Roughing It* (New York, 1903), Vol. 1, p. 101.
5. *Journal of Discourses*, Vol. 11, pp. 268-9.
6. *Millennial Star*, Vol. 28, p. 190.
7. Lorenzo Snow, *History of Utah*, Vol. 3, p. 471.

8. Kimball Young, op. cit., p. 146.
9. Ibid., p. 438.
10. O'Dea, op. cit., p. 140
11. John J. Stewart, *Brigham Young and His Wives* (Salt Lake City, Mercury Publishing Co., 1961), p. 14.
12. Ibid., p. 41.
13. Loc. cit.

CHAPTER 9

1. *New York Times* (Aug. 1, 1962), p. 17.
2. Weston, op. cit., p. 34.
3. Loc. cit.
4. Loc. cit.
5. *Journal of Discourses*, Vol. 1, p. 136.
6. Kimball Young, op. cit., p. 444.

CHAPTER 10

1. *New York Times* (Aug. 1, 1962), p. 17.
2. *Church News* (May 4, 1963), p. 3.
3. Jerald Tanner, *Mormonism* (Salt Lake City, Jerald Tanner, undated), p. 199.
4. Neil Morgan, "Utah: How Much Money Hath the Mormon Church?" *Esquire* (August, 1962), p. 91.

CHAPTER 11

1. James E. Talmage , *The House of the Lord* (Salt Lake City, Bookcraft, 1962), p. 89.
2. Eliza R. Snow, *Biography and Family Records of Lorenzo Snow* (Salt Lake City, 1884), p. 11.
3. Talmage , *The House of the Lord*, p. 123.
4. *Journal of Discourses*, Vol. 14, p. 275.
5. N. B. Lundwall, *Temples of the Most High* (Salt Lake City, Bookcraft, 1956), p. 234.
6. *Deseret News* (June 15, 1901).
7. Lundwall, op. cit., p. 82.

CHAPTER 12

1. S. H. Goodwin, *Mormonism and Masonry* (Washington, D.C., Masonic Service Association of the United States, 1924), p. v.

2. E. Cecil McGavin, *Mormonism and Masonry* (Salt Lake City, Bookcraft, 1956), p. 13.
3. George B. Arbaugh, *Revelation in Mormonism* (Chicago, University of Chicago Press, 1950), p. 159. Copyright by the University of Chicago.
4. Orson F. Whitney, *Life of Heber C. Kimball*, p. 26.
5. McGavin, op. cit., p. 17.
6. O'Dea, op. cit., p. 57.
7. H. Calvin Rich, *Some Differences in Faith*, p. 31.
8. Goodwin, op. cit., p. 50.
9. Fred L. Pick and G. Norman Knight, *Pocket History of Freemasonry* (New York, Philosophical Library, 1953), p. 15.
10. McGavin, op. cit., p. 41.
11. *Church News* (May 18, 1963), p. 3.

CHAPTER 13

1. Hyrum M. Smith and Janne M. Sjodahl, *Doctrine and Covenants Commentary* (Salt Lake City, Deseret Book Co., 1950), p. 226.
2. Joseph F. Smith, *Gospel Doctrine*, p. 279.
3. Widtsoe, *Rational Theology*, p. 147.
4. Thomas F. O'Dea, "The Mormons: Strong Voice in the West," *Information* (March, 1961), p. 19.
5. Wayne J. Anderson, "Child Rearing—The Mormon Viewpoint," *Improvement Era* (January, 1963), p. 37.
6. *National Observer* (June 17, 1963), p. 9.
7. John A. Widtsoe, *Program of the Church*, pp. 76-7.

CHAPTER 14

1. Hyrum Smith, *The Life of Joseph F. Smith*, p. 73.
2. Ibid., p. 76.
3. Melvin R. Brooks, op. cit., p. 76.
4. Ibid., p. 75.
5. *Improvement Era*, Vol. 19, p. 833.
6. Joseph Smith, Jr., *History of the Church of Jesus Christ of Latter-day Saints* (Salt Lake City, 1930), Vol. 7, p. 101.
7. *Journal of Discourses,* Vol. 13, p. 139.
8. Ibid., Vol. 12, p. 37.
9. Leonard J. Arrington, "An Economic Interpretation of the 'Word of Wisdom,'" *Brigham Young University Studies* (Winter, 1959), Vol. 1, No. 1, p. 43.
10. O'Dea, op. cit., p. 146.

CHAPTER 15

1. *A Uniform System for Teaching Investigators* (Salt Lake City, Church of Jesus Christ of Latter-day Saints, 1961), p. 3.
2. Loc. cit.
3. Loc. cit.
4. Ibid., p. 15.
5. Loc. cit.
6. Ibid., p. 26.
7. Ibid., p. 75.
8. Ibid., p. 89.

CHAPTER 16

1. John J. Stewart, *Mormonism and the Negro* (Orem, Utah, Bookmark, 1960), p. 45.
2. Ibid., p. 34.
3. Ibid., pp. 52-3.
4. Horace Greeley, *An Overland Journey* (New York, 1860), p. 211.
5. *Journal of Discourses,* Vol. 7, pp. 290-1.
6. Ibid., Vol. 11, p. 272.
7. Ibid., Vol. 10, p. 110.
8. *Time* (April 13, 1959), p. 96.
9. *New York Times* (June 7, 1963), p. 17.
10. *Wall Street Journal* (Aug. 2, 1963), p. 6.
11. *Chicago Tribune* (Oct. 27, 1963), Sec. 1A, p. 2.
12. *Time* (Oct. 18, 1963), p. 83.
13. *Look* (Oct. 22, 1963), p. 79.

CHAPTER 17

1. O'Dea, op. cit., pp. 228-9.

CHAPTER 18

1. Elbert A. Smith, *Differences That Persist Between the Reorganized Church of Jesus Christ of Latter Day Saints and the Utah Mormon Church* (Independence, Mo., Herald Publishing House, 1959), p. 30.
2. Ibid., pp. 30-1.
3. Joseph Fielding Smith, *Origin of the "Reorganized" Church* (Salt Lake City, Deseret News Press, 1909), p. 116.
4. Elbert A. Smith, op. cit., p. 13.
5. Joseph Fielding Smith, op. cit., p. 87.
6. Ibid., p. 80.

7. Ibid., p. 115.
8. Ibid., p. 102.
9. *U.S. Census of Religious Bodies, Latter-day Saints* (Washington, D.C., Bureau of the Census, 1940), p. 39.
10. Ibid., p. 39.
11. *Newsweek* (Nov. 21, 1955), p. 99.
12. Samuel W. Taylor, *I Have Six Wives* (New York, Greenberg, 1956), p. 13.

CHAPTER 19

1. *Christianity Today* (Sept. 28, 1962), p. 44.
2. *Church News* (Jan. 26, 1963), p. 16.
3. *Christian Century* (May 16, 1962), p. 621. Copyright 1962 Christian Century Foundation. Reprinted by permission from the Christian Century.
4. Albert L. Zobell, Jr., *Improvement Era.* September, 1959, pp. 664f.
5. *Deseret News* (July 22, 1963), p. 10A.
6. *Journal of Discourses,* Vol. 12, p. 272.
7. Ernest Sutherland Bates, *The American Faith* (New York, W. W. Norton & Co., 1940), p. 346.

BIBLIOGRAPHY

Anderson, Einar, *Mormonism*. Chicago, Moody Press, 1956.

Anderson, Nels, *Desert Saints: The Mormon Frontier in Utah*. Chicago, University of Chicago Press, 1942.

Arbaugh, George, *Revelation in Mormonism*. Chicago, University of Chicago Press, 1950.

—— *Gods, Sex and Saints*. Rock Island, Ill., Augustana Press, 1957.

Arrington, Leonard J., *Great Basin Kingdom*. Cambridge, Mass., Harvard University Press, 1958.

Barney, Gwen Marler, *Mormons and Their Temples*. Salt Lake City, Bookcraft, 1959.

Bates, Ernest Sutherland, *The American Faith*. New York, W. W. Norton, 1940.

Beardsley, Harry M., *Joseph Smith and His Mormon Empire*. Cambridge, Mass., Houghton Mifflin, 1931.

Bennett, John C., *The History of the Saints; or, an Expose of Joe Smith and Mormonism*. Boston, Leland & Whiting, 1842.

Bennett, Wallace Foster, *Why I Am a Mormon*. New York, Nelson, 1958.

Braden, Charles S., *These Also Believe*. New York, Macmillan, 1953.

Brodie, Fawn M., *No Man Knows My History*. New York, Knopf, 1945.

Brooks, Juanita, *The Mountain Meadows Massacre*. Stanford, Calif., Stanford University Press, 1943.

—— *John Doyle Lee*. Glendale, Calif., Arthur H. Clark Co., 1962.

Brooks, Melvin R., *LDS Reference Encyclopedia*. Salt Lake City, Bookcraft, 1960.

Budvarson, Arthur, *The Book of Mormon—True or False?* Grand Rapids, Mich., Zondervan, 1959.

Burton, Sir Richard, *The City of the Saints*. London, 1862.

Call, Lamoni, *2,000 Changes in the Book of Mormon*. Bountiful, Utah, 1898.

Campbell, Alexander, *Delusions, An Analysis of the Book of Mormon*. New York, 1832.

Caswall, Henry, *The City of the Mormons, or Three Days at Nauvoo*. London, 1842.

Cerza, Alphonse, *Anti-Masonry*. Fulton, Mo., Missouri Lodge of Research, 1962.

Clark, Elmer, *The Small Sects in America*. New York, Abingdon-Cokesbury, 1949.

Clitheroe, Eric, *The Mormon Religion*. Unpublished manuscript.

Cross, Whitney R., *The Burned-over District: the Social and Intellectual History of Enthusiastic Religion in Western New York, 1800-1850*. Ithaca, N.Y., Cornell University Press, 1950.

Davis, Inez Smith, *The Story of the Church*, 4th rev. ed. Independence, Mo., Herald Publishing House, 1948.

Deseret News, various issues.

Dwyer, Robert J., *The Gentile Comes to Utah, A Study in Religious and Social Conflict (1862-1890)*. Washington, D. C., Catholic University of America Press, 1941.

Fife, Austin and Alta, *Saints of Sage & Saddle*. Bloomington, Ind., Indiana University Press, 1956.

Flanders, Robert Bruce, *Nauvoo: Kingdom on the Mississippi*. Urbana, Ill., University of Illinois Press, 1965.

Flint, B. C., *An Outline History of the Church of Christ (Temple Lot)*. Independence, Mo., Board of Publications of the Church of Christ (Temple Lot), 1953.

Gates, Susa Young, *The Life Story of Brigham Young*. New York, Macmillan, 1930.

Gerstner, John, *The Theology of the Major Sects*. Grand Rapids, Mich., Baker Book House, 1960.

Goodwin, S. H., *Mormonism and Masonry*. Washington, D. C., Masonic Service Association of the United States, 1924.

—— *Additional Studies in Mormonism and Masonry*. Salt Lake City, 1932.

Harrison, G. T., *Mormons Are Peculiar People*. New York, Vantage, 1954.

Hield, Charles R. and Ralston, Russell F., *Baptism for the Dead*. Independence, Mo., Herald Publishing House, 1960.

Hinckley, Gordon B., *What of the Mormons?* 4th ed. Salt Lake City, Church of Jesus Christ of Latter-day Saints, 1953.

Hoekema, Anthony, *The Four Major Cults*. Grand Rapids, Mich., Eerdmans, 1963.

Holloway, Mark, *Heavens on Earth, Utopian Communities in America 1680-1880:* London, Turnstile Press, 1951.

Howe, E. D., *Mormonism Unveiled*. Painesville, Ohio, 1834.

Improvement Era, various issues.

Jonas, Larry S., *Mormon Claims Examined.* Grand Rapids, Mich., Baker Book House, 1961.

Journal of Discourses, 26 vols. Liverpool, 1854-1886.

Kirkham, Francis, *A New Witness for Christ in America, the Book of Mormon.* Independence, Mo., Zion's Printing and Publishing Co., 1951.

Lee, John Doyle, *Mormonism Unveiled.* Omaha, 1891.

———— *A Mormon Chronicle.* San Marino, Calif., Huntington Library, 1955.

Linn, William A., *The Story of the Mormons.* New York, Macmillan, 1902.

Lundwall, N. B., *Temples of the Most High.* Salt Lake City, Bookcraft, 1962.

McGavin, E. Cecil, *Mormonism and Masonry.* Salt Lake City, Bookcraft, 1956.

McMurrin, S. M., *The Philosophical Foundations of Mormon Theology,* Salt Lake City, University of Utah Press, 1959.

Martin, Walter R., *The Maze of Mormonism.* Grand Rapids, Mich., Zondervan, 1962.

Mead, Frank S., *Handbook of Denominations,* 2nd rev. ed. New York and Nashville, Abingdon Press, 1961.

Meyer, Eduard, *Ursprung und Geschichte der Mormonen,* 1912.

Mulder, William, *Homeward to Zion.* Minneapolis, University of Minnesota Press, 1957.

———— *Among the Mormons.* New York, Knopf, 1958.

Mullen, Robert, *The Latter-day Saints: The Mormons Yesterday and Today.* Garden City, N.Y., Doubleday, 1966.

Nelson, Lowry, *The Mormon Village.* Salt Lake City, University of Utah Press, 1952.

Nibley, Hugh, *Lehi in the Desert and the World of the Jaredites.* Salt Lake City, Bookcraft, 1952.

———— *No, Ma'am, That's Not History.* Salt Lake City, Bookcraft, 1946.

———— *An Approach to the Book of Mormon.* Salt Lake City, Deseret News Press, 1957.

———— *The Myth Makers.* Salt Lake City, Bookcraft, 1961.

O'Dea, Thomas F., *The Mormons.* Chicago, University of Chicago Press, 1957.

Paden, W. M., *Temple Mormonism: Its Evolution, Ritual and Meaning.* New York, A. J. Montgomery, 1931.

Pearson, Glenn L., *Know Your Religion*. Salt Lake City, Bookcraft, 1961.

Pratt, Parley P., *Key to the Science of Theology*. Liverpool, 1855.

Quaife, Milo M., *The Kingdom of Saint James*. New Haven, Conn., Yale University Press, 1930.

Richards, LeGrand, *A Marvelous Work and a Wonder*. Salt Lake City, Deseret Book Co., 1950.

Riley, I. Woodbridge, *The Founder of Mormonism: A Psychological Study of Joseph Smith*. New York, Dodd, Mead and Co., 1902.

Roberts, Brigham H., *A Comprehensive History of the Church of Jesus Christ of Latter-day Saints*. Salt Lake City, 1930. 6 vols.

—— *A New Witness for God*. Salt Lake City, George Q. Cannon & Sons, 1895.

—— *Succession in the Presidency of the Church of Jesus Christ of Latter-day Saints*, 2nd ed. Salt Lake City, Geo. Q. Cannon, 1900.

Rosten, Leo, *A Guide to the Religions of America*. New York, Simon and Schuster, 1963.

Rumble, Leslie, *The Mormons or Latter-day Saints*. St. Paul, Minn., Radio Replies Press, 1957.

—— *A Reply to the Mormon Counter Attack*. St. Paul, Minn., Radio Replies Press, undated.

Shook, Charles A., *Cumorah Revisited*. Cincinnati, 1910.

—— *The True Origin of the Book of Mormon*. Cincinnati, 1914.

Smith, Elbert A., *Differences That Persist Between the Reorganized Church of Jesus Christ of Latter Day Saints and the Utah Mormon Church*. Independence, Mo., Herald Publishing House, 1959.

Smith, Ethan, *View of the Hebrews; or the Ten Tribes of Israel in America*. Poultney, Vt., 1823.

Smith, Hyrum M. and Sjodahl, Janne M., *Doctrine and Covenants Commentary*. Salt Lake City, Deseret Book Co., 1950.

Smith, John L., *Has Mormonism Changed?* Clearfield, Utah, Utah Evangel Press, 1961.

—— *Hope or Despair?* Clearfield, Utah, Utah Evangel Press, 1959.

Smith, Joseph, *The Book of Mormon*. Salt Lake City, Church of Jesus Christ of Latter-day Saints.

—— *Doctrine and Covenants*. Salt Lake City, Church of Jesus Christ of Latter-day Saints.

—— *Pearl of Great Price*. Salt Lake City, Church of Jesus Christ of Latter-day Saints.

—————— *History of the Church of Jesus Christ of Latter-day Saints,* ed. by B. H. Roberts. Salt Lake City, 1902.

Smith, Joseph F. and Evans, Richard C., *Blood Atonement and the Origin of Plural Marriage.* Salt Lake City, Deseret News Press, undated.

Smith, Joseph Fielding, *Origin of the "Reorganized" Church.* Salt Lake City, Deseret News Press, 1909.

Smith, Lucy Mack, *Biographical Sketches of Joseph Smith the Prophet and His Progenitors for Many Generations.* Liverpool, 1853.

Snowden, J. H., *The Truth About Mormonism.* New York, George H. Doran, 1926.

Sperry, Sidney B., *The Book of Mormon Testifies.* Salt Lake City, Bookcraft, 1952.

Stegner, Wallace, *Mormon Country.* New York, Duell, 1942.

Stenhouse, T. B. H., *The Rocky Mountain Saints.* New York, B. Appleton, 1873.

Stewart, John J., *Mormonism and the Negro.* Orem, Utah, Bookmark Division of Community Press, 1960.

—————— *Brigham Young and His Wives.* Salt Lake City, Mercury, 1961.

Stone, Irving, *Men to Match My Mountains: the Opening of the Far West.* Garden City, N. Y., Doubleday, 1956.

Talmage , James E., *A Study of the Articles of Faith,* 27th ed. Salt Lake City, Church of Jesus Christ of Latter-day Saints, 1952.

—————— *The House of the Lord,* Salt Lake City. Bookcraft, 1962.

Tanner, Jerald, *Mormonism.* Salt Lake City, Jerald Tanner, undated.

Taylor, Samuel Woolley, *I Have Six Wives.* New York, Greenberg, 1956.

—————— *Family Kingdom.* New York, New American Library, 1961.

Turner, Wallace, *The Mormon Establishment.* Boston, Houghton-Mifflin, 1966.

Uniform System for Teaching Investigators. Salt Lake City, Church of Jesus Christ of Latter-day Saints, 1961.

Van Baalen, J. K., *The Chaos of Cults.* Grand Rapids, Mich., Eerdmans, 1955.

Velt, Harold I., *The Sacred Book of Ancient America.* Independence, Mo., Herald House, 1952.

Wallace, Irving, *The Twenty-seventh Wife.* New York, Simon and Schuster, 1961.

Webb, Robert C., *The Real Mormonism.* New York, Sturgis & Walton, 1916.

Werner, M. R., *Brigham Young*. New York, Harcourt, Brace and Co., 1925.

Weston, Joseph H., *These Amazing Mormons!* Salt Lake City, Weston Publishing Co., 1948.

Whalen, William J., *Christianity and American Freemasonry*. Milwaukee, Bruce, 1958.

Whitmer, David, *An Address to All Believers in Christ*. Richmond, Mo., 1887.

Widtsoe, John A., *A Rational Theology*. Salt Lake City, 1915.

———— *Priesthood and Church Government*. Salt Lake City, Deseret Book Co., 1939.

———— and Leah D., *The Word of Wisdom: A Modern Interpretation*. Salt Lake City, 1938.

Young, Ann Eliza, *Wife No. 19*. Hartford, Conn., 1875.

Young, Brigham, *Journal of Discourses*. Liverpool and London, 1854-1886, 26 vols.

Young, Kimball, *Isn't One Wife Enough?* New York, Holt, 1954.

Index